GRIT

The Battle Within

ANKIT GUPTA

RUPA

First published by
Rupa Publications India Pvt. Ltd 2022
7/16, Ansari Road, Daryaganj
New Delhi 110002

Sales Centres:

Allahabad Bengaluru Chennai
Hyderabad Jaipur Kathmandu
Kolkata Mumbai

ISBN: 978-93-5520-335-9

First impression 2022

10 9 8 7 6 5 4 3 2 1

Printed by Parksons Graphics Pvt. Ltd.

Dedicated to my parents and to
all those who struggled and fought.

CONTENTS

1

DOORSTEPS

When life brings the battle to you,
You bring the battle to life,
Rise, warrior, rise.

I took a few deep breaths, trying to get through a panic attack, desperate to jumpstart my cold body lying in a fetal position on the floor. I tightened my eyes and clenched my teeth as hard as I could to stop my heart from pounding so hard. It was September 2008, the dawn of the financial meltdown. As I was lying in my luxury apartment in Irvine, Southern California, my mind was consumed by thoughts of a fast-approaching freight train bringing in bankruptcy and ruin. At the prime age of 30, I was sinking into darkness, into the nadir of my life.

The battle was supposed to be over. This was to be the first day after the 'happily ever after', a new beginning of my life—a content and happy life that I had yearned for so long. What went wrong?

That morning, I woke up to the noise of angry winds knocking at my bedroom window. It was quite dark outside. Being jet-lagged and tired, I could not tell whether it was day or night. I had picked up my phone from the end table and saw it was 10.23 a.m. It was an uncharacteristically cloudy and dark day in Southern California. I stretched my limbs to the four corners of my queen bed and crawled underneath the comforter.

I had arrived the previous evening from my vacation in India. I could now take as much time as I wanted to recover from the jet lag and the 24-hour journey. A vacation after a long vacation is the best feeling in the world. I could still hear the angry winds howling at the window. I felt the chill outside as I touched the window glass; though they were sealed, the noise was annoying like an unwanted guest. I rested my head against the pillow and tried to go back to sleep. But it was too late now, as a plethora of thoughts had now barged into my befuddled head.

I took a deep breath and stared at the ceiling. The four-week vacation in India had been a good break. It was, in fact, a pilgrimage as I had taken my parents to temples across the country. The travelling part was challenging with the constant crowds and chaos, but it was worth it.

One of the special moments of the trip flashed in front of my eyes. As I was standing in the compound of a temple in mental and physical agony, I had felt deep peace, something akin to satori. For a moment, I had felt as if I had moved beyond the physical and mental field and had touched the spiritual. It was one moment of transcendence when my whole life flashed in front of me. I had a glimpse of something from another realm, something just beyond the battlefield of my life. It was a space of complete acceptance where I could finally trust and let go of myself, my will and my flapping resistance. Stripped of my former self, I had felt lighter in that moment. My entire being was in complete harmony.

During that epiphany at the temple in India, I could see beyond the struggles I had faced since childhood. I had been familiar with adversity since I was 10 years old when my Dad lost his job in Mumbai. Images of hired goons burning our possessions in front of our eyes and mercilessly evicting my family from our apartment still haunted me. We moved into a single-room apartment, which was so small that my Dad had to sleep in the kitchen.

Each of us, including my brother and sister, fought hard at every turn of our lives so we could define our paths and not let adversity dictate us. I completed my Bachelor of Engineering, with, thankfully, a scholarship and minimum tuition fees. My goal, to make a genuine contribution to the field of technology, brought me to the US in 1999, nine years ago for further studies. I came to the US to do my masters in computer engineering with empty pockets and no clear means to pay my tuition fees. I earned my degree from Texas A&M University, College Station, one of the best American universities. Despite multiple layoffs and challenges, I blazed through the maze to make a genuine contribution in the field of chip design. The company I worked with designed the main processing chip, which functions as the brain of the iPhone. I was very proud of my contributions.

My next battle was to climb the challenging mountain of prosperity through stock market investments. All I wanted was to ensure that poverty and hardship should not steal the childhoods of my subsequent generation. That battle in the stock market had been fierce and mentally draining. I had put everything into it, materially and emotionally. My investment grew steadily and I was on the way to reach my financial goal to become a millionaire.

However, engaging with the stock market felt empty and joyless. The anxiety and pressure of borrowing huge amounts of money to experiment with the volatile stock market had taken its toll and I ended up suffering from insomnia and hypertension. I was mentally exhausted and was close to having a nervous breakdown when I decided to take some time out—a spiritual sabbatical. During that journey, I disconnected myself from both the real and the digital world to question whether there was a way out of my misery.

Like a soldier returning after winning in a war, I was still scarred from all the battles I had fought, both willingly and unwillingly. The ghosts of these battles were constant company and something I could not dispense with.

That day at the temple in India, that moment of satori had shown me a path to absolute freedom—a new path in life. I had decided from that day onwards that the compass of all my pursuits would only point to peace and happiness. I would cash out of the stock market, focus on enjoying my new dream job which I was to start with, and enjoy my life in San Diego.

Just remembering that moment in India filled my heart and the room with joy and peace. I took a deep breath to absorb it. But, oh, the winds! The winds kept howling at my window.

Is there a storm coming? Do I need to prepare for it? I thought, looking outside and feeling the lashes of the unrelenting wind. *Relax Ankit,* I told myself. *Stay in the monk mode and not the warrior mode. Remember to focus on peaceful thoughts.* It was tricky controlling my sensitive mental compass.

My stomach now started growling, resonating with the external noise. I had not eaten anything since the previous night. *Hmm, got to eat something. It's lunchtime in the US and dinnertime in India.* I walked towards the living room putting my phone in my pocket.

I turned on the lights. With one eye still closed and the other only half open, I looked at the living room admiringly, taking in the quiet of the large space of my beautiful rental apartment. It was a top-storey apartment with high ceilings and minimal furniture: a couch, a small coffee table and a 46" flat-screen TV. I wanted a calm, minimalistic space as my bachelor pad. I was glad to be back in quieter surroundings, away from the hustle and bustle in India.

I looked at the packed suitcases lying in the corner. Unpacking those and putting things back in place was going to be a task, I thought. No worries. I had a few weeks more to get into the groove. I opened my suitcases and rummaged through the neatly packed things. I found a white pillow cover stitched at both ends. On one surface, the following words were written with a blue marker, 'Sweets, Biscuits, Choklats.' I smiled at the misspelling. It was my

Mom's way of full disclosure for the US Customs. I tore through the stitches and started munching on the goodies. I remembered Mom saying, 'You need to take food from India that would last at least a couple of days. You would get none in the US.' She was right. I started munching on the peanut chikkis, feeling a sudden stab of homesickness and loneliness. I was missing my family.

I walked to the other end of the room towards the French windows. I glanced at the dust on the TV screen in the centre of the room. Underneath the TV table was my laptop, which was also gathering dust. As an engineer, I loved technology, but it had been such a relief to be disconnected from the Internet for the past four weeks. Despite its benefits, I felt that the Internet had an uncanny way of changing one's mental state. I would get up fresh as a flower, read something alarming or bad on the Internet and feel restless for the rest of the day.

No more Google alerts today. Compass still pointing to happiness.

I was glad to just walk by and not dust my abandoned laptop.

I opened the French windows and could feel cold air hit my face. The gust of wind whooshed by, assaulting my eardrums and blinding me momentarily. I braced myself as I absorbed the ambience of my resort-style apartment community. I looked outside at the faux classic Italian architecture; even the Italian statuettes seemed to be feeling cold. The majestic palm trees were swaying, resisting the unforgiving wind. After a few quiet moments of admiring the artificial beauty, my jumbled thoughts came rushing back.

I should check the Internet, it's been a while. I need to check if there are any emails about my joining date for the new job. They should have contacted me by now, it's been a while since the interview. I had had the interview before I left for my vacation and I had not checked my emails since then.

I also thought of checking the status of my stock brokerage account. I had not checked it for a while. I was sure that with everything the financial markets had gone through over the last few weeks, there must be some new update about the ongoing turmoil.

No Internet, Ankit. Remember the pursuit of happiness. Stay centred. I chastized myself, knowing my mind could be easily distracted like that of a small child.

But I did need to at least check my starting day for the new job.

There were two conflicting voices in my head with opposing views in every situation. One voice was gentle and kind and the other was the harsh critic, the punisher. I could only act once a compromise was reached between the two. I smiled at the thought that for enduring peace, I would need to silence the two voices in my head.

As I started to wipe my laptop with a napkin, I sneezed five times, making my eyes watery. *Damn, dust allergies.* Now, I was wide-awake.

I turned on the laptop, sat down on the couch with my feet on the coffee table.

Wi-Fi detected. Ah, thank you.

I opened my Yahoo email and started to browse the inbox. There is so much spam these days, I thought as I scrolled through my inbox. Then I found what I was looking for—an email with the subject line 'Interview for engineer position'. A rush of excitement went through my veins. This was it. This was the result of the interview I appeared for in India. This was just not any ordinary position—it was the perfect position at my dream company and that too at my dream location, San Diego.

A few years back, I had heard this company's CEO speak at a conference. I was both impressed and inspired by his vision of connecting the world through technology. I had heard some great things about the company's work culture from a friend who was employed there; I knew that I wanted to work and eventually retire from this company. The position was also an excellent fit since that team had been using the computer models and tools that I had developed. My manager knew the director of the new group and he made a strong recommendation for me. The director was very interested in having me on his team. Though I had thought of the interviews as just a formality, I prepared for them and all eight went really well.

I started to read the email and was very excited at the prospect of the new beginning and the new turn that my life was about to take.

I wondered when they would ask me to join, hoping it would not be too soon. I needed a few more weeks to recover from my jet lag.

San Diego, here I come.

The email read: 'Thank you for the interview. We are not able to offer you a position at this time but will keep your resume in our database if a more suitable position opens up.'

Wait, what? I was a bit confused.

I read the email again. Was that a rejection or did they just want to hold off? My mind was still trying to deny the obvious. Maybe they're just holding off on the position with the economy going through a downturn, I told myself. But soon the realization dawned on me.

Damn, I am rejected. I gave a big sigh, feeling absolutely dejected. I took a deep breath. I was still trying to find an interpretation of the email that would somehow mollify my disappointment. Within moments my emotions went from denial, despondency, anger to acceptance of the painful reality. I got up and started pacing the living room—one of the reasons I did not have much furniture in the house. Walking and thinking hard was part of my DNA. I had started this ritual during my engineering days in India when we lived in a one-room apartment. It was one-fourth the size of my current living room. For studying, I would walk across on the terrace with just one thought in my mind—how to achieve my dreams and elevate my life. Pacing back and forth had worked for me for the last 15 years. I had achieved every goal I had set my mind on.

As I continued to pace the floor, I was a bit worried but determined. I started thinking.

Ok, what should I do? Let me send an email to the director. Since that director was not present at my interview that day, maybe I should arrange for an interview with him now. Though I don't know if that is possible. I need to work at that company. It is the perfect company with great leadership and a great future. I can do great things if I can get my foot in the door. How can I get in? Maybe there is another position. But that position suited my skill set so well. Will I be able to fit in another position? Ahhh! That was a bad miss, Ankit.

C'mon, we'll try again. I need to improve my interview skills as well. I am horrible at interviews. What a great fit that job position was! Should I go take the job offer from the other company? My disappointment was overwhelming.

I had worked for five years at my previous company. It was a UK-based company and had office in Irvine, California, a city not all that far from San Diego. Our division was being transferred to another company. The day it was announced, I got a call from the UK division to come join them in Cambridge, England, along with an offer of a promotion and better pay. Also, the company that bought our division had offered me a much better position and better pay. But I acted like a maverick and rejected both offers simply because I wanted to work for my dream company in San Diego.

My benevolent friend Arun had advised, 'Ankit, don't take a risk. Accept the job from the new company and then you can interview with your dream company later.' I remember responding, 'Arun, my heart is like a child, and either it wants everything or nothing at all.' I had closed the door on two job opportunities in the pursuit of my dream job. Now, the third door had just been slammed shut by this rejection email.

Oh damn, I am jobless now.

I paced the floor briskly from one end of the living room to the other, determined to find a way out of the unexpected situation.

My cell phone rang and I rushed to the bedroom to see who was calling. It was a number I did not recognize. Hoping it would be from the company's HR, I picked up the phone.

'Hi, this is Steve from your stock brokerage firm.'

'Hi, Steve.'

'How are you doing, Sir?' he asked.

Hearing that greeting, I got a bad feeling. It was one of those sensations when you're speeding, and the cop catches you and first thing he asks is, 'How are you doing, Sir?' You have a feeling that something bad is about to happen.

'Sir, have you checked your stock account?' he asked.

'No, I was on vacation for a month.'

'Sir, you should. You are on margin call. You will need to deposit some funds within three business days or we will need to take some action.'

'Okay,' I said trying to keep my reply as terse as possible. I knew what a margin call was, but I was receiving it for the first time. I was overleveraged on my stock account by taking loans based on the value of my stocks. Though the value of my account was more than $200,000, more than $100,000 was on margin loans. I had never received a margin call as my stocks had been doing so well.

'It's been chaotic in the market over the last few weeks. Good luck.'

'Thanks, Steve.'

I hung up and hurriedly logged into my stock account. There was a sea of red. Most of my stock value had lost more than half its value in one month. I looked at the bottom row; it showed negative $25,000.

Okay. So, from the net profit of more than $100,000, I am down $25,000. Hopefully, this is just a knee jerk reaction from the market. Mr Market being manic depressive as Warren Buffett often said.

I quickly shut down the laptop trying to get back to my peaceful state of mind. I did not want to be dragged around by the storm of stocks just like I had been in the last few years. A loss of $25,000 is fine; I will cash out whatever is left.

As I stood still for a few moments, staring into nothing, I recalled the webpage of my stock account that I had just seen a few moments ago. Something did not seem right about my evaluation. I could sense a feeling of dread followed by the sound of a fast approaching train. I wish it weren't true, but the truth hit me.

Wait, if I'm down just $25,000 in my portfolio, why did I get the margin call.

I began to imagine the worst-case scenario, still hoping it was not true. I opened the laptop and looked again at the account.

Oh, no...no...no...no.

I put both my hands on my face and gasped loudly. I realized that the negative $25,000 in my account was the net number that was owed after selling all my stocks at the current market value. So, at this time, if I sold all my stocks and walked away, I would still owe the brokerage firm $25,000. I was in utter disbelief.

I looked at CNN.com. It had a picture of a stock broker and the headline informing the public that the stock market had collapsed. The stockbroker looked aghast with his head resting on his hands, echoing my current feelings. I browsed through other websites and saw the same headline everywhere: the stock market had collapsed.

I began to sweat profusely. I could not believe that in just a few moments, my life savings of more than $100,000 had been wiped out. To top that off, I still owed more than $25,000 to the brokerage firm. Ah, and to add to the misery, I had no job.

After a few moments of staring at laptop and then the ceiling and biting my nails, I got up and started pacing the floor of my living room. I was hoping to find a solution to my dilemma.

There has to be a light in this darkness. I've got to fight it out.

As I started walking briskly, I tried to focus on the problem.

My analytical mind was getting into action.

I had just lost more than $100,000...my savings of eight years in the stock market. On top of that, I have to pay $25,000 in three days.

Arun was right. Why do I take all these risks in life? Maybe because I am an idiot. But I must take risks. You have to risk everything when you start from nothing.

Don't digress. Focus. Focus harder. What is the immediate problem?

The immediate problem is to pay $25,000 in three days. I should try to solve this problem.

But I lost all my life savings today!

Just focus on the immediate problem. How do I return the money in three days?

Do I have money anywhere else?

I checked my bank account. It had a few thousand dollars, but I also owed a lot of money on my credit card from my vacation. And I still have to pay rent, so putting more on my credit card was not an option.

Do you have any other accounts? You have worked for seven years. Do you have any other assets?

I had diluted all the company stocks to invest in the stock market. I had poured everything—pay cheque and income—into stocks.

Think…think, Ankit, there has to be a way. There is always a way.

Can I take a personal loan? The bank could give me a loan since I have a good credit history. But wait, they would require me to have a job. I need to reapply at that dream company. I have to get a job in that San Diego company.

Just take any job you can get now.

My next thought was that the economy seemed to be heading towards a recession. All job openings would be frozen. *Remember the 2002 economic crisis? This recession could be like that.*

This was not looking good for me.

Focus. Focus Ankit! There is always a way. You just have to find it.

Ok, where can I get the money? Can I sell something?

I had the Mustang. That should go for $5,000. The Jeep Wrangler was old but that should get another few thousand dollars. I tried to figure out if I could sell my surfboard.

However, on second thoughts, vehicles take a long time to sell and the surfboard will fetch only a few hundred dollars on Craigslist.

I was walking quickly with my shoulders feeling heavier and heavier with a load of anxiety. I was tumbling headfirst towards a bankruptcy. As I walked, I could feel the ground shaking. I could imagine a dark pool bubbling under my feet. In it, I could see my demons in the form of black octopus-like creatures with long tentacles reaching out, trying to grab and pull me down. I had been able to fight them off and keep them at bay. But this time around they looked stronger and hungrier.

I'm a fighter; I'm not going to lose. I kept pacing the floor as fast as I could. I tried to calculate again if I could use my credit card. I had a good credit history and account balance on a few of my credit cards.

But then, stockbrokers don't take credit cards. *Can I ask somebody for some money?*

I was aware of my family's situation in India. And none of my friends had that kind of money. When working on the trading website, the thousands of dollars were just numbers on my balance sheet. Now they had shifted from the virtual to the real world and had taken on a large, destructible form.

Will they cancel my green card if I am not able to pay the money?

I was not sure, but the prospect sounded scary.

Do they put you in jail? Do creditors come to your house in the US if you can't pay? Do they harass you like they do in India?

My mind was whirring with thoughts of impending doom.

It was bursting with my childhood memories of the time when my father lost his job and also a fortune in various businesses. Creditors used to bang on our doors repeatedly and we had to keep quiet inside the house with the lights off, waiting for them to leave. The night we were cruelly evicted from our house and the goons burnt all our stuff came back to me in flashes again.

Oh God, I won't be able to go through that ever again. I am ruined. Now, I started getting frantic by the minute, trying to stop from imploding. I was only a few feet away from the balcony when I felt this sharp darting pain in my chest and numbness in my feet. I stopped walking, trying to grasp this sensation and check my bearing. The cold winds engulfed my body. The pain in my chest was intensifying; my heart seemed to be pushing against my ribcage and it felt as if it was about to rip out of my chest.

As the shooting pain was becoming increasingly unbearable, I lay on the floor, hoping that the soft carpet would support my seemingly heavy shoulders and chest. Now, I was gasping for air with my mouth wide open and hoping to get some air from the open balcony. The rest of my body was beginning to feel numb. My stomach was coiling inside; it felt like someone was kicking me in the pit of my stomach. I got into a fetal position in a bid to protect myself. The pain in my chest was intensifying like a needle was being inserted into my heart. It was unbearable. *Oh God, I'm having a heart attack.*

My mind drifted to thoughts of another near-death experience I had while surfing a few years ago. I remembered feeling the sensation of drowning in the Pacific Ocean and gasping for breath and flailing to get out of the strong undercurrents. That day I was able to swim to the shore and save my life, but today I was feeling paralysed—my limp body being of no help.

Oh God, I am going to die.

I wanted the pain to stop.

Come on Ankit, you are a warrior. You have always risen after falling. Do not give up now.

My body was not cooperating—it was crying out in pain and did not want to go to battle with me anymore.

A moment from my childhood flashed in front of me—my older brother and I used to take turns acting out boxing scenes from the movie *Rocky* with its inspiring music playing in the background. Initially, Rocky would get hammered and fall to the floor. After a bit of melodrama, he'd get up. We would make our sister, Anamika, who was three years younger, play the referee and do the countdown. For this, she would be angry complaining that we took her away from her dolls and kitchen games. She would count very quickly from one to ten before Rocky completed the motivational dialogue. The fight would end with Rocky lying defeated on the floor.

My heart was doing the countdown at a fast pace, not giving my mind the time to push my body back into action.

The chest pain was relentless, unforgiving to the point where I was just hoping it was not a stroke but a heart attack. Maybe it was time to cross over to the other side. It was time to finally let go.

Let go, Ankit.

Maybe this was the ultimate peace I was yearning for.

In those fading moments, I regretted not having a child of my own, whose little fingers would have grabbed mine, whose giggle would have filled my heart.

With the one last ounce of energy l had left, I looked searchingly at the sky for some sign of hope. But there were just dark clouds all around. *Where is the light?* There was always a light guiding me.

As I let my consciousness sink into the abyss of darkness, I could hear fireworks far away.

2

JOY

I felt the glow as one lamp lit another.

The brightness pressed against my eyelids. In that radiance, I could see my mother's face as she held a lit diya (clay oil lamp) in front of the unlit one in my hand. It was the night of Diwali, the festival of lights.

This was in the mid-1980s in Mumbai and I was about seven years old. As I looked outside at the skyline from the kitchen of our fourth floor apartment, there were a lot of fireworks spectacularly lighting up the sky. I could hear the fireworks exploding everywhere. It seemed like the entire city of Mumbai was celebrating this festival.

'Ankit, go and place your diya on the other kitchen window.'

'Mom, why do we place the lamp on the windows?'

'Diwali is the celebration of the victory of good over evil, of light over darkness. We light these lamps and place them at the doors and windows of our house to attract more light. This is the light of knowledge and we invite it in so it can drive away our ignorance. Having cleared the darkness within, we fill our hearts with faith so we see things in a better light and with more hope.' It was easy to fill our hearts with faith then. We lived in a kind of a paradise, with our loving family, protected by financial security.

As I placed the diya on the edge of the kitchen window, I could see my whole apartment complex. Our housing society had eight buildings with five to seven floors. From one of our kitchen windows, we could see the buildings and the central complex.

As I looked around, most of the windows had colourful lights or diyas on the windowsills. On the ground, residents were starting to gather to enjoy the fireworks.

'Ankit, let's go. The fireworks are going to start.' Despite the fact that my brother Abhishek was about 18 months older than me, we were similar in height and build, both being thin and slender. We had similar interests in sports and other hobbies. He was more of a friend than an elder brother except when our parents scolded us. During those times, my sister and I would take a step back letting Abhishek take the brunt of the scolding.

Leaving the kitchen, we were joined by Anamika, then not even five. I noticed the rouge on her cheeks and the gloss on her lips.

I asked her, 'Did you apply Mom's make-up? Is that lipstick?'

'Make-up? Who dare put make-up?' she started to look around jokingly.

'You did, silly girl,' I pointed to the rouge on her cheeks, 'I'm going to tell Mommy.'

'It's Diwali night. We are supposed to wear new clothes and put on make-up.'

'Not sure about that last part,' I said, smiling at my sister.

'It's okay, Ankit. It's Diwali. Let's hurry,' Abhishek intervened.

We took the elevator and rushed outside. Holding hands, my siblings and I tried to make our way through the big crowd. A tall gentleman with a deep voice tapped my shoulder and asked, 'What is going on?'

We instantly recognized him. He was one of the movie stars who lived in our apartment complex.

'There is a fireworks spectacle that is about to start,' Abhishek replied.

'Who is the person bursting the firecrackers?'

'That would be my Dad,' I said. My heart filled with pride at the thought that movie stars would be the audience in awe of my Dad's Diwali show.

'My Dad told me the display of fireworks this year was going to be great. The fireworks are important from China,' Anamika said.

'Not important. Imported from China,' Abhishek quickly corrected her.

'Uncle, we saw your movie on our coloured TV,' Anamika said bursting with pride. Most of the TV sets in India at that time were only in black and white. That month we had replaced our black-and-white TV. It was amazing to watch all the programmes and movies in colours.

'Anamika, shhh! Don't show off. I'm going to tell Mom,' Abhishek cautioned her.

As we moved to the front of the crowd, our Dad looked at us and smiled. He had been waiting for us. He picked up an eight-inch cylindrical box from the cardboard container and placed it on the ground as our eyes followed him in awe. He had a commanding presence. He was a well-built, muscular person and had an aura of confidence that marks an Army man. He had maintained a mustache since his Army days. As he lit the fireworks, everyone could see his expensive watch and gold ring. There was a certain joy in his face having his family next to him. His sense of achievement was intensified having reached a particular level in society after putting in years of hard work. The Diwali fireworks were a celebration of life for him and had slowly become a much-awaited annual tradition in our apartment complex.

As my father lit the cylindrical box, eight fireworks erupted in rapid succession. They went up in the sky and exploded spectacularly, each having a unique pattern. There was a collective 'wow' from everyone in the crowd. None of us had seen anything like this before. There were three such cylindrical boxes and when the fireworks ended, everyone clapped. 'Happy Diwali, everyone,' my Dad called out as we began to head home. Mom, who was watching from the balcony, quickly moved into the house, ready to serve a sumptuous festive meal to my family.

After the fireworks, Dad asked us, 'How did you like it?' as he took Anamika in his arms.

'It was amazing,' we responded in the elevator. My father assured us that the night was not over yet.

'Really, what are we planning to do?' I asked, wondering what else was left to be seen on that splendid night.

'I have planned something exciting but only for Abhishek and Ankit. Anamika, you are young. So, you can only watch.'

As we went inside, there was a box of sweets waiting for us. Abhishek and I were very eager to know what Dad had in mind. After quickly finishing dinner, Dad called us into the kitchen. He asked Mom and Anamika to wait in a different room.

As my Dad went to one of the bedrooms to get the surprise, my mind raced with ideas—what could it be? Was it a Diwali gift? But we never had a tradition of gifts in our home. And why was Anamika kept out of it? She is always the first one to get a gift!

Maybe it's a reward for some achievement in school, I thought.

But Abhishek and I barely used to get passing marks in the qualifying exams we needed to advance to the next grade.

Definitely no reward for academics, I was sure of that. Nothing else barring academics came to mind.

Maybe it was some kind of punishment, I thought, since our principal constantly reprimanded us and Mom was frequently called to school. She, however, never relayed any of that to Dad. Or did she?

I looked at Abhishek. He shrugged his shoulders not knowing what to expect.

Dad came back holding three anaar (flowerpots). Instead of the floor, he placed those in our hands and said, 'Let's light it up towards the window.'

I felt a rush of fear and frantically thought, *What if this thing explodes in my hand or sparks start coming out from the side or if it gets heated and catches fire from the bottom? Oh, boy!*

I remembered the mishap involving my friend Sanju. It was a

day after the previous Diwali when four of us—Abhishek, Sanju, one other friend and I—had collected the leftover gunpowder from the fireworks the night before. We had put the gunpowder in a piece of paper and lit it. It was a random collection of gunpowder from different fireworks and thus it was exciting to imagine what mix of sparks it would produce. But when Sanju lit the gunpowder, it exploded with an uncharacteristic bang, and badly burnt his hands and legs. His hair, also burnt, had a smoky white look.

For the next three weeks of Diwali vacation, I spent most of my time giving him company at his house, since he could not step outside. We played chess all day long, waiting for his wounds to heal. I longed to go outside and play soccer or cricket but I had to be a good friend. I improved dramatically at playing chess. *Now if this anaar was to burst, I would be spending my time this Diwali too playing chess*, I thought. Maybe I will become a young disfigured chess grandmaster. My heart started to pound with fear.

Abhishek tapped my shoulder and asked me to look towards the door. Mom had her eyes closed and her hands folded as if praying to God. She would not have intervened when Dad was in his element and in such fervor. I nervously smiled at Abhishek; I could feel that he was afraid too.

'I am going to teach you boys about guts and courage. You know courage is not about having no fear, but having fear. It is about those moments when fear grips your mind and beats in your heart. Many people will run away from that feeling but the brave walk with it. They say to fear, "I will walk the distance with you but I will not change my path."'

He handed me one anaar. It was heavy as it was filled with gunpowder. I realized that my heart rate was going higher and higher at the thought of spending another vacation playing chess.

'Are you feeling fear beating in your heart?' my Dad asked.

'Yes,' we both replied.

'Good. In 1971, when I was in the Army, we were sent to the enemy lines during the war. We used to walk in the swamp in the forest. The entire area was paddy fields laden with mines and booby traps. The water came up to our shoulders and we held our rifles high above our heads. I used to be afraid of a potential enemy shooter hiding in the trees taking shots at my head. My heart would be beating at a rapid rate even though my chest was submerged in water. I would feel out of control.'

'The only thing that kept me going was the belief that I was doing this for my country. I knew that even if I died, I would be remembered fondly back home. It was the feeling that I was dedicating my life for something greater than myself. It was that very feeling that kept me moving forward on that long journey, with fear as my companion.'

'Always run towards your fear and not away from it. Feel the fear beating in your heart and use the power of your soul to go beyond it. Boys, are you ready to light it up?'

I was fearful for sure, but I knew I had to do it if my Dad wanted us to. Should I tell him about the incident involving Sanju and why I was so fearful? Maybe not. I decided that the Sanju story would be no match for his war story. So, I just held the anaar.

'Yes,' we both replied.

Dad lit those with a lighter. Initially, the sparks went up about a foot and then they caught momentum. In a few seconds, they were as high as six feet. I could feel the heat of the anaar in my hand, but at the same time I was mesmerized by the closeness of the shooting sparks. They were like prisoners of light escaping and gushing out of the container, celebrating their new-found freedom in the air. I looked at Abhishek and then at Dad. They were enjoying the sight as well. It was a glorious burst of sparks from our balcony. There were some astonished and truly appreciative observers nearby, but there were also some angry neighbours downstairs who seemed irritated at the commotion. Overall it was an exhilarating end to a wonderful and memorable night. That lesson about fear from my father that Diwali night was something I carried with me through many battles of my life.

The next day when Dad was at work, the four of us relaxed in the bedroom. Mom was a quiet, gentle woman and remained silent, especially in my Dad's presence. Afternoons were the time when she was alone with her kids and also the time for her to educate us. Mom sat with her back resting on the headboard of the bed, Abhishek lay with his head on her leg and mine on her other leg. Anamika lay facing my Mom's feet. This afternoon lounging was part of our everyday routine. Ordinarily she'd get a book or newspaper and talk to us about it.

This afternoon Anamika asked, 'Mommy, when did you meet Dad. Was it during his Army days or after?'

'Well, it was after he had returned from the war of 1971. He had served in the Indian Army for more than five years. He'd had enough of the fighting and had taken an early discharge from the Army.'

'Did they harass him when he came back from the war? Like they did with Rambo?'

I looked at Abhishek since he was the only one who had seen the movie with me. He smiled, confirming that he understood the reference.

'Who is Rambo?' Anamika quizzed.

'C'mon, you don't know Rambo? That is Rambo,' said Abhishek as he pointed to the poster of Sylvester Stallone in *First Blood* on the wall. Next to it was another poster, of Arnold Schwarzenegger in *Commando*. We gushed looking at our idols.

'He is the big brother of Bruce Lee,' Abhishek joked and winked at me acknowledging how cool we were to know about Bruce Lee and Rambo.

I winked back at him with one of the Bruce Lee's martial arts stances, shouting, 'Waakaaaww!'

Vacation time was for watching a lot of Hollywood and martial arts movies.

'We are talking about Dad here,' Anamika replied.

'Nobody harassed him after the war, but they got him married. Close enough,' Mom laughed and we all joined in.

'How did you meet?' I was curious to know.

'Well, Dad's family was in Dehradun, a small town in North India in the foothills of the Himalayas and we lived in the neighbouring village. We knew their family through some common family members. There were no movie theatres in our town, so we used to take a horse carriage and go to the cinema in Dehradun, which was the only one in the area.'

'Wow. You took a horse carriage to go see a movie?'

'Yes. Watching a movie was a special occasion. My aunt and I were big movie buffs. Once a month, we used to watch a movie, do some shopping and eat at the bazaar in Dehradun. It was an all-day event. Sometimes we stopped at your Dad's home since his Mom and my aunt were friends.'

Mom's father had passed away when she was only a few years old. She had to complete her schooling and college living at her aunt's place since her mother did not have a source of income and lived in a mere one-room cottage.

'Your dad was never home in Dehradun. He was in the Army and was placed all around India. I would get to hear interesting stories about him. He was quite a hot-blooded man. There is this story about him that one day his sister came home from college and told her mother how on campus the college student body president and his friends had teased her by passing some lewd comments. Your dad overheard this conversation.'

'Oh… what happened then?' I asked as we turned our heads around to listen attentively.

'That night he snuck out of the house and went to the college dorm all by himself. He proceeded to beat up the student body president and, for good measure, his roommates as well. Dad came back home and quietly went back to bed without telling anybody about what he had done. It was only when the student body president appeared at our home the next day with his blackened eyes and apologized to Dad's sister that his family found out what had happened.'

'He did not like school and college and felt that he had bigger goals. He left home at the age of 18 and got enlisted in the Army.'

'I don't like school either,' I said, trying to find some commonality.

'He was a sharpshooter in the Army. He had this long air pistol that he used when competing in the national-level shooting competitions. His brother would point to a mango on a tree and Dad would shoot it down with one shot.'

'Ah, that's why he has so many shooting medals.' In the living room, there was a frame containing about 15 such medals.

'He won many shooting championships at the national level during his Army days.'

'Wow that's so cool,' we responded in awe.

'So, when his marriage proposal came and I saw his picture in the Army uniform and his big mustache, I agreed without hesitation.'

'Dad looked like a hero,' my brother added referring to Dad's black and white pictures from his younger days.

'Like in *An Officer and a Gentleman*,' I said, still drunk on the movies.

'Mom is like Miss India. Pretty...like me,' my sister added.

'Then what happened? How did you both end up in Bombay from Dehradun?' I asked.

'After our wedding in 1974, Dad worked in the oil fields as a roughneck, just a labourer drilling oil. He worked on oil rigs in the sea for months. We travelled to multiple places around India. We were in the western state of Gujarat when Abhishek was born. Your dad was very hard working and dedicated to his company. When he returned home from the oil rigs, his body would be completely drenched in oil and sweat, and his face would be completely blackened. At the start, we lived in small towns around India and then the company moved him to the outskirts of Bombay. We lived there in a small one-room apartment. Then we moved into the city to a one bedroom flat and that is where Ankit was born. It was difficult living in a new city with young kids with Dad away for months at a stretch on the oil rig.'

'Dad kept climbing up the corporate ladder in the company. He helped set up the new office in Mumbai and hired over 50 people. Now he is a big manager in a multinational oil company. Dad had a large team reporting to him. He was a valuable employee, and this is why the company had given us this big apartment with all the perks in a posh locality near the beach. It is all about working hard in life. A good life has to be earned,' my Mom said emphatically trying to derive morals which her kids could take away.

'Are a lot of Dad's employees from Dehradun as well?' Abhishek asked.

'Yes, he has hired a lot of young guys. Many of them are misguided youth from small villages. He thinks he can give them direction by employing them.'

'Ah. That's why we have so many guests in our house.'

Our house was always full of guests. A lot of them were young people who were coming to the city to look for employment. We had a few of our cousins living with us for many years until they were settled in their careers. Even casual acquaintances would stay for a few weeks. Once while coming back from Dehradun on a train, Dad made friends with a family. The entire family stayed with us for three days since they didn't know anybody else in the city.

'I guess hosting guests is our way of giving back,' Mom said.

'We should put up a sign saying "Guesthouse" outside our door,' I suggested. 'There are too many guests. And the worst are the ones who come from the US.' There were many friends from Gujarat who had NRI (non-resident Indians) relatives living in the US. Since Mumbai had one of the few international airports in the country and our house was in the vicinity, it became the hub for not just friends but even friends of friends. Dad used to pick them up from the airport in his car and Mom would cook delicious meals for them. They would feast at our place for a couple of days before leaving for their destination ahead. And then they did the same thing flying back to the US.'

'With their huge and heavy suitcases?' Abhishek asked.

'Oh yes. Those are so heavy. Last time when Patel Uncle came, the elevator was not working. Abhishek and I had to carry his luggage up three floors. They were heavy as hell! Dad made sure that we were part of the free hospitality services he was offering; he would ask us to bring in the groceries too.' I said.

'We don't even know who Patel Uncle is,' Abhishek added.

'He is a very successful businessman in the US,' Mom said.

'So he is a friend of Atul Uncle,' I said. Atul Uncle had become friends with Dad in Gujarat when he was staying as a paying guest at their place.

'No, Patel Uncle is best friends with Dhruv Uncle, who is the business partner of Atul Uncle,' Mom clarified.

'But why do we have to carry things for them—a friend of a friend of a friend?' I questioned, clearly not happy with the situation.

'It is more than that. It is about doing good karma. In life, you must do good deeds for others. Helping people in need is our way of giving back to this world.'

'But why?' I asked, still not convinced.

'Because all the good deeds come back in the circle of life. That is the law of karma.'

Back then, I did not know how future events could violate the laws of karma and my parents would soon be punished for their kind deeds. I believed that my mother was a person of character who saw it as her job to provide us a good moral foundation.

'Mom, what is the difference between karma and dharma?' Abhishek queried.

'Karma is what one does in life, the human deeds. Dharma is the compass that guides one's life.'

'Is this part of the Hindu religion?' I asked.

'Religion is just a pointer to understanding one's own self and one's dharma, but not an end in and of itself. I think karma and dharma are principles or values that are above religion.'

'All religions together form one big pyramid. If you are at the lower end of that pyramid, you will only see differences and distances between religions. As you come to understand your religion more deeply, you elevate yourself in the pyramid and soon become aware of the commonality among religions. You become closer to other humans who practise other religions. You understand that there is more that binds us all together than what separates us.' Mom would always encourage us to respect all religions and she would often read stories from other religions.

'We just need to make sure we offer good service to all people and ensure we are on the right path, guided by the correct principles at every moment.'

'How do we know what the correct path is?' I asked.

'When you ask for guidance earnestly, a quiet voice within you will whisper in your heart and point you in the right direction. But the guided path may be difficult and your fears might try to subdue that voice. And that is the time when you must fight your fears, as Dad explained to you yesterday.'

'I can't hear that voice, Ma,' I said closing my eyes, taking a few quick breaths.

'It will come to you in time. The question is will you be strong enough to walk that path or not. How you face the storm will define the person you become in life.'

'I won't run away from it,' I promised her.

'Me neither,' Abhishek added.

'I want to be on the fashion ramp,' Anamika joked. 'Can we talk about movies or about the upcoming Miss India pageant?'

'Mom, can you read some stories about the mafia?' Abhishek asked.

In the mid-1980s, the mafia was quite rampant in Mumbai. Every other day, there were stories in the newspaper about killings among the rival gangs or about police encounters executing mafia gang members. On some afternoons, Mom would read such articles with great dramatic effects to heighten the excitement. The stories were interesting but not scary because the narratives sounded so distant and separated from our lives. Little did we know that they were on a course of collision.

'No, Mom. Tell us about the time when we adopted Anamika,' I urged, winking again at my brother. My brother and I used to tease my sister that she was the daughter of Shakuntala, our domestic worker who had been working for us for 10 years.

'She is Shakuntala's daughter,' my brother added.

'Not Shakuntala...say Shakuntala Aunty...treat her with respect,' Mom said in a stern voice. She always asked us to treat everybody with respect, irrespective of whatever work one did.

'Yes, Shakuntala Aunty,' Abhishek added.

'Isn't that the reason why Shakuntala is so fond of Anamika and takes more care of her than us?' I questioned.

'That is true, she does adore Anamika a lot,' Mom said, now in on the joke with Abhishek and me.

'No, Mommy. I am your daughter only,' my sister started crying, hugging my Mom's legs harder, as the rest of us laughed.

'It is too late. You must do your homework now. We will talk more about this tomorrow afternoon. You kids should take a nap. Close your eyes.'

She then moved her hands from my forehead to the top of my head. I don't know what charm it was, but my mother gently tapping my head would put me to a deep slumber.

~

Our daily routine on weekdays began with Mom waking us around

7.00 a.m. Waking up involved multiple stages. The first attempt was a call from Mom, 'Kids, get up. It's morning. Time to go to school.' This was then followed by wiggling our toes under the bedsheets. It would persist with moving into a fetal position. If we wouldn't be awake even by then, the comforters would be pulled off. And if somehow we managed to stay in bed, there would be a splash of cold water in the face. That would jump-start us for sure.

Our school was a 15-minute walk from home. We always felt a sense of excitement going to school. It was probably because we never went there with the idea of studying; it was more about meeting friends and playing sports during the physical training class on the beach across the road. It was a small private English medium school owned by two idealistic and disciplinarian brothers. We had a very strict uniform code—each student was required to have clean white and grey uniform, a tie and canvas shoes, a badge and a handkerchief. Each student was required to have oiled their hair, which we faked sometimes by putting water just before the class monitor would touch our heads to check.

When we would enter class, we would pick small pieces of chalk and sit at the back benches. As the teacher would turn around to write on the blackboard, we would throw the chalk pieces at our classmates. Before the teacher could turn back, we would return to our 'following the class lecture attentively' pose.

But the teacher was smarter. Sometimes, she would turn her head while writing on the blackboard and catch us red-handed as we stood up, ready to throw the chalk pieces.

'Ankit, you wretched scoundrel, get out of my class.' My favourite English teacher Mrs Chauhan would yell at me. Sometimes, as I was thrown out of the classroom, I would see Abhishek standing outside his classroom waving at me with white chalk residue on his hand as well. We were two peas in a pod.

We would return home around 1.00 p.m., have lunch, listen to Mom's well-prepared lecture of the day and take a short nap.

After that, we studied and completed our homework which was a prerequisite for going outdoors to play at 5.00 p.m.

The tradition in our apartment complex, as in most housing societies in India, was simple—kids would go outside in the evening to play. As many as 20 to 25 kids would assemble and participate in sports together in the garden or empty areas between the buildings until 8.00 p.m.

We would then finish our dinner and be ready to go to bed by the time Dad came home from office. He would be very tired so we would not have much conversation except the normal greetings. Dad depended on Mom for communicating with the kids. Dad would sometimes joke that our mother had a PhD in everything and so it was important to listen to her.

On the weekends, we would play cricket on the beach with the residents of a neighbouring housing society, and later help Shakuntala Aunty and Mom with chores, which involved removing cobwebs from the flat's high corners and watering Dad's houseplants.

During our house chores, we would hear songs on the radio. Whenever there would be a good song, Anamika would turn up the music and start dancing. She loved dancing and performing. She would drag Abhishek to join her and he would break into a dance move; I would self-consciously join them a little later. Anamika would pull Mom to join them and after a few 'no, no', Mom would dance to the tune of the songs from 1970s. We would sing the lyrics loudly and groove on the song with Mom leading the charge. Anamika would get Shakuntala Aunty in the circle who would shyly join us, performing her traditional steps. Enacting the lyrics with hand gestures was a lot of fun and would quickly turn into a game of dumb charades. Such moments were carefree joys of childhood that I remember vividly to this day.

After lunch on Fridays—the most exciting part of the week for us—it would be time for an English movie. A small group of friends would chip in and get a video cassette of a good Hollywood movie or a karate movie. We loved the karate movies with Bruce Lee as well as the ones with Shaolin monks. Since only one boy in our circle of friends at the housing society had a VCR, we all went to his house to watch movies. It was exciting to wait as the black video cassette slowly rewound the movie. With all the curtains drawn, there would be complete attention as the movie started. Everyone sat motionless and focused. We watched without batting an eyelash. Even if we had to pee, we would hold it to avoid breaking the concentration of our friends. We were so completely absorbed in the movie that by the time it was over, the spirit of the Shaolin monks would be embodied in us and we would be talking to each other in funny Chinese. When Abhishek and I walked home, we would practise the actors' karate moves on each other. We would pick up sticks from the bushes using them for sword fights.

Sometimes we would take the wooden baton from the watchmen's booth. In our apartment, there were about six to eight security guards who took turns patrolling the area on foot or monitoring visitors from their respective booths. Sometimes in the afternoon, when they were not there or were sleeping in the booth, we would sneak in and take their wooden baton. Those four-foot-long sticks worked well as props for our martial arts fight scenes. Our favourite watchman to prank was this guard who would sometime be drunk on the job and remain asleep in his booth. People called him Bengali because he was from West Bengal. Soon, after we stole his baton, we would see Bengali running after us demanding for it to be returned. Bengali was bald and a little drunk and he resembled the drunken monk in the Shaolin movies. We would throw the baton away at the entrance and run back home.

At home, we would continue to act out the movie scenes. Sometimes, we would use Anamika as a prop. We would ask her to play the hostage or the damsel in distress, and Abhishek and I would take turns playing the hero and the villain. Other times, she would play the refree from Rocky, while one of us turned into Rocky. We had many toy guns in the house and caused a lot of collateral damage when we bumped into things, broke a few treasures or made a mess as we played out our fantasies.

In return for playing her part, Anamika would ask us to be a prop in her games. She had a big kitchen set and she asked us to be guests at her house party. She would have her makeshift house with pillows and a bedsheet in place and when we knocked on her pretend door, she answered as the hostess. She served us tea in small pink plastic teacups. We would still be in our Shaolin monk zone, accepting the tea with the Shaolin greetings. We would sit upright and drink the tea as Shaolin monks did.

'Biscuits for the guests,' Anamika said as she brought us biscuits in a plate.

'Shaolin eat no biscuits,' we would act as angry monks.

'Hey. This is my turn. You have to be my guest. You are not in your movie. We already did that.'

'No. Shaolin monks don't eat biscuits.'

She would begin to cry and start to call Mommy.

Abhishek would then agree, 'Ankit, let's be fair. Let's be good guests. Eat the biscuits.' We would eat the biscuits and the meals at the make-believe tea party.

In another one of her games, one of us had to put the crown on her head as she would win her imaginary beauty pageants and wave to the imaginary crowds. Sometimes, there was a ramp walk. Abhishek loved it and would join her walking on the ramp.

'Shaolin monks no walk on fashion ramp. Shaolin monks walk on the bodies of their enemies,' I said from the sidelines, as Anamika and Abhishek walked on the ramp practising different walking styles and facial expressions.

Sunday lunch was special too since it was the only time during the week when we ate non-vegetarian food at home. Mom was pure vegetarian and did not even eat eggs. But she made the best omelettes and chicken dishes. There was only one condition for

Mom to cook the non-vegetarian meal—she would not touch raw meat and so Dad would cut the meat and put it in the cooker. Mom then would add all the amazing spices. When Dad joined the Army, he had been pure vegetarian as well, but it was tough to survive being one. He soon decided to start eating non-vegetarian in the high-altitude areas. From that experience, he encouraged us to eat non-vegetarian food so that we could become good travellers and not be limited by our food choices.

Sunday afternoon was Dad's relaxation time. He would turn on the AC in the bedroom and close the blinds and go to sleep. We remained quiet in the other room so that Dad got his much-needed rest since he worked round the clock, six days a week. Once awake, he would take us to his office. Dad's office was part of a sprawling compound. He worked in a new three-storey building with plenty of indoor and outdoor space, surrounded by beautiful glass offices. It was a big compound with a lot of greenery in vicinity. Dad had hired a lot of gardeners and he loved planting trees. He loved showing us the new trees that he added to the landscape.

Dad encouraged us to meet all the engineers who were from other places, including the US and Europe. He would urge us to talk to them and learn from them. 'Just be frank with them,' he would tell us. We were a bit shy to talk openly but Anamika was not. She talked to them in her own version of Hinglish.

Sometimes Dad's manager, Mr Dastoor, would take us on a tour of the office. He was slightly younger than Dad. He was sophisticated, had studied abroad and had worked in many countries around the world. On one such day, we met Mr Dastoor in Dad's office.

'How is your school going?' he asked.

'Good. We like school. It is the studying we find boring.'

'What do you want to do when you grow up?'

'I want to be a sportsperson,' my brother said.

'Me too,' I added

'I want to be Miss India,' Anamika said.

'Mmm. Don't you want to become engineers and work in oil rigs with the cool electronics? It is a lot of fun. C'mon, let me show you the tools we use.'

Then he took us to the tools department and showed us the assembly of large metal pipes. There were open metal pipes with all the electronic gadgetry in it. 'The pipes are drilled into the sea floor and the tools inside provide information on whether there is oil in the sea bed. This is where we log the data and study it.'

'Wow!' Anamika and I found the instrumentation and electronics very interesting and would ask questions about their functionality.

'Can we work with these without studying?' I asked.

'No. You have to study a lot to get an opportunity to work on them. You will, right?'

'Mmm.' We were not sure about studying 'a lot'.

'Dad did not study but he is very successful,' I would add.

'Your Dad is a successful manager because he works very hard. In the seven years that I have worked with him, I have not seen a more disciplined and principled man. He is never late. Even when he lived two hours away from the office, he was always on time. He works hard so that you kids can get the chance that he never got. The opportunity to study, get a good education and make a good life. You have this opportunity. Study hard and choose a good career. Abhishek, how is your Math tuition coming along?'

Abhishek was very weak in Math and so Dad had got him a private tutor. Despite that, he would struggle with numbers.

'Uncle, you know, actually I love Math but I…I just cannot understand Math.' This was his oft-used line and we would all have a good laugh about it.

Mr Dastoor was a cool uncle and a very mild person. There was just one time I had overheard him speaking to Dad in a harsh tone. He was saying, 'Pramod, you have to keep your subordinates in control. The higher-ups will not tolerate forming unions in our company. There will be consequences…bad consequences. Get a grip on the situation.' Dad was trying to assure him that everything would be okay.

On Sunday evenings, Dad would drive us around the city and we'd eat at some fancy restaurant. On some days, he would take us to simple but popular food stalls set up on roadsides. Though it was street food, the taste of the dishes was amazing. Many cars would be parked outside these stalls, all waiting for food. Once the food would arrive, hood of the car would serve as the dining table. When we finished eating, we would buy ice cream or sweets. Driving through Mumbai on the roads hugging the coast of the Arabian Sea, we could see the bright lights, the big hotels. There were also many sleeping on the streets. The contrast highlighted the city's creed—'the City of Dreams' where dreams were made for some but broken for many. Upward mobility was a slow grind and downward slide was rapid as we were about to find out.

❧

Anamika, Abhishek and I were cuddled in Mom's lap when we got the news. I had just finished class VI and it was our summer vacation. It was during one of Mom's afternoon sessions when I casually asked, 'Why does Dad leave late and come early from work these days?'

'Well, there is a reason, kids. I have to tell you something important.'

Shifting from our relaxed position, we sat up and paid close attention.

'Unfortunately, Dad has lost his job.'

'Oh no!'

'This is a just a temporary situation,' and after a long pause, she added 'Dad is trying his best to work it out with the company's management.'

'But whatever happens, as a family we have to come together

and support him and each other in this difficult time. This is our dharma. Will you do that?'

'We promise, Mom,' we replied in unison.

I was just 10 years old when I rushed towards my first call of battle. At that moment, I did not look back. Had I looked back, I would have seen my childhood waving me goodbye.

3

TURNING OF THE TIDE

'It is just a misunderstanding. It will clear up soon,' Mom tried to give us hope about Dad's new reality at work. 'Dastoor Uncle left the company to work abroad and now there is a new management. Also, the employees are forming a union, much to the dislike of the new management.'

'But what has Dad got to do with that? He was always opposed to unions,' I inquired.

'Yes, that's true. However, many of the employees were hired by him and management now thinks he is somehow responsible for the formation of a union. Plus, they want to show their power,' Mom replied.

'But they are trying to exert power in the wrong way,' Abhishek asserted.

'Management should be asking for Dad's help to reign in the unions. He is the perfect go-between for the management-employee relationship,' I added.

Mom responded, 'He is trying to explain to them to allow him to handle the situation while trying to clear the misunderstanding.'

'He has worked hard for this company for more than 10 years. His loyalty should count for something,' I added.

'Hopefully, it will clear up in a few days and they'll reinstate him.'

Days became weeks and weeks became months but there was no change. Management stuck to its decision. Dad looked more and more worried. He would leave home in the morning and come back early evening. He did not talk much to us except the usual greetings; most of his communication with us was through Mom. At home, he'd either be on the phone or in the other room standing by the window. There were some changes in our routine as well. No more weekend parties or restaurant visits. Mom tried to compensate for the loss of these activities by cooking new dishes on Saturdays and Sundays. Our parents tried to ensure minimal changes in our lives so that we would not feel anxious or deprived. The flow of guests into our home reduced drastically as well.

It was during this time when my class VI final examination results came. The school required Dad to sign my report card. We were never interested in studies and it reflected in my report card. There were many red marks to indicate that I had failed many subjects. The only reason I could go to the class VII was due to the grace marks I received from my teachers and the principal. Generally, bad grades did not matter to us as long we got to move to the next grade with our classmates. My feelings about this changed because of the situation back home. There was tension in the air. I tried to defer showing the report card to my Dad. On the very last day, I somehow mustered enough courage as I needed to get his signature.

That afternoon he was standing by the bedroom window. I approached him cautiously and asked, 'Dad, can you sign my report card? I need to return it today.'

As I handed it to him, he opened it and saw the red marks and the barely passing grades. He was already in despair and this just added to his sadness. He was stone faced, but I could sense his sadness when he signed it and handed it back to me.

He looked into my eyes and said in a low tone, 'Ankit, you should know this. You kids are my pride and joy. Even if I lose everything in this world, I don't want to lose that feeling.'

Though he said those words softly, they hit me hard. Generally, Dad did not have long conversations with us and when he did, each word carried a lot of weight.

I went to school and showed the signature on the report card to my teacher. When I returned home with it, I stood next to the window in our living room. Dad's words still echoed in my mind and I could feel their weight on my shoulders. This was probably the first time in my life that I had felt as if my actions had actually hurt somebody. Life had just been a breeze until then. It had been a journey where I went from one fun thing to the next and never had to think about the past. But, at this very moment it felt as if my life had been paused and was asking me some very serious questions.

As I kept staring out the window, I felt guilty about hurting my Dad, and especially at a time when he was already disturbed. As the breeze blew, I could see the folded sheet of my yellow report card fluttering with the red marks inside. I stared at it in anger and started to tear it. First, I tore one half of it and then the other half into smaller and smaller pieces until it could not be torn any further. Then I let the shredded pieces fly with the wind. As the pieces of the report card fluttered in the air, I made a promise to myself, 'Never again.'

❧

It had been months since Dad started explaining himself to the new management, but they refused to budge from their stance. They must have believed that they would appear weak if they changed their stand. Meanwhile, the employees went ahead and organized a union. To recruit more union members, they needed to have a specific cause. They offered to help Dad fight his cause, since most of the staff sympathized with Dad's fruitless struggle to get his job back. He agreed to let the union file a lawsuit for the wrongful termination on his behalf against the management.

The union hired some big shot lawyer for Dad. The lawyer was confident in a quick resolution. He advised my Dad not to take a new position in a similar company until the case was settled. We were hopeful and counting on the Indian judicial system to deliver prompt justice. But months became years. Most court hearings of the case were adjourned. On every court date as Dad left for the court, we wished him good luck and hoped that that was the day when our ordeal would end. But he would come back later in the day and inform us that he 'just got another date after two months'. Sometimes the judge did not turn up at all and sometimes the other party or their lawyers didn't turn up. When all of them did show up, they would just set the next date to reconvene. It was a normal court procedure for lawyers and judges, but the delay was sheer anguish for us. We wanted to be as supportive as we could be.

When Dad was employed, he drew a healthy pay cheque, but he had not saved much. He often argued with his friends about the value that people put on money. In contrast, his friends believed that money was everything in life. He challenged their position with the assertion that 'Money is not everything. It is only a means to have a meaningful and productive life. So, we should spend the money on ourselves and on our families rather than just putting it in the bank or buying gold. Living miserably so that one can have a false sense of financial security is a morbid disease.' Following his own line of thinking meant he had not saved for a rainy day. As months became years, his small savings began to dwindle.

The only significant investment he had was in a plot of land in an upcoming town. He had bought the land in partnership with our previous neighbour who had already moved to another state. They had two daughters and one son, about our age, and we used to play together as kids. It was a big plot of land whose value had appreciated over time.

Dad said, 'I will go to Gujarat and tell Mr Sampat to sell our joint property. That will provide us with some much-needed cash.'

He left by train and came back dejected three days later.

He said, 'Sampat has run away to Bahrain leaving his family

behind. His wife and kids are still at his place waiting for him to come back. They have no idea where he is. They are now living in dire straits. I could not think of asking them about my property. I gave Mrs Sampat some money to help with the kids' school fees.'

I mustered a smile in reaction to the irony of the situation. Selling that piece of land at that moment was extremely critical, but there was no humane way to do it. And Dad had originally gone there to get some cash and ended up giving Mr Sampat's wife and kids some money to help them in their desperate situation.

Dad lost his job in 1988 when I was in class VI. As years passed, all the parties, dinners and long rides had dried up. The three of us were careful not to make any frivolous demands. We acted cautiously to avoid adding to our parents' misery. The monthly school fee was a big component of the expenses, but our parents decided to continue with the private English medium school. I began to focus more and more on my studies. It was my way of giving joy to my parents, since their children's education was a big deal for them. I was able to pass all my subjects in seventh grade with no red marks on my report card. I also got the 'Best Endeavour' award on Annual Day, which was for the student who had shown the biggest improvement in studies during the academic year. By the eighth grade, I had developed a strong disposition for Math and Science, and achieved the highest score in the former.

One day when I entered my empty classroom, I saw two kids teasing an autistic student. They were mimicking how he spoke and laughed hysterically at him. I quickly intervened and told them, 'Don't you do ever that to my friend again.' One of those bullies was running for the school student body association election and I decided to compete against him because it was the right thing to do. I won the election with one of the biggest margins in the school's history. I became the school head boy and part of the student council. My first decree as representative in my class was that no one was allowed to make jokes at anyone's expense and no one was allowed to laugh at anyone's physical disability. In addition, I made it clear that bullying would not be tolerated. Anyone not following this order would be boycotted from our class and no one in our class would talk to them. Being actively involved in academics, sports and extracurricular activities in school was a good distraction for me from what was happening at home. The only downside was that as part of the student body, I had to check all the boys' hair for oil.

By the ninth grade, I got the highest marks in every subject but one, and got the first rank in class. On the school's Annual Day, I collected my prize, which was a stack of books from the celebrity guest. But I decided not to collect the official photograph of it since we had to pay for it.

⁂

At the start of the 1990s, India was experiencing a major transformation when it opened up its economy to global investment. Suddenly, there were important international products in the markets. A noticeable change was the introduction of cable TV. Until then, there had been only one TV channel called Doordarshan with a few hours of programming. Now there were many international and Indian channels with round the clock airing of interesting programmes. Since our outgoing activities were restrained, we were entertained with the diverse programmes on TV. Among the new channels we liked was MTV, which played music all day long. Our favourite channel showed pirated Hollywood movies. Our fascination for this new revolution in TV broadcasting did not last long, since my parents decided to discontinue cable as one way to reduce our household expenses. Abhishek and I accepted that decision, but Anamika was less agreeable.

'I want the cable. I wanted to see the Miss World Beauty pageant this weekend. Miss India is participating. She is going to win,' she insisted.

However, our cable was already cut.

Abhishek told Mom, 'We should have waited until Monday so Anamika could have watched her show.'

'I guess so. We can't control certain things. I wish we could have done that,' Mom agreed.

Seeing Anamika sad that day made me feel low too. Over the last few years, we had accepted the situation that we could not ask our parents to take us out or buy new clothes. This was the first time that something we had or liked was being taken away due to financial duress. I did not readily accept that idea. I felt it was not fair for Anamika to feel sorrow at the mere age of 10.

That Saturday morning as I was leaving home, I saw an extra cable wire running between my house and my neighbour's. It seemed to be not carrying any signal and therefore I thought I could use it to create a path for our cable signal. With a hammer and a nail, I pierced the neighbour's cable and then put one nail through the dead wire and another through its other end and our cable. When I turned the TV on, there was signal, but with a lot of noise. I adjusted the position of the nail quietly, hoping the neighbours did not open their door. After a few adjustments, I finally achieved success. Every channel could be watched crystal clear.

I called out to Anamika and Abhishek. Anamika was super excited to see that the TV was working. 'Yeah, we are going to be able to watch the beauty pageant.'

I flexed my arm and shouted, 'Waakaww' with the Bruce Lee pose. I felt that it was a small victory against the odds—it was a glimmer of light in view of the dark shadows that had been cast over our family for far too long.

After the moment of exhilaration ended, Mom took me aside and said, 'You did smart work on the cable. Anamika is happy that she can see her show. But we have to do the right thing. You know that, right?'

'Yes, Yes Mom. I will remove the nails and the cable once her show is over.'

'Good,' she said.

'Mom,' I said in a reflective tone, 'I think I am going to be an engineer. I will be an electrical engineer and work on electronic equipment, just like the ones in Dad's previous company's lab.'

'That's great, Ankit!'

'I will not just be any engineer. I will be an engineer who will make both you and Dad proud.'

That was the day I made my life's most significant decision. Over the next few days, I charted out the path to achieve my goal. I had to score very well in my class X board examinations. Based on that score, I would get into junior college for class XI and XII. There were three options in junior college: science, commerce or arts.

To get into the science stream in junior college, I needed to score well in my class X board examinations. I was required to score very high marks in math, physics and chemistry in class XII board exams to get a seat in the College of Engineering for a bachelor's degree. There were many good students and only a few merit seats generally available for engineering. The competition was fierce.

After years of waiting, Dad realized that his court case was not going anywhere, and his savings were down to nil. Based on his contact with a friend in a different oil venture, Dad started a trading company to supply goods to that oil company with things like cleaning supplies and items like engraved mugs and pens. Dad asked us kids to come up with a name for the company. Since one of my favourite subjects was French, I came up with *Ami*.

'*Ami* means friend in French and our trading business would be like a friend to the companies.'

'That's a good idea, Ankit. Ami Enterprise it is,' Dad proclaimed proudly.

Within a year, the business started to take off and the goods

Dad was supplying started to increase. Things were getting better, which resulted in a stable flow of money. The oil company, he was supplying to, appreciated the quality of Dad's work and they asked him to supply specialized goods. They asked if he could provide the special logging paper that was used on the oil rigs for logging data collected from underwater. There was only one company in North India that specialized in manufacturing this paper. Dad would have to get this product from North India and transport it to the company in Mumbai.

The special logging paper was very expensive and specialized. There were a lot of initial investments required, but the margins were good. We all knew that after a few successful deliveries, we would be out of financial trouble. It was highly risky in terms of investment, but it came with rewards. Dad decided to accept the offer. He borrowed a lot of money and went to a factory in Haridwar, North India, where the paper was manufactured and made an agreement with the supplier. Upon returning to Mumbai, Dad had completed all the arrangements for delivery, paid the money and initiated the process. The company would load the papers in a goods compartment in Haridwar and fax the delivery papers to Dad. He would then collect the papers once the train arrived in Mumbai the following day. Packaging was the key. This specialized paper had to be handled with great care. Any minor damage would make the entire lot unusable.

That night, Dad received the confirmation fax from the company that the huge order of papers had been dispatched and was on the train. As a family we were thrilled about the prospect of Ami Enterprise's first major delivery. Finally, there was a glimmer of hope and everybody was excited. We ordered take-out from a good restaurant, which we hadn't done in a very long time, and we enjoyed the chicken gravy watching the rain outside. The next morning Dad and some helpers left for the train station. Together they were to unload the paper from the train and load it into the taxi and bring it home.

We were waiting at the window watching the rain when Dad arrived in the taxi with huge bundles of paper. As I looked down, even in the rain, I could see that he looked tense and was sweating profusely. The package looked wet, especially on the bottom. He asked the helpers to bring the package in the house and gave them some money and asked them to leave. He was trying to wipe off the sweat from his forehead. Mom gave him a glass of water and a towel to dry off. He was clearly shaken up, staring anxiously at the package. Then he thrust himself onto the couch. Everyone was staring at him in silent anticipation of his next words. It did not look good. With his hands still on his forehead and over his eyes, he said, 'The paper has been spoilt by the rain. There were leaks in the goods compartment of the train and the rainwater seeped in and damaged all the merchandise. The whole bundle of paper is wet. It is now completely useless.'

'But isn't supply the company's responsibility?' I asked.

'No, once it is dispatched and loaded onto the train, it is on us. There is no insurance and I don't think the Railways is going to reimburse us,' he said, still staring at the wet cargo. 'This is our bad luck, this is a huge loss. I have taken out big loans for this. The creditors are going to be all over us.'

Everybody felt sad and no one said a word. We knew that the creditors would soon come knocking at our doors. In the quiet of our home and the noise of the rain outside, we braced ourselves for the next battle ahead us. The persistent rain now felt like a big annoyance, whereas it had been such a great childhood companion. I began to reminisce about it as I looked from the window.

The first rain of the monsoon season was an experience each Mumbaikar, rich or poor, enjoyed. Everyone would be looking up to the sky for rain, because the weather forecaster had no idea when it would come.

The unpredictability of the rain was one of its mythic traits. One afternoon, it would rain magically when no one was expecting it. It would start with some strong winds, then just a few drops for some time. 'Was that a rain drop or is someone drying their wet clothes on the top floor?' one would wonder. After that, it would start pouring. People in the streets and in their homes would all yell with excitement. What is beautiful about rainfall in India is that the temperature does not drop much once it rains. So, it makes for a perfect weather to be enjoyed.

Abhishek and I would run outside and stand in the rain to experience the heavenly show. With our hands outstretched, we would look up, open our mouths and taste the rainwater with our tongues. With the dust on the ground settled, there would be a pleasant scent from the wet mud. Raindrops would do a tap dance in the puddles. There was something divine about the raindrops and I would often look up in the sky to see the source of the drops.

'Who turns this shower on? I might be able to see something if I look intently.' The rain drops would fill my eyes. We would get completely soaked. As we looked around the building complex we would see women and domestic workers rushing to the windows to remove the clothes that were left to dry on the windowsill. Some clothes flew off the sill due to the strong winds.

We would walk outside the apartment gate to the narrow street that led to the main road. From the main street, we could see a lot people enjoying themselves in the rain. They were happily chatting, laughing and walking around having a good time.

Sometimes, songs on rain would start playing in some of the shops and people would dance on the streets. We would pass our school and wish that it would be closed the next day if it was still pouring. Next, a walk to the beach would follow. As we walked on the sand, grains of sand would blow in our faces. We would push our way through the gusts of the wind and walk through it. It was a fun and challenging game. The wind along with the rain would slap our faces with great intensity. We felt like superheroes resisting the evil forces. We were pitting ourselves against the natural elements.

Growing up near the beach, I had a special bond with the sea. The calmness and violent nature of the waves, the high and low tides and the beautiful sunset were something I could watch in awe for hours. I would feel this innate urge to be a part of the violent churn.

'Let's jump in the water,' I urged my brother.

'No, it's too risky.' My brother was very circumspect and aware of his responsibility as the elder brother. He was naturally calm, just like Mom. I was more impulsive and inherited Dad's risk-taking tendencies.

'C'mon, one dive in the water. In and out.'

'No. Mom said no to swimming in the water. We can walk along the shore and splash water like this,' he said surprising me by splashing water on me. I ran and chased after him.

Somehow battling against the force of the wind and rain, we were finally able to reach the end of the beach. From there, we would turn around and walk in the direction of the wind. Before starting back, we would pause, close our eyes and spread our hands. We would hold our position as the wind would push us from behind urging us to move forward. I would then let go of the resistance and let my body be one with the wind.

The wind would take control of our bodies and swiftly transport us. With the winds guiding us, we swirled and spun. The force of the wind was so strong that our feet touched the ground very lightly. For brief moments, we flew like a plastic bag in the wind. With the wind as our carrier, we trusted it to take us home. Abandoning myself to wind and rain, I found complete freedom and joy.

By the time we came back, all the streets were clogged with water up to a foot high. We would get loose book pages from the grocery store and make paper boats and put them in the stream of water and chase them as they quickly floated towards the drain. In the rain, earthworms came out from the ground and we'd pick them up with thin sticks and put them on the paper boat and give them a free but unwanted water ride.

We would be completely drenched, and our faces covered with mud and sand. Sometimes, Mom and a neighbour would be standing outside the building buying vegetables from the street vendor or just chatting. As we approached from a distance, her friends would ask, 'Mrs Gupta, are those your children? I can't even recognize them. 'Yes, those are my boys,' she answered. We would then dry ourselves and settle with a warm glass of chocolate milk.

The rage I felt at our losses due to the rainfall belied those beautiful childhood memories.

A few days later, during a somber lunch, the whole family sat at the table while Mom served food. Everyone was silent.

As Mom was putting the food on the table, I noticed that she was not wearing the gold bangles or rings or her gold necklace that she had always worn. I looked at Dad. He had his eyes lowered and was deep in thought. I looked at his hand. He was neither wearing his gold ring, nor his gold chain.

I was in complete disbelief and anger. As I was about to say something, my brother pinched my hand and shook his head forbidding me from opening my mouth. So, I finished lunch quietly, still trying to make sense of what I was seeing and how to alleviate my feelings of claustrophobia. I got up from the table after finishing lunch and went to the other room to look outside. I was still angry at the rain. I was hoping that the rain would somehow quell my inner rage.

Abhishek came in and put his hands on my shoulders. I shrugged it away.

'Where is all of Mom's jewellery? Even Dad's favourite ring is gone.'

'Dad and Mom had to sell them to pay off the creditors.'

'Damn. This is not fair. Let me at least talk to her about it and tell her how sorry I am. I feel so bad.'

'Your feeling bad will not make her feel better. It will only make her feel worse.'

'So, what should we do?'

'Absorb it. Sacrifice is the truest form of love, Ankit. As a family, we are tightly bound to each other. Each of us will encounter adversity of one kind or another. The more we absorb the pain, the less we will pass on to our family members.'

'This is not fair. I hate this. You know Mom had worn those bangles at her wedding.'

'Our parents made this sacrifice for us and now we have to make sacrifices as well. Just don't talk about it. Let's face this hardship quietly and bravely. Let's do everything we can to make them proud.'

'I can't explain my feelings at this moment. I feel so awful seeing Mom and Dad in this situation,' I said, sadness writ large on my face.

'I know, Ankit. I know. We just have to fight it out,' Abhishek encouraged me as he put his arms around my shoulders.

For a while, both of us stood silently looking expressionless at the rain outside as if we were in someone's mourning ceremony. A part of us died that day. I pledged to myself that my parents' sacrifices will not go in vain and got back to my studies. The next day as I was studying, Dad gave me a thick stack of paper. It was the damaged logging paper which had dried out but still had the watermarks. 'Now that it is useless as logging paper, why don't you use it for your studies? Make it valuable again.'

Those papers were useful for my class X examinations as I used them for notes and writing practice tests. Besides, I used them as a symbol of my fight against the turning of the tide. I topped my school with the highest score. I scored 95 in French, which was one mark less than the highest in the state.

Mrs Chauhan, who taught us French and English, was my favourite teacher. She was in her 60s, was petite and had white hair. She reminded me of a female Santa Claus except that she was always angry with the kids. But, she was a very good teacher. Some days, she would ask me to read aloud in class from the French textbook. As I would begin reading in French, she would put her hands on her ears and say, 'Ankit, please stop. I can't take it anymore. You are single handedly killing the sweet French language with your pronunciation.' I would say, 'Oui Oui Oui Oui, Madame,' in my best French impression and the classroom would explode into a fit of laughter.

Even when I was struggling with my studies in class VI, though she always scolded me in public, in private she would encourage me, 'Ankit, you are barely making the passing grade in most subjects. You are so much better than this.'

After my class X results, I went to meet and thank her. I thanked her in French as well with a 'Merci Beaucoup, Madame' which brought a rare smile to her face. She was very proud that I had finally realized my potential.

⁂

My class X board score was good enough to get me into science stream of a good college. I picked a prestigious junior college, which was about a 30-minute bus ride from home. All my school friends were excited at the prospect of going to junior college. 'No more uniforms, beautiful girls not in ponytails, skipping class and no more oil in our hair. College is going to be so much fun!' my best friend exclaimed.

'And the class XII board examination results in two years will decide our careers. That is super important, man.' I tried to stifle the pleasant but distracting thoughts in my mind and concentrate on my studies. Though my resolve kept me focused on the next challenge at school, thoughts of having fun did enter my mind.

No longer having to wear a school uniform was a welcome change. However, the school uniform had served us well when we needed to conceal our dire financial situation from our friends.

When everyone wore a uniform, no one knew who was rich or poor. But that was about to change in junior college. I looked at the jeans I was wearing. For the last few years, Abhishek and I had had just two pairs of jeans between us. We had decided that we would share them and wear them on alternate days so that it would appear to our friends that each of us had two pairs. Also, we had worn the same ones for years now and these jeans were worn out. Instead of asking our parents for a new pair, we would get the tears fixed by getting the tailor to put a patch. Also, our shoes had worn out, but we got them fixed by the cobbler.

On my first day of junior college, I stopped by the cobbler on my way to school. We had known him since we were kids and we always exchanged greetings.

'Uncle, please fix the shoes. They are torn on the bottom by the toe. Just put a piece of leather at the base from the inside and stitch it up. Just make sure that the stitches are not visible, please.'

'Okay. Wow, Ankit baba, you are in college now. I remember you and your brother used to walk to school from here when you were five or six years old and always said hello to me. How you have grown!' he reminisced.

'Yes,' I answered kind of abruptly. I did not want to chat fearing I might be late for classes.

'College will be fun. Will you have a girlfriend?'

'Why not? Why won't I?' I snapped back somewhat defensively. Perhaps he doubted me because of my torn shoe. 'Please. Hurry, I will miss my bus. Just stitch up the shoes so nobody can see the stitches.'

On the first day in bus, my heart fluttered at the thought of seeing some beautiful girls in my classes. I was not disappointed. There were some very pretty girls who wore very fashionable clothes. I thought about talking to them, but I was not sure what to say. They were always with a group of cool guys who were from very rich families. Some of the guys drove their own cars to college and they took the girls for a spin.

C'mon Ankit. Talk to the girls, I would say to myself. *You are decent looking, the topper of your school, your former school's head boy and great in sports. They might find you interesting.* I egged myself on.

Doubts crept further in as I looked at my jeans and shoes.

Hmm, I don't know. Wonder if the stitches on my jeans are visible. And what about my shoes? The cobbler has done a good job but the stitches are still visible from some angles. I thought as I adjusted my stance to hide the stitches.

Maybe not. If they go for coffee, I won't have money to pay for them. I only have enough money for bus fare, I realized as I checked the coins in my pocket.

Forget it, focus on your studies. Remember that you have to become an engineer. The class XII board exams are in two years.

With those thoughts, I did not approach a single girl. I was not part of any group and generally sat by myself. One day, when I arrived early to class, this group of beautiful girls and rich guys had already arrived and were sitting, chatting and having fun in the classroom. I resolutely prepared to talk to them, but in the end my inferiority complex got the best of me. I went to a corner of the classroom and sat alone. It was a large room and the desks were placed on small elevated steps to provide better visibility. I sat on the very last bench on the top, not knowing what to do alone while the rest of the group was having fun. To avoid looking foolish, I opened a textbook and started reading it. One of the cool dudes approached me.

'What are you reading?' he asked teasingly.

'Chemistry,' I said, though I wasn't really reading anything at all.

'Guys and girls, we have a studious student here studying before the class starts,' he mocked. The rest of the group laughed.

'He is studious and good looking. Are any girls interested?' he asked.

I ignored him while I continued to stare at my book and waited for him to disappear.

'Here, let me sit with you and get enlightened as well,' he said, smirking from ear to ear. As he tried to move in close and touch my book, I was tempted to react.

I stood up and said, 'I am the son of an Army man. Do you really think you can bully me?'

I stared straight into his eyes and took a step towards him. My aggressive approach surprised him, and as he took a step backwards, he slipped on one of the steps. He recovered his bearings and rushed away from me. It appeared that I had pushed him but I had not. He rejoined his group, who were now looking at me with surprise and contempt.

I walked out of the classroom.

There goes my chance with the girls in this class. They will think I am some kind of an aggressive freak and better to be left alone.

Dejectedly leaving the room, I noticed a brochure for the college cricket team posted on the message board. It read, 'Try-outs for the cricket team.' This was a prestigious junior college and it had a very good cricket team that was renowned throughout Mumbai. I thought it would be great if I could be part of the sports team. I was confident that I was talented enough to get on the team.

Maybe that is the way to get the girls to recognize me and cheer for me. Maybe we could become friends that way, I thought with a smile.

As I read further, it stated that the trials were the following week and players had to come dressed in sports attire: white shirts and white pants. I had a white T-shirt but no white pants.

I'll just wear jeans. Not a big deal. I will not ask my parents for white pants.

On the day of the trials, I went to the cricket grounds. I was wearing a white T-shirt and light blue jeans and sport shoes. It was afternoon and the sun was at its peak. The grounds were big and they had a batting pitch in the middle surrounded by blue nets. There was a big line of students trying out for batsman positions and then there was a separate line for bowlers.

I joined the long line for batsmen waiting for my turn. I would get to face six balls to showcase my talent. I started thinking of the shots I wanted to play. I started to do some shadow practices of hitting the ball.

A head coach and his assistants were trying to organize everything. As the coach glanced at our line from afar, he gestured his assistant to call someone from our line. It seemed like he was pointing towards me.

'The coach is calling you,' the assistant said and motioned me to come with him.

Has the coach seen me play before? Maybe he saw me at the beach. I had played some good match innings at the beach. Not sure why he is calling me over. I was confused at the early call.

As I walked towards him with the assistant, I could see the coach walking towards me in a haste. His expression surprisingly was one of anger. As he approached me, he stood uncomfortably close; his face was centimetres away from mine, his toes less than inch apart. He stared into my eyes.

'Did you read the trial brochure, boy?' he shouted.

'Yes, coach. I did.'

Then he removed one from his pocket and pointed to the line stating, 'Come in sports attire: white T-shirt and white pants.'

'Do you think you are above the rules?'

'No, Sir. I did read it.'

'Then why are you in jeans?'

'Aaah…hmm…'

'You guys…You think that you are in college now and so you can do whatever you want. No respect for rules and traditions.'

He was raising his voice which seemed amplified by his proximity. His face was so close that I could see spit coming out of his mouth. He was creating a scene with all his gestures and shouting, and all the students were now gathering around us. Some were passing comments that I was trying to be cool by wearing jeans to the trial. I could also hear some boos and jeers from other hopefuls who were frustrated with the pause in the selection process.

'Sir, please let me do the trial. If I qualify for the team, I promise I will buy white pants.'

'So you think you are someone special, don't you? Why are the other students dressed appropriately?' he snapped.

'No. Please sir. It is my circumstances.' I said courteously.

'What circumstances? You are just making excuses.'

'No Sir, please try to understand. It is my circumstances.' I was really hoping he would catch my drift.

'What is your problem, boy?' he shouted again in a very harsh and insulting tone.

I looked in his eyes and searched for empathy. There was none. It was just misdirected anger and his need to assert power over the new recruits.

I hesitated. I had so far kept my personal situation hidden from everybody. I was not going to tell anyone about my family's financial problems, and especially not to this stranger.

'Nothing, Sir,' I looked down at the grass.

'Then don't waste my time. Get out of my field,' he shouted. With his hand outstretched pointing to the exit gate, he kept shouting, 'Just get out' with disgust. I felt a sense of humiliation, like someone had pierced my chest and was tugging at my heart. The words of the coach and the laughter and jeers around felt like a knife was prodding my body. I felt profound pain. I had never been insulted like this and never known humiliation as deep as that. I thought, 'The coach could have just asked me to leave politely and I would have left. Why did he have to insult me like that?

I accepted the situation and started to walk towards the gate. I wanted to run away from that place and disappear. As I approached the exit gate, I looked up to the sky and felt the blaze of the afternoon sun. I closed my eyes and took a deep breath. I questioned myself. Is this what suffering felt like? Is this what the struggle was meant to be like?

As I touched the gate, I turned around and looked at the ground.

You have to face this suffering. You have to embrace this rejection and endure this. You have to take this in your stride. There is no running away, Ankit.

So, for the next two hours, I stood at the gate of the ground watching the selection process. I saw the students turning elated on being selected. I looked at the setting sun and felt the evening breeze on my face and asked the higher powers to give me strength to absorb this humiliation and make me stronger after this experience. After enduring those bitter hours standing in isolation, I left for home.

Abhishek opened the door and excitedly asked, 'Tell me, you got selected, right?'

I took a pause, looked at him and was unsure about whether to share the bad news or just stay quiet.

'No, I was not good enough. Those guys were so much better than me,' I decided to spare him the pain. Before he could ask for more details, I told him that I had to go to the bathroom. I went to the bathroom and sat down on the tiled floor with my back up against the wall. I sat there trying to pull myself together. I made sure I absorbed that hit and did not pass it on to my family members.

To hell with having fun at college and playing sports. From now on Ankit, focus solely on your career.

From that point on, I barely went to college. I skipped most of my classes and for the classes that had stringent attendance requirements, I showed up just long enough to have my attendance recorded, and then I jumped from the window, which was just six feet above the ground.

I started my coaching classes for the class XII board exam even before the session started. The exam results were to determine whether I would become an engineer. I had started feeling awkward about going to college, especially around the students who seemed to be having fun.

The general mood in the house was a quiet resolve with everyone working hard and supporting each other. There was not much verbal communication, but there was a deep understanding and respect for what each of us was pursuing. Even though the resources were very limited, there were never any conflicts, with a deep understanding among us. Each of us was trying to climb a mountain beyond his or her capacity. We as family members lent our support in confronting and overcoming each other's barriers.

On some nights, it did get tough. It happened when our landlord started harassing us. Mr Roshan, a Muslim businessman, had leased the house to Dad's former company and he was responsible for collecting the rent. The company, in turn, had taken a large deposit from Dad for this apartment and it had been cutting an additional amount besides the rent from his salary. When things were good and Mr Roshan was getting his rent from the company, he was my Dad's good friend and would often come over to have dinner with us. He often complimented my mother for her excellent culinary skills. But now that Dad was in the middle of a court case, Mr Roshan started getting impatient.

Dad explained to him many a times that we did not want his house. Furthermore, we were prepared to leave once the case was settled and our initial deposit was returned. The deposit paid to the company was a large amount. The court had issued a stay order which allowed us to continue living there until the case was settled. Unfortunately, Mr Roshan would not listen and became quite agitated.

Once every three months he arrived, often after drinking too much, and banged on our door, shouting bad words and threatening us. Our parents kept the door locked and kept us safe inside, but we could still hear him shouting. He used to threaten us saying, 'You don't know who I am or what I can do. I have connections with the underworld. One phone call to Dubai and your family will disappear from the face of the Earth.' Dad would get riled on his family being threatened and would want to confront Mr Roshan, but we would restrain him and beg him not to open the door. Things would have only gotten worse if a brawl broke out as Mr Roshan was an old man. On those dark nights we would turn the house lights off, hoping that he would think we are away. We would be cowered quietly inside with Mom holding back Dad while Mr Roshan cursed our family outside. We would pray for a quick end to those nights, but they lasted long. As word of such event would spread rapidly through the housing society, it would get quite embarrassing for Abhishek and me to go out and play with our friends.

There were no Diwali celebrations any more. We did not ask our parents to buy firecrackers. We did not go outside on Diwali night. We just looked from the windows as our friends lit up the firecrackers.

Our TV had stopped working and we never asked our parents to repair it or to get a new one. For around three years, our only source of entertainment was a small music system. We did not celebrate birthdays either. We went out of our way to hide our birthdays from our friends. In India, it was a tradition for the birthday boy or girl to give treats to their friends. So, in addition to buying candies for your classmates, your closest friends would pester you for a treat at a decent restaurant. Since we did not want our parents to spend anything unnecessarily, we tried our best to keep low profile, so nobody would know it was our birthday. On our special day, we just visited the temple and spent a quiet day at home.

After the supply business came to an end and the creditworthiness was gone, Dad had to close down Ami

Enterprise. Dad was never the one to give up, and hence he started another business venture with some friends. This business managed an entertainment troupe of artists and organized cultural dance events for Indians living abroad in the Middle East. The dance troupe sometimes practiced at our home. The troupe's first event was in Dubai since many Indians lived there. All the arrangements were made. Some of Dad's partners went with the troupe, but my Dad stayed back to save money. The troupe arrived in Dubai four days before the event. Within two days of arriving, they started getting calls from the Indian underworld mafia demanding a private performance of the female dancers. This 'request' was unexpected, and my Dad would be on the phone discussing with the partners whether they should comply or not. Private performances were definitely unsafe, especially for the young female performers, but turning down the calls had its risks as well.

My Dad was opposed to any private performance, whatever the consequences might be. So, it was decided that they would not comply. But then the threats kept coming. And on the day of the practice performance, the goons came to the hall, created a ruckus and hurled threats. Fearing for the safety of the troupe, the partners decided to cancel all the shows scheduled for different cities and brought everybody home immediately. Though it was the right thing to do, it was another financial blow for my Dad. He and his partners had to pay for the arena, the plane tickets and they also had to compensate the troupe. All the money invested in this venture sank.

After that failed venture, the next plan to earn an income for our family was to lease out Dad's car. Our car was a white Fiat sedan modified into a hatchback. In those times, a car was a rare luxury and renting it out could provide a good source of income. Dad made arrangements with a friend who had some contacts in South India. He agreed to take the car there to rent it out and assured us of a small but steady monthly income. We were all attached to the car as it had been part of our family since our early childhood. On the evening when it was going to be taken away, our family went for a quiet ride. We did not want to part with the car, but reluctantly accepted our new reality. During the ride in the car, we talked about the memories we had of the car. How when we were small, the three of us would sleep in the trunk of the hatchback during long rides. How in some mornings, we would take the key and start the ignition to warm the engine before Dad left for office.

Abhishek and I took turns being the driver and the passenger. We would press on the accelerator and feel the car roar. We would enact some car chase scenes from movies such as *Mad Max*. We would sometimes pretend that we were chasing thieves or sometimes played the thieves running away from the police.

Anamika would sit in the backseat. Hanging from the rear-view mirror was her toy, a Hello Kitty doll. One of Dad's friend had gifted this to us upon his return from Japan. When one pulled on the doll, it played nice oriental music for a while. When Abhishek and I would be in the middle of our intense car chase scene, turning the steering right and left and accelerating the car, we would be interrupted by Anamika. She would lean in from the backseat and pull on the Hello Kitty. The slow melody coming from the doll was an odd interruption in our intense speed-chasing fantasy.

As we finished our last ride that evening, Anamika took down her doll from the rear-view mirror and asked, 'Can I keep this, Daddy?'

'Yes, of course,' Dad said remorsefully.

The next day Dad's friend, Mr Badran, came and took the car. The following day we got a call from Mr Badran's friend, 'Mr Badran had a car accident.'

'Is he okay?'

'He has some fractures and head injuries. He is in the hospital. His injuries are not life threatening.'

'What about the car?'

'The car is badly damaged. It is unsalvageable. It's total junk now.'

We were in complete shock.

For the next few days, Dad was very sad. He had tried his best to bring his family out of this difficult situation, but every business venture he had tried had failed—the trading business, the entertainment business and now the car.

Dad's brothers lived in Dehradun and when they heard about their brother's bad fortune they encouraged us to come live close to them. His oldest brother suggested forcefully that we leave Mumbai and return to his native town, Dehradun. At least, we would have the support of Dad's family and the cloud of uncertainty would be less daunting. Dad's large family would be there to help, should we continue to face adversities. Also, his dad had two rooms in a big building in his name, so at least we would have our own place to stay instead of a rental place. They also suggested that they could help us open a stationery store which Abhishek could manage. And since I was better in academics, I could enroll in a pharmacy course and open a pharmacy next to it. At this time, Dad had become very despondent for obvious reasons. He was unable to envision how to sustain the family in Mumbai. Things were just not turning out right and expenses were increasing. The more he tried to get ahead, the more losses he incurred. And worst of all, his bank account was bone dry.

So, he finally decided he had had enough. He was 18 years old when he had left home to make a life for himself and work hard in the Army, in the oil fields and starting new business ventures. Now, it was time to go back home.

Dad called a family gathering. We all sat down as Mom walked in and out of the kitchen, listening to everything Dad said. 'I have decided we are going to move to Dehradun. This house is rented and we have to vacate it once we get our deposit back. You know how our landlord Roshan has been behaving. I have a home in Dehradun and my extended family can help us. They own shops and they can help us set up a shop of our own and we can again earn a steady income.' We all were in a state of shock as we looked at Dad. The prospect of moving from a large city to a small town and becoming a shopkeeper was unfathomable. What about my dream of becoming an engineer? I remained silent. We as a family had never questioned our Dad's decisions; his decisions were always final. I thought that it might have been the right thing to do and I had to accept it silently.

'No, we should not. We will not,' Mom interrupted. We turned around and saw Mom approaching us. We were all surprised at her stern tone. 'We always said that education is the most important thing for our kids. I will not and neither will you see your kids become shopkeepers.' We were surprised at Mom's objection. This was the first time in her life she had talked back at Dad. Mom had always given our education the highest priority. Fearful of her children abandoning their dreams, she revolted against Dad. Even Dad was taken aback by Mom's disagreement.

'We have to give them a chance to make a career for themselves. As a family we will go down fighting. I am ready to face any challenge. We will get through this. I will not let anything get in the way of their education.' We were all surprised seeing her aggressive side. Dad, after some thought, relented and decided to remain in Mumbai and face what was in store for us in the city of broken dreams.

Witnessing what my family was going through, I started focusing even more on my studies. I had decided I was going to be an engineer and I was not going to open a pharmacy. To achieve that goal, it was imperative to get good scores in physics, chemistry and math in class XII board exams. I studied and prepared zealously for the examination each day. It became an obsession for me. I barely went out to play sports. I knew that I had to score very high in those subjects to get a seat in an engineering college.

The engineering colleges had opened admission for a few merit seats only; the remaining seats were not free. I knew we could not afford to pay ₹32,000 a year. I did not want to be selfish and not leave any resources for my siblings. So, getting 90 per cent was my primary goal. I studied very hard with a focus on becoming an electronics engineer. My family supported me a lot and I could feel how much each of them wanted me to succeed.

And then came the day of my class XII board exams. After taking the first exam, I walked back home with my friend Umesh. He lived close to my house and we were assigned the same exam centre. Umesh was from a very rich family and often came to our house so we could study together. He was an average student, so I used to help him with some subjects. When we were returning after appearing for our first exam, which was English language, he showed me a piece of paper on which all the questions which had been asked in the exam could be seen.

'Look Ankit. I had this leaked paper before the exams. I knew all the questions that were going to be asked.'

I looked at the paper and though the paper colour and quality were very different from the exam question paper, it had the exact same questions. I could not believe it.

'I know some people who sell these leaked papers on the morning of the exam. They are going to provide me the papers for the rest of the exams as well, especially the important ones of physics, chemistry and math,' Umesh bragged.

'Wow, it's unbelievable.' I was in disbelief that something like this could happen.

'Well, my family paid a lot of money to get those papers. But I can share them with you for free since you have helped me prepare.'

'Hmm,' I said, trying to comprehend the situation.

'It is very simple, Ankit. I get the leaked paper early in the morning; we sit together and look up the answers in the book. Then in the actual exam in the afternoon, you put in the correct answer,' he said matter-of-factly. I listened attentively, still in shock that something like this could happen.

'Ankit, this guarantees your success in the exams. A sure shot at becoming an engineer. What do you say?'

'Hmm, let me think about it.'

As we continued walking back, I kept thinking about it. Umesh didn't let up.

'Look, you don't have to pay the high fees for the engineering seat. I know that your family has financial problems.'

I looked at him in surprise, as I had never told him or anybody else about my family's situation. 'Ankit, I know, okay? I visit your house regularly. I know.'

I continued walking and thinking of his proposal. It was a moment of reckoning for me. I thought to myself, 'Life has been unkind and unfair to me and my family. Maybe this is a sign from God to even out the score. The engineering admission itself was unfair. A person with a lower score than me could get an engineering seat because he is rich. They can exploit their benefits and I would be denied my engineering dream and end up becoming a shopkeeper for the rest of my life. Maybe this was my edge to balance the scale.'

The argument in favour of taking Umesh up on his offer was beginning to make sense in my head. But there was a voice in my heart that kept nudging me from the inside and would not be silenced: 'This is not the right thing. Remember your dharma. Your dharma.'

As we were about to reach our respective homes, Umesh asked, 'What did you decide? Should I come to your house tomorrow morning with the leaked exam paper?'

'No, I can't. I can't cheat. I have to have a clear conscience. I will accept whatever I fairly deserve. If I don't become an engineer, so be it.'

We parted ways. During the remainder of the exams, I avoided Umesh because I did not want to be tempted. I needed to remain focused on what I had to do. When the exam results came out a few months later, I scored 96, 95 and 94 in math, physics and chemistry, respectively. I lost 2 per cent in the science practical exams. I had been skipping my classes at college and the labs and that 2 per cent on top of the 95 per cent would have ensured me a merit seat. Though slightly disappointed with that score, I felt very proud that I had not cheated. I was hopeful that I would get into some engineering college.

The admission to all engineering courses in our state was centralized. All the students in the state were ranked sequentially according to their scores. So, the students who were ranked higher would get to pick which college and which engineering stream they wanted. Students were asked to bring cheques of ₹4,000 and ₹32,000. When their turn came, if any merit seats of their liking were left, they could select one of them and then deposit the ₹4,000. If not, they would have to pick the non-merit seat and deposit a check of ₹32,000 to finalize their admission to the college. Since it was on a first-come-first-serve basis depending on merit, the merit seats in the best colleges of the most sought-after engineering streams like computer science and electronics would fill up first. I knew our family did not have the money for the non-merit seats, so I told Dad to get a cheque for ₹4,000. I hoped that when my chance came, there would be some merit seats left and we would need to deposit only ₹4,000.

I went with Dad to the admission centre. In the first round, as we were watching the results on display, the pool of available merit seats in all good colleges was limited. There were quotas and each college had reserved seats for certain communities. The net effect was that there were very few merit seats and the ones from the good colleges were rapidly disappearing. It was looking like there wouldn't be any merit seats left for electronics by the time my turn would come. There was a lunch break after the first round and my turn had not come yet. The chances of getting a merit seat looked slim. If I did not get one of the few remaining merit seats, I could not even try for the non-merit seat either as we did not bring along a cheque for ₹32,000.

Dad and I sat quietly in the cafeteria. The prospect of becoming an engineer was looking bleak. I tried not to think about how I could possibly miss out on an engineering career and instead focused admiringly at Dad and how he was eating so adroitly with a spoon and fork.

Suddenly Dad shouted loudly, 'Ankit, why didn't you tell me that there were payment seats? I would have brought a ₹32,000 cheque with me.' Dad's loud voice startled not just me but a few other students and families sitting nearby. I looked at my Dad. Our eyes met and there was this moment of silence, then an understanding followed without me saying anything. In those few seconds, I saw his expression change from anger to the realization why his son had not told him about the paid seat—there was no way our family could afford it. This realization led to a feeling of despair in him for not being able to do what was needed for his son's career, the feeling that he could not provide for his son's future. His expression of despair soon turned to harrowing pain as he could feel his son's future shattering right before him. I could now see the corner of his eyes getting moist.

I quickly grabbed his hand and held it as tightly as I could. I did not want him to shed a tear. As I continued gripping his hand, he finally became aware of it and my presence. 'Dad, Dad it's going to be okay. I will get the merit seat,' I assured him.

I was not sure whether I was going to get a seat, but I was sure that I did not want to see my brave Dad tear up. As we walked back to the hall dispiritedly for the second round, I pondered if I had made a mistake when I rejected Umesh's offer. That would have guaranteed higher scores and an engineering seat. As we walked through the aisles, I looked up to the sky and prayed, 'God, please make me believe.'

In the second round, when my turn came I saw that there was an open merit seat for electronics in one of the newer colleges.

Not many students before me had picked that college since they did not want to risk being admitted to a new college with no ranking. I had done some research beforehand regarding all possible colleges, and I knew that though this college was new, the management and board were good. Also, it was only about 30 minutes from home and close to my junior college.

So, when my turn came, I picked a seat for electronics engineering in this new college. It later would turn out to be the right decision since that college, after many years, would become one of the best engineering colleges in Mumbai. As we took the bus home, I felt joyous in knowing that I was going to become an engineer. We did not talk much, but there were moments when we exchanged smiles. I was excited about my future and so was Dad. He was relieved after having carried the burden of guilt for long. He could now feel a sense of pride. We both returned home happy and never mentioned that moment of despair in the cafeteria. Mom was particularly proud that her son would become an engineer. I would be the first engineer in our extended family.

I was elated to start my first year of engineering college. It felt that all my hard work for the last few years had finally paid off. I promised myself that I would not be a recluse like I had been in my junior college and that I would immerse myself in experiencing college life.

With this attitude, I participated sprightly in the class activities with my batchmates. I was elected the class representative and became the captain of my class football team. That year we won the intra-college football championship. I was also part of the class cricket team and was batting in the key position. I actively took part in the technical quizzes and debates. Most importantly, I did well in my studies. Out of the four years, the first year engineering syllabus was the toughest as it was intended on filtering out students not suited for engineering. But I was able to grasp all the new concepts and enjoyed the subjects. The logical and rational thinking that was required seemed to come naturally to me and I excelled academically. I was much more relaxed, being secure in the knowledge that I would one day graduate as an engineer.

It was during my first engineering examination when there came a night that rocked the very existence of our being.

4

FALL OF THE NIGHT

There was a loud thumping at the door and there was something odd about it. My mind was trying to decipher what was happening as the noise kept on getting louder. The answer came too late.

It was around 9.00 a.m. and we had already finished dinner. Mom, Abhishek and Anamika were watching TV in the living room. Dad was in the kitchen since he never enjoyed watching anything other than news. I was about to start my last session of preparations for my first exam, engineering drawing. I was seated at my study table in the living room calibrating and practising with my mini drafter.

When the ringing of the doorbell was followed by loud knocks, we looked at each other and wondered who could it be, so late in the night. Maybe it was an unexpected guest. Abhishek, almost as a reflex, opened the door. As his hand reached for the doorknob, I realized why the knocking seemed strange. The oddity of the knocks was that it was coming from multiple people and not just one person. It was definitely two people, maybe three. Who could it be?

I failed to warn Abhishek in time. Just as he opened the door, there was a big push from the other side shoving him back. Suddenly a group of about 10 young men, mostly in their 20s, barged into the house. One stocky person with a long beard shouted, 'Throw them all out! Throw everything out!' At first, they looked at each of us and then glanced around the room to take stock of the place.

Abhishek and I rushed towards the door to push the intruders out. Mom quickly grabbed Anamika and hurried to the opposite corner of the room. The first couple of young men to enter threw us back with force. These guys were much bigger and stronger than we were. As we tried to defend ourselves, they pushed back again. This time the bearded man, who seemed to be the leader, removed a small knife and pointed it towards us.

'Stand back!'

Mom shouted, 'Abhishek, Ankit, stop!' It was so sudden and reflexive that we didn't realize that we were pushing and shoving. We stopped and took a few steps back moving closer to Mom and Anamika.

'What are you guys doing? Why have you barged into our house like this?' Mom asked the bearded guy.

'This is not your house, Madam. This is Roshan's house. We are his men and we are going to throw you out of the house.' Shouting to his guys, he said, 'Throw everything out!' They hastily started to remove things from the living room. They started with the pictures that hung on the cabinets and on the walls in the living room. They pulled the telephone connection and took the phone. Then they started to empty all the drawers and take all the documents.

As five men started emptying the house, the bearded guy directed the next intruders to move towards the kitchen. 'Bring Gupta out. I know he is at home. He must be in the bedroom or in the kitchen. Drag him and throw him outside!' They rushed to the kitchen and called out, 'Where are you Gupta? Come out!' When Mom saw the knives, she stopped us from engaging with the guys. While one group was emptying everything from the room, the other five guys came in and started replacing some of our things. In total, there were around 15 guys, all working very quickly. They replaced our photographs with photographs of another man who we recognized as Mr Roshan.

We were absolutely shocked. Our minds were trying to get some grip on the insanity that was unfolding in front of us. Why were they doing this?

'Roshan is dead and we are his family. We are here to take back his property,' a voice that came from behind the bearded guy answered. As the bearded guy stood aside, a guy in white trousers and a bright silk shirt made a somewhat deliberate entrance into the apartment. He was in his mid-30s, had a slight build and stood about 5'4". He had squinty eyes, a mustache and a big mole on his face and spoke in a husky voice. He seemed to be the leader and the bearded guy seemed to be his muscle man.

'We don't want this house. We just want our deposit back. The case of this house is in dispute and we are waiting for a settlement. The court has asked us to stay in the house. Please check with the court,' Mom tried to explain.

'No, Madam. The courts will no longer decide this case. Do you understand?' he responded as he approached us. Each word was uttered slowly for maximum impact. It seemed like an eternity, given the chaos that was going around us.

'We will decide it now. Tonight, it ends...tonight.' I could feel the horror of his words in my spine. 'Throw their belongings outside. Leave nothing behind,' the guy angrily ordered with full authority.

The young guys now started to take away the TV and the music system. By now, our neighbours had opened their doors to see what all the noise and commotion was about. They stood in the hallway, outside the house, looking in but afraid to interfere. But our next door neighbours, an old couple, did snatch our music system from one of the guys as he was leaving. They grabbed it and took it into their house.

We started to hear a lot of thumping noises and shouting coming from the kitchen. There was the noise of things falling and things being thrown against the wall and worst of all the sound of people in pain. It seemed that some kind of fight was going on. Our thoughts suddenly drifted to Dad and the guys carrying knives who had entered the kitchen. We were very worried about our father's well-being. Abhishek looked at me and I looked at him. I gestured to him and we ran into the kitchen dodging the guys who were standing in front of us.

As we ran towards the kitchen, we saw Dad holding the edge of the wall of the kitchen entrance. Two guys were pushing him out from behind, trying to remove his grip from the wall and three other guys were pulling him by his legs. Dad was kicking them and they were in turn hitting his stomach, legs and face. I could see that his face had bruises, but the faces of some of the other guys were worse. The guys were brandishing their knives and slashing at Dad while they were trying to avoid Dad's kicks. Dad ended up with bruises and cuts on his thighs. Without further thought, we jumped on top of Dad to protect him. The guys continued hitting him. Abhishek and I got punched in the back as we shielded Dad's stomach. At this time, the five other thugs from the living room came into the kitchen. By now, 10 guys were dragging the three of us through the hallways. With his grip loosened from the edge of the kitchen wall, Dad was now being dragged by his legs with his body sliding on the floor with us on the top. We were trying hard to push back, trying to hold onto anything we could see in the hallway. We got dragged from the kitchen along the alley to the living room. As we were close to the front door, our neighbour Anil rushed in. He was young and very tall. He aggressively pushed some of the guys, but then he noticed their knives.

He pleaded, 'Pramod, you have to leave the house. They will kill you and your family. Please.'

Dad heard his words and as the words sank in he stopped resisting.

'Come to my house downstairs and get your injuries taken care of. There are too many of them,' Anil advised.

Anil then pushed the rest of the guys away from Dad,

shouting, 'He is leaving, okay? Just get away from him now.' Anil then put one of Dad's arms around his shoulders and started to carry him as Dad limped alongside.

Dad looked at us, still grimacing with pain and said, 'Abhishek and Ankit, go get the police, tell them everything and bring them with you. Hurry!'

He then looked at Mom who was cowering in the corner of the living room with Anamika. 'Vijaya, under no circumstances are you to leave the house.' Dad knew whatever these hooligans could do to the men of the house, they would not dare touch the women. To do so would create serious problems for these intruders.

On his orders, Abhishek and I moved towards the door. We glanced at Mom and signalled her that we would be back soon.

We ran down the stairs as quickly as we could, jumping three steps at a time. We wanted to inform the police and return home immediately. As we rushed outside our building entrance, we were taken aback as the bottom of our feet felt the heat rising from the pavement. We then realized that we were barefoot.

A few steps from our building, there was a huge bonfire. Our belongings: family photographs, important documents and clothes were up in flames. As I looked at the fire I saw all my engineering books being burnt. One goon, who was completely oblivious to our presence, continued unloading suitcases full of clothes into the bonfire. With the clothes catching fire, the bonfire grew bigger and bigger. He then threw the empty suitcase over the wall and into the creek on the other side. I looked at him, hoping that we would make eye contact. They could have at least spared us the photographs and the books. He quickly walked by us and went up to get the next load to burn. I looked around and noticed that the things that could not be burnt had been thrown into the trash bin close by.

The bonfire was about eight-feet high, fueled mostly by the books and clothes. As I looked into the fire, our possessions, one by one, identified themselves in the light as they were consumed by the fire. 'Oh, that's the book I read this morning, that's our family album, that's Anamika's dress that she wore on Diwali, that's our poster of Rambo.' Each object was bidding its final farewell as it was being slowly consumed by the flames. As I looked at the fire, my instinct was to at least save something, maybe a book that I needed for the upcoming exam.

I saw one photograph of us three kids when Anamika was a one-year-old baby holding a comb and Abhishek and I in matching red shirts were sitting with our arms around her. We were all smiling. For that photo, Mom had gotten us all dressed up with new clothes and taken us to the photo studio. That was Mom's favourite picture of us as babies and she had hung it up in the living room.

I found a stick from nearby bushes and tried to pull the photo out of the fire. It was a thin stick and it forked into two branches at the end. I put my hand as close to the fire as I could bear, and I tried to drag out the picture. From the light of the fire, I could see that the picture was already half burnt. It was the part of the picture that contained my face and now it was burning towards Anamika's image in the centre.

C'mon Ankit, try harder. I encouraged myself as I tried to push my hand further into the fire. I tried to drag it across the ground, but the stick's grip on the picture was not strong enough. It was losing leverage as the photo was turning to ash.

You can do this, Ankit, you can do this. C'mon. I kept trying and I could feel the heat on my hand and body as I was sweating profusely. I had to stretch just a little further, but the fire was relentless. Anamika's face in the photograph was burning as the centre of the photograph disappeared before my eyes. I desperately tried to save some small part of the photograph as the last third bit of it burnt. Abhishek threw me a pair of mismatched slippers and then said, 'Ankit, put these slippers on. Let's go. We have to get the police and bring them back with us.' By now that picture had almost completely disintegrated under the heat of the fire. Resignedly I threw the stick into the fire and put on the slippers. We ran towards the exit of our apartment complex to get help.

The police station was a good 30-minute walk. We knew where it was since we always passed it on our way to the library. We ran most of the way and then walked to catch our breath. It was a quiet night and the only thing I could hear was our heavy breathing. We were in a state of shock. Everything had happened very quickly from the moment Abhishek had opened the door till then. None of us had any idea about what had just happened and why. Some people walked by us and looked at us in confusion, not understanding why the two boys wearing mismatched footwear were running at night. We didn't care. We were focused on getting the police to come to our home as quickly as possible, so they could throw those hooligans out. We hoped the police would come and put a full stop to this senseless chain of events.

The police station was an old single-storeyed building at the corner of the main road. We quickly identified what looked like the main entrance with a flapping door that we pushed to enter. A guard came running quickly imploring us to stop, 'Wait. What do you want?' he asked annoyed.

'Sir, some goons have forcibly entered our house. They have burned all our stuff. They injured our Dad and now they have taken over our place,' Abhishek explained.

'So what do you want us to do?' he asked with a complete lack of concern.

'We want the police to come to our house and throw those thugs out,' I said.

'First you need to talk to the big Sahib and only then can we do something. But the Sahib is busy right now.'

We could see where the inspector was sitting and talking on the phone. He was of an average height with a moustache. He was having a casual conversation and we could hear his laughter. He could see us standing outside waiting for him.

'How much time will it take?' Abhishek asked.

'It will take some time. Yours is not the only work we have, do you understand?' he shouted.

'But Sir, those goons are still at our house. We don't know what they are doing to our father, mother and sister. It is dangerous and we need protection,' I added.

'Just wait until Sahib is ready to speak to you, okay? Go sit over there.' He pointed to the bench outside the room.

Reluctantly and disappointedly, Abhishek and I sat on the bench. I could not sit still for even a minute because I was feeling rattled at the thought of Mom and Anamika stuck in the house. My mind filled with thoughts of the absolute worst. I started pacing the floor.

'What are the police doing? They should be rushing now. Their job is to protect civilians. It is late at night. There is nobody around. I don't know what work is more important than this,' I said looking at the door.

'I just hope everything is okay at home. I wonder if Dad has come back home yet,' Abhishek said.

'Let's keep pacing outside the door so the inspector knows we are waiting,' Abhishek suggested as the guard was still inside.

So, we kept taking turns walking outside the door, hopeful that they could see us moving. Two young boys walking in front of the door in mismatched slippers should get the inspector's attention.

After more than 20 minutes, which felt like hours, the guard asked us to come in. It was a big room with multiple tables and chairs where different sub-inspectors were sitting. There was also a big table with a pile of papers for the main inspector. The walls had peeling paint and the room had a feeling of neglect.

As we walked in front of the main table, the inspector looked at us. Sitting in his chair, I could see his protruding stomach as his shirt buttons were barely able to contain it. His eyes were red with anger as he asked us to sit down and questioned impatiently, 'What is the problem?'

Abhishek repeated what he had said earlier.

'Please come with us and throw them out of our house,' I pleaded.

'Hmm. We will have to investigate. You can go,' he said dismissively.

'Sir, at least write a report. We want to file a complaint,' Abhishek said.

'I said we will investigate. We cannot file a report hearing kids who come in and say anything. How can we believe you and your side of the story?' he angrily shouted. 'Give your address, go back home and we will come.'

'Our family is in imminent danger. They were carrying knives. You have to protect us,' I begged.

'Don't tell me about my job. We cannot leave the police station just like that for any property dispute.'

'Sir, we will not return until you come with us,' Abhishek insisted.

'Then you wait outside. We have other works to do. We will let you know when we are ready to leave.'

'Go! Wait outside!'

He signalled to the guard, who then moved towards us. We got up and walked outside and sat on the bench again. As I sat down on the bench, I was confused by the inaction and apathy of the police.

'They knew,' Abhishek said thoughtfully.

'What do you mean?'

'They knew that our house would be attacked.'

'What?'

'We just complained about a few goons entering the house, but the inspector said it was a property dispute. How did he know that it was a property dispute, unless he knew from before?'

'Oh no! The police are in it as well.'

'Yes. Roshan's family most likely bribed them.'

There was a pause. The new development took a long time to sink in.

'I just hope everyone is safe. We should just vacate the house. Material things don't matter,' Abhishek said.

'At least they have shown some restraint towards Mom and Anamika. I am concerned about Dad. I hope he doesn't start fighting them again but knowing him, he will.'

'Oh look over there. Now they're having tea. Our house is burning down and they are having tea,' I said as I saw a young tea vendor enter the room with a kettle of tea.

'We should be at home. The police should be there as well. What nonsense is this? Are we living according to the law of the jungle now?' I asked.

'Abhishek, let's go home man. They are not going to help us. They are just wasting our time.'

'No, Ankit. Dad said to bring the police and that is what we will do, even if it takes the whole night. We will not move from here.'

We started to walk outside the door again. None of our neighbours had landlines and our telephone had been pulled out of the wall, so we couldn't think of any other way to call home. I could hear the laughter when some of the cops were horsing around inside. When the phone rang the inspector spoke softly talking to the caller, so I was unable to eavesdrop.

After half an hour of waiting, Abhishek barged in and demanded, 'Can you come with us?'

'Should we all just leave the station empty because two kids are here? Who will take care of the station? We will leave when we are ready. I told you to wait outside.'

By now, we had turned very fearful and were just hoping that our family was safe and sound. We heard the phone ring and after a few minutes of conversing, the inspector came out with two guards. He looked at us as though we were the criminals.

'What is your address?'

We gave it to him and he said, 'Okay. We are going. I will sort out the matter. We will file the report later.' A police jeep pulled up outside the station. There were four people sitting in the jeep: the inspector, the driver and two more guards. The back was empty. We asked the inspector if we could go with him.

'Do we run a taxi service or what? Find your own way home.'

I looked at him. I was surprised by his harsh retort and watched as the jeep rushed by us.

'Let's just run back,' Abhishek said pulling my arm.

As we ran back home, our thoughts were filled with dread. What would have happened at home since we left a couple of hours earlier? Was our family safe? How would the cops sort things out? As we ran back, this time we were more fearful and less hopeful than when we had gone to the police station.

As we reached our building, there was an eerie silence. I could detect the weird quietness of the night. At the entrance of the building, the cars that had brought the goons were gone. There were no bystanders. The police jeep was parked on one corner and one of the guards was standing expressionless. It felt like nothing had happened.

The bonfire and everything else had been cleaned up. On the ground, we could see the black burn marks left by the fire and the broom marks showing that the ashes had been swept away. All the scattered material had been put in the trash or possibly thrown in the creek on the other side. The silence of the night was scary as we climbed the stairs. The only thing we could hear was our breathing and the voices in our head whispering the worst-case scenario. We were hoping that there were no incidents or 'encounters' as the police would term it.

As we entered from the open door of the house, we saw a huddle in our living room. Our eyes searched for Dad and we found him among the people crowding around the inspector.

Our eyes searched for Mom and Anamika. They were standing in the corner looking at Dad. I thanked God and gave a sigh of relief.

The inspector was surrounded by Dad on one side and the ring leader with the mole and a lady who we had not seen before on the other. Mom and Anamika had disappointed looks on their faces as they listened to the animated conversation going on. There was no trace of the bearded man or the thugs who had stormed into the house.

The lady was showing some court stamped papers to the inspector. 'I am Roshan's daughter Shabnam. This is his property. Here are our papers. I have been staying in this house with my husband Salim,' she said, pointing to the slimy ring leader. Shabnam was a short plump lady in her early thirties. Salim, her associate in crime, had a mischievous look and was the only one who seemed to be enjoying the events of the evening.

'My father Roshan has passed away and he handed the property to me, his heir,' she stated as she pointed to the picture of Roshan on the wall. For the first time, we looked at the picture and then everything else in the house. We saw that none of our possessions were left. Everything had changed and now their pictures, showpieces and other objects had replaced our possessions.

'It is this bad guy who has forcibly entered my house with his family,' she said signalling towards Dad.

'Sir, this is a country of law. We can continue having this argument the whole night. However, the courts have issued the stay order for us to live in this house. Once the court case is settled and we get our deposit back, we will leave this house. But, it has to be done legally.'

'Okay. Then where is your proof? Where are the court papers?' the inspector asked Dad.

He replied emphatically, 'These people brought goons who stole all our papers.'

'You were talking about the rule of law, right? The law wants proof. Where are your papers, Sir?'

'We don't have them now, but I can get them when the courts reopen tomorrow morning.'

'Do you have any other proof that you have the right to live here?' the inspector asked.

Dad thought for a moment but could not come up with an answer. Anamika interjected, 'We have a ration card.' I immediately stopped her from suggesting it since I had seen it burn in the bonfire.

'I have my property papers,' Shabnam showed her document.

'So, it seems like they don't have the property papers, right?' slimy Salim chimed in smugly, since he knew that all the goons had burned our papers, 'and we have our property documents. So, we are the ones who should be staying here, since we have proof.' There was something maniacal about Salim, who was getting a sense of thrill and joy from this awful situation.

'I don't want the house, but we want our deposit back. It is a huge amount of money that we paid the company upfront and we need to get it back. The courts are reviewing the situation and they will decide. Roshan's agreement is with the company and not with us. They should address the company and the courts. I don't understand why they would forcibly and illegally enter this house and attack my family.' Dad was beside himself with anger and frustration.

'Attack? We have done nothing to your family. I don't know why they are imagining that someone could attack them, beat them and take away their kids,' Salim indirectly threatened us and Shabnam smiled coyly.

Hearing this threat, Dad walked towards Salim. The inspector raised his right hand to block him and push him back.

'I am here. Don't do anything. Control yourself, okay?' the inspector scolded Dad.

'So you don't have the house papers, but they do. How can we know who has been staying in the house? We need to investigate,' he stated in a matter-of-fact way.

'Look around Sir, everything in the house belongs to us. Shabnam started to show the family pictures and the showpieces.' She opened one of the drawers and removed some of her things.

'Okay,' the inspector seemed to agree. We were in complete shock how easily the cop was lapping up their story and poking holes in our truth.

'Sir, they are all lying. We have been living here for more than 10 years. You can ask the neighbours,' Dad implored.

'We will conduct an investigation,' the inspector responded authoritatively.

'Sir, we have shown you the papers. We live here,' Shabnam asserted.

'Enough is enough,' the inspector raised his hand as if he had reached the final judgement. 'They have the proof. The police have no choice but to go with the concrete evidence. So, I have decided that Salim and Shabnam will stay in the living room, your family will reside in the bedroom and the rest of the living space will be shared. That is what I have decided, and it will remain so until we complete our investigation. Everything is now settled.'

'What? How can they stay with us? What is happening? I am going to complain to your higher-ups. This is not a country that is ruled by the law of the jungle,' Dad protested.

'Okay, you go and complain to whoever you want. I am just trying to be fair,' the inspector explained defensively.

'You can go. You can take your family with you. Otherwise something could happen and this time the kids and lady may not be spared,' Salim chimed in staring threateningly at Dad. Dad had had enough of these threats and this time he grabbed Salim's shirt collar and tried to lift him up. 'What did you say about my kids?' he shouted.

The inspector again pulled Dad back and said, 'I don't want

any violence. I told you to control yourself and you have not followed my instructions.'

'But he is threatening us. Can't you see that?' We were all very surprised to see that the inspector was siding with Salim.

'Listen Mister, you see this baton?' the inspector angrily pointed it towards Dad. 'I will shove this up your ass and remove it from your mouth.'

This whole chaotic night came to a screeching halt for a few seconds as the inspector's gross words filled the air. There was dead silence. All of us were in complete shock. Nobody uttered a word. We were in total disbelief that the inspector would say something like that to Dad. Nobody had ever spoken to Dad like that. It was really disheartening to see an Army man who had fought for this country be treated that way. Even Shabnam and Salim who had been using cuss words at liberty seemed shocked by the crassness of those words. The silence was deafening.

Dad's head bent down in complete dejection and he said, 'There has to be justice in this country. I am going to complain.'

'I don't want any ruckus until our investigation is over. And you are very violent,' he said as he pointed his baton at Dad. 'You get out now and complain to whoever you want. Salim and Shabnam will be in this room and the kids and their Mom in the other room. If there is any ruckus I will come personally and throw your family out. Is that clear? Take him outside,' he ordered the guard.

As the guard accompanied Dad, he was so embarrassed that he did not even look back at us.

The inspector looked at Mom, 'Madam, you stay in the bedroom with the kids. The living room is for the others. The rest of the living space will be common area, as I have already said. I don't want to hear anything more until the matter is resolved. Is that clear?'

Mom agreed as she did not have any choice. We started to walk towards the bedroom.

I just wondered about the 15 goons. Where did they go? Maybe they were hiding on the top floors and would just rush back in once the police left.

'Sir, can you leave a guard at the door for our protection?' I asked the inspector as a last-ditch effort.

'Are we your servants? No. Go!' I gave a sigh as I looked at Abhishek. This inspector did not like us at all.

As I was walking towards the bedroom I glanced back and saw the inspector and Salim leave together. The inspector seemed to ask him with a hand motion, 'Did I do all right?'

'Yes,' Salim said very quietly with a wry smile, acknowledging a job well done.

Being of the view that he was starting to become violent, the police took away our protection, our Dad and now we were sitting ducks with this horrible couple who were going to stay with us. The couple had control of the living room and the entrance of the house, so they could invite anyone they wanted into the house anytime they wished. Our bedroom door didn't have a lock, so we wondered what else the night had in store for us.

The cops left the house, so it was just Salim and Shabnam sitting in the living room, with the four of us inside the bedroom. Hoping that the night would be uneventful, we lay down to rest. As we slept, Mom, wanting to keep us safe, stood by the door keeping watch.

When I woke up, I had flashes of goons barging in, beating us up, the bonfire, the police station visit and the insults hurled at Dad, especially the inspector's foul mouthed threat. I thought that all these events were just a bad dream until I opened my eyes and saw it was daylight. As I was sleeping at the edge of the bed facing the bedroom door, Anamika was in the middle and Abhishek was at the other end. I was still hoping that it was all a dream and could be undone.

Waking up, I saw Mom sitting down on the floor with her back and head along the bedroom door. If someone wanted to enter our room, it would be through her. As I looked at her, she smiled. Her eyes were droopy, and I could tell she had not slept all night and stood guard. I looked at her tired eyes for a few moments and I saw acceptance and pain, but also the resolve not to accept defeat.

She gestured me to come close to her. I sat next to her as she held my hand and said, 'Ankit, it is your engineering exam today. You have to take your exam.'

'Hmm,' I hadn't even thought about the exam.

'You cannot miss the exam and lose your engineering year. I will take care of the house.'

'But Mom...'

'Anamika is going to be here with me since she is preparing for her exams and does not have to go to school. I am concerned that they will go after you kids to further scare us. Abhishek can drop you off safely at school. He will wait outside until you finish your exam.'

'No, I will go alone. Abhishek should be here with you and Anamika. Shabnam and Salim are here. They are evil and they will attack you.'

'Yes, Ankit is right. I will stay here with you,' Abhishek said. He had just woken up and was sitting on the floor next to us. Anamika was awake too now. We all sat closely together.

'Dad came to visit this morning with another inspector. Currently they cannot get these people out of the house since they have the court documents and we don't. So, Dad left to get the court documents as soon as the courts open.'

'Was he okay?'

'Yes. I suggested to him that he should stay out as much as possible since Shabnam and Salim will continue to taunt him or possibly attack him. We can manage here.'

'Yes, I can take care of things here,' Abhishek said.

Mom said, 'They will try to scare us and do whatever they want, but we should not be scared. I will not leave the house. If

I do they will close the door and not let us back in. It is going to be an ugly fight. They will cause further trouble and create fear. We have to get back the deposit that is rightfully ours.'

'You have to take the exam today. Focus on the exam and we will take care of everything else,' she said.

'Yes, Ankit, we will handle the situation here. Just don't fail the exam,' Abhishek said.

'Okay,' I nodded. I was still disoriented and trying to align to the new weird reality.

I made a mental check of the things I needed for the exam. Most of the things like books and clothes had been taken and burnt the previous night. Luckily, some of the clothes that I wore to college were left hanging on the peg on the back of the bedroom door. They were not noticed by the mobsters and hence saved from being burnt. But my textbooks were all gone, either burnt or thrown away. I could buy a pen and pencils.

It was engineering drawing examination. I needed the mini drafter to do the technical drawing. I remembered that the goons had taken that as well.

'Mom, I need the mini drafter for today's exam. They took it.'

I knew it was an expensive instrument and buying another one was not an option.

'The guys threw some stuff over the wall into the creek as well, the things they could not burn. Maybe it is there,' Abhishek suggested.

'Let's go and find it,' I added hopefully.

Mom thought for a moment and agreed, 'Okay, go very quietly.'

So, Abhishek and I moved towards the door as quietly as we could. We saw Salim and Shabnam sleeping and snoring in the living room. We opened the door quietly and went outside but were aware that our movement had awoken them. We did not look back and engage with them in any way. We just wanted to find our things and immediately come back, so we did not lock the door.

When we went downstairs, the black marks from the fire downstairs were even more visible in the morning sun. They reminded us of the horrors of the previous night. About 15 metres from our building entrance was the boundary wall of our complex. Beyond was the creek where the seawater rolled in during high tide. The water was very dirty because it brought in garbage and trash that the people living in the complex threw into the creek. We found Bengali and asked him for the key to the steel door that gave us access to the creek.

'Why were you not on duty last night, Bengali?' He lowered his eyes. He looked embarrassed. He tried to avoid looking at us as our eyes followed him. We had known him for many years, from the time we were kids. Dad had helped him financially many a times. When his kids got sick or when he had to send money to his village during festivals, Dad gave him money. He avoided making eye contact and just opened the gate. 'If possible, please forgive me kids,' he murmured and walked away.

The creek was connected to the nearby beach. When there was a high tide the water level of the creek would also rise. As we entered the creek, the water from the sea mixed with mud and the trash created a filthy sight. As we stepped in deeper, our feet sunk into the dirty mud. Up close, the smell was really bad, but we were focused on the task of finding the mini drafter. We could identify some of our things which were now mixed with mud and ash. We quickly moved the pile of dirt. We could see a lot of our possessions scattered around and some of it was now floating in the water. There were shoes and some personal objects. I saw the marbles that were lying around from an opened box in which we had stored some of our childhood mementos. The marbles were reflecting the light from the sun.

As I looked around, I still could not find my mini drafter. Abhishek's hands and legs were getting dirty as he rummaged through the filth. I felt we should stop. Maybe the tide had swept it away. As I was about to call Abhishek, a gleam of light caught my eye. Was it another marble? As I approached it, I saw a piece of glass protruding from the water. It was the glass edge of the mini drafter. I shoved my hands in that pile of muck and lifted the mini drafter out of the water and held it above my head.

'I found it!' I said ecstatically. I smiled at my achievement and at the thought that I would now be able to appear for my exam.

Abhishek gave a sigh of relief at our small victory.

'Let's hurry back. Mom and Anamika are by themselves,' Abhishek said collecting the few things he could salvage.

We were both very dirty and we hoped that none of our friends in the building would see us, especially our friends from the cricket team. As we walked back, we took the stairs to the fourth floor. We were hoping that things would be somewhat peaceful at home. Our hopes were dashed when we heard a commotion in the kitchen.

Upon entering the kitchen, we saw Shabnam, with Salim at her side, throwing all our utensils on the floor and shouting at Mom. 'This is not your kitchen. This is not your house. You cannot cook here. This is ours,' she said as she pointed to the gas burners.

'I have to cook for my kids,' Mom said.

'That is not my problem. I can't believe you guys are so shameless and have not left yet.'

Shabnam removed the connection from the gas cylinder. 'This cooking platform belongs to us.'

'Okay. We will cook in this corner. We do not want any fighting, so please stop,' Mom appealed, trying to keep the situation calm.

Abhishek entered the kitchen and stood by Mom's side. I stood outside the kitchen holding my mini drafter. The goons had taken the dining room table, so there was now an empty space in the corner of the kitchen facing the window.

Abhishek took the steel gas range and put it on the ground

in the corner by the window. He moved the cooking cylinder and began to reconnect it.

'You don't get it. You won't leave easily. You don't know who we are or who we know.' She was muttering cuss words just as Roshan had used in our tense encounters with him. The apple didn't fall far from the tree.

'We are professionals at this. We throw people out of our houses on a regular basis. We have contacts with the underworld,' Salim declared proudly.

Shabnam advised, 'You don't know how dangerous we are and what we can do. You will be responsible for that. That is why I am saying as a woman, just take your kids and leave the house now. You don't know what you are getting yourselves into.'

'We are not leaving. We just want to live peacefully until the matter is resolved in the courts,' Mom countered with determination.

Annoyed, Shabnam started to pick up and throw the utensils from the cupboards onto the floor and against the wall. As they bounced off the walls, the utensils made a lot of noise. To distract myself, since I was standing at the wash basin outside the kitchen, I turned on the tap and started to clean my mini drafter. I knew I had to focus on my pending exam somehow. I took the soap and started scrubbing off the dirt from the drafter. I could still hear all the noise and Shabnam shouting bad words. Mom and Abhishek were just listening but not reacting, hoping that she would go away.

With no response from our side and exhausted from their own aggression, Shabnam stormed off with these final words, 'Just watch what we will do.' Salim followed her out.

I looked at the mirror in front of the wash basin and could see Shabnam walking behind me towards the hall. I kept scrubbing the mini drafter, not wanting her to unleash her fury on me. I was relieved to see her move towards the living room.

'Going to school today, kiddo?' I was surprised to see Salim looking at me in the mirror. I saw his eyes staring at me. There was an unusual evil look in his eyes. He spoke with conviction when he declared himself a professional who had contacts with the underworld. Fear ran down my spine. It was as if a big weight had moved from my chest to my stomach. I opened my mouth in disbelief, shocked and frozen stiff. Terrified, I just closed my eyes. But he continued looking at me in the mirror and jingled the words, 'Good. Good.' I glanced at him and he seemed to be enjoying deviant thoughts. I was really scared and felt trapped, so I quickly ran into the bathroom next to the basin and closed the door behind me.

As I entered the bathroom, I was quaking with fear. I put the mini drafter in the corner, turned on the hot water heater on the tap and sat down on the stool next to the bucket. I tried to distract myself by looking at the water falling into the bucket, but it didn't help. I sunk my head into my hands but was unable to stop my body from shaking. I could feel knots in the pit of my stomach. I tried to inhale deeply, but my breathing felt heavy.

'This is real. They are going to kill us.' I was certain after having seen the sadistic evil in Salim's eyes. His aberrant wickedness could let him kill or maim a person, and he would feel nothing, no remorse, no sympathy, no humanity, just sheer pleasure from the torture.

In contrast, I felt weak. Every fight that Abhishek and I had since childhood had actually been imaginary. But this was real. We kids had never been in a real fight. We had never had a physical altercation with any of our friends at school or in our housing society. There was never a good reason to fight. We always had more than we wanted, and Mom had always taught us to be good people and not hurt anybody physically or verbally.

But the violence of the last night was real. I knew that their threat of ensuring our disappearance was a genuine one. My breathing became even more laboured.

Where are those guys who were here last night? Where did they go? They must be waiting outside, waiting to pounce on us. They have seen our faces. What will they do if they catch me when I leave for the exam? Should I skip my final exams today?'

I closed my eyes and took deep breaths.

Come on, Ankit. Be brave. Be strong. Mom is counting on you. Do the right thing. If you don't go today, they will think they have won and will make our lives more difficult. Walk the difficult path. Agnipath.

I started to recite the poem 'Agnipath' by Harivansh Rai Bachchan, an Indian poet which translates as,

If there is comfort in trees, shady and huge,
Don't ask for the shade of a single leaf
Walk on the Path of Fire, Walk on the Path of Fire.
Never tire. Never stop. Never turn back,
Take this oath, take this oath, take this oath.
Walk on the Path of Fire, Walk on the Path of Fire.
O imagine the glory of that sight
A human soaked, swathed in his tears, sweat and blood.
But still walking on the Path of Fire, the Path of Fire.

I kept reciting as I poured water all over my body. With each recitation, I could feel the fear gradually leaving my body and freeing my spirit.

If we must go down, we will go down fighting. I made a fierce resolve. I took my bath praying to find strength from a higher power.

I can do this. I will do this, I thought as I stepped out of the bathroom.

In the bedroom, Mom had made tea on the stove, sitting on the floor and she had served bread and jam. As I sat down, I could see Anamika in the corner quaking with fear. Mom's eyes showed the confusion and conflict she was fighting, risking her son's safety for education. Abhishek was also very concerned. It had been bad enough so far and we did not know how much worse it could get.

'I am going for the exam,' I said determinedly, trying to dispel the fear that was now permeating the room.

I looked at each of them to give them confidence. After I finished my breakfast and picked up my mini drafter, I could see that Anamika and Mom were still feeling shocked and confused, tormented over the dilemma of whether to allow me to leave and take the exam. Finally, Mom calmly said, 'Take care of yourself, Ankit. We will wait for you.'

I bid them goodbye.

As I walked outside, Salim noticed me leaving. I did not look at him. My mind was focused on getting to school and taking the exam.

Ok. If those hired thugs are waiting for me, they will either be standing outside the society gate or at the bus stop on the main road. What if I take an alternative route and completely avoid them?

As kids, we had jumped and climbed many walls of our apartment complex and knew all the secret alternative routes. So, instead of going the usual road, I climbed a side wall next to our society garden. It was a 12-foot stone wall, but it had some pegs on it where stones had been pulled out leaving small holes. When we played in the garden, sometimes our ball would go beyond that wall and we would climb on it to retrieve it. On the other side was an old defunct movie theatre and next to it was the bus stop I used to stand at. During the bus ride this day, I vigilantly looked out for any suspicious people following me.

I reached school, completely determined to take the exam. When the exam started, I was standing next to the inclined drawing board. The examiner gave me a big blank white sheet that hooked onto the drawing board of my mini drafter. Using it, we were supposed to work on the drawings on the sheet.

As I started to calibrate the scales by straightening the mini drafter, a piece of dirt came out from the mini drafter on the white sheet. Fear overtook me once again as my mind recalled the horrors of the previous night and this morning's events.

Was my family okay? Have they been hurt? Mom, Anamika and Abhishek. Is Dad okay?

C'mon Ankit. Focus! You cannot fail. You will not fail.

As the examiner handed me the paper, I was still blankly staring at the sheet and focusing on that piece of dirt. I took the exam question paper and looked at it. I went through the questions, but they were not getting registered in my consciousness. They were not making any sense as my mind was racing around like a wild horse.

C'mon focus! I looked around. All my classmates had already started their drawings and I was still holding the exam paper, staring at it, not knowing what to do. I just wanted to run back home and make sure that my family was fine.

You can do this. Remember Agnipath. Do not fail. Okay? Just try to get a passing grade so you don't lose the year. Just finish quickly and leave immediately afterwards, I thought. To pass, I had to get 40 out of 100. I went through the paper and started to mark the questions that I thought I could answer correctly, hoping that that would allow me to get at least 40. As I went through the questions, I began to realize I knew more answers than I needed to pass. I quickly got into action and set my mini drafter and started to work on my drawings. I finished the paper 30 minutes early and handed it to the teacher without even reviewing my answers. I picked up some books from the library for the next exam and ran to the bus stop, anxious to see my family.

As I reached home huffing and puffing, I rang the bell and Abhishek opened the door. Just by his facial expression, I could see that things were all right. Salim was sitting in the living room reading a newspaper. As I walked behind Abhishek towards the bedroom, Salim and I exchanged stares. But this time, I maintained the eye contact with him. I kept looking at his eyes and didn't look away until he looked down at the newspaper. I wanted him to look into my eyes and see that I had no fear. I raised my mini drafter over my shoulder and walked away.

My family could breathe a collective sigh of relief seeing me safe at home, and Mom went into the kitchen to get some fruits as I changed my clothes.

In the evening, Dad came back and said he had filed the case in court and there was a hearing scheduled for the next day. We were cautiously hopeful that the matter would be resolved quickly. After we finished our dinner in the bedroom, Dad stood by the window. We could hear loud noises from the living room. It appeared that Salim and Shabnam had brought men into the house and they seemed to be partying, eating, drinking and laughing.

I asked Abhishek, 'What is that funny smell? Hookah?'

'No. I think that it's ganja. They're doing drugs.'

'What the hell, man,' I said as we braced for the worst. Though the bedroom door was closed, we could hear them laughing loudly.

'Ankit, you don't have any exam tomorrow, right?' Abhishek confirmed.

'No. The next exam is the day after tomorrow.'

'Can you stay at home? I don't trust the courts or the police. I want to talk to some of my friends who may know someone influential who could help us with our situation.'

'Sure. I will stay with Mom and Anamika.'

Then there was a loud thud on the door and someone could be heard shouting. His voice was unfamiliar. It was not Salim's or the bearded guy's voice. It was someone else.

'Hey soldier. You like to grab people's collars? You come out and hold mine,' the voice taunted. Abhishek and I ran to hold the door. Dad turned away from the window, walked towards the door, hands clenched to form a fist.

Mom stopped him from going closer to the door. 'They are just trying to instigate us. Just hold back. It is just a matter of a few days. It will get worse for all of us if we open the door…' Mom said pointing to us and added, '…think about the children.' Dad restrained himself.

After some more knocking and hurled abuses, we heard Salim's shout, 'Let's go buddy, we'll take care of them afterwards.' The voice went away, and we slept in the bedroom, hoping for no more incidents.

Dad and Abhishek left early the next morning for the court. I was home studying for the next exam. The book from the library was not exactly the textbook that I had used for studying, but I tried to grasp the best I could. I closed my eyes and tried to recollect what I could from the textbook that I had read a few weeks back and started making notes. There was a commotion in the kitchen and it was distracting.

As I rushed to the kitchen with my book, Shabnam was again shouting and abusing Mom, who was listening quietly, trying to deescalate the situation. But this time Shakuntala Aunty who had come to work, stepped in and was now talking back on Mom's behalf.

'You are bad people. You are evil and are harassing this good family, a gentle lady and her kids.'

Shabnam and Shakuntala Aunty kept arguing back and forth. Shakuntala Aunty had always been quiet during the few years with us, but her true fearless nature came out at that moment.

It was good to see Shakuntala Aunty fight back on our behalf in a verbal duel with Shabnam. Finally, Shabnam, irritated by the rebuttals, gave up and walked away with the threat, 'I will take care of you later.'

Once she left, Shakuntala Aunty took out a small bundle of money from her blouse and handed it to Mom saying, 'You will need this money now. Please take it.' The money was about two month's salary.

'No, I cannot,' Mom said.

'Please. You are like an older sister to me. Just take it for the kids to buy their books and food for the family.'

Mom thought for a moment. This was true. We did need the money for food since we no longer had our bank documents.

'I will return it as soon as this case wraps up.' Anamika and I couldn't help but admire Shakuntala Aunty for her kind act. We had never known a domestic worker who gave money to her employer. It was truly unusual.

'Ankit, there is too much commotion in the house. You won't be able to study. Why don't you study at the neighbour's? I can handle it. I have also asked Dad to be home as little as possible to avoid their taunts. I can handle it here.' I looked at her in surprise, not sure how she was able to manage with the recent abuses. Yet, she persisted without losing her composure.

'Abhishek is going to be home soon. Shakuntala is here.'

'Okay, I will be next door. If there is any trouble, just call out to me from the kitchen window.'

'Okay.'

I agreed and went to our next-door neighbours. Mrs and Mr Arora were an elderly couple. I rang the bell. 'Uncle, is it ok if I study at your house for a few days for my exams?'

'Of course, please do. We are so sorry about what happened to your family last night. We have never seen such lawlessness,' Mrs Arora lamented.

'I was able to grab your music system from one of the thugs,' Mr Arora said pointing to our music system, clearly proud of his achievement.

The music system meant nothing to me at that time. 'Can you keep it for a few more days? You know how the situation is at our house right now.'

'Can I go to the room that is next to our kitchen window? Just in case, you know.'

'Yes, you can use that room to study,' Uncle responded as he showed me to the bedroom.

As I sat alone in the room and looked out the window, I closed my eyes and tried to recollect what I needed to know for the exam. I had studied the material before. I also made a mental note to get a book from the library or make copies of the textbooks for other exams.

The next day I took the exam, once again choosing the alternate route to reach school. My immediate goal was to score enough to pass the exam. I answered the questions I was sure of with certainty and then I completed the rest. I tried to finish the exam early so I could go to the library and borrow the books I needed.

I came back from the exam and checked with Abhishek on the status of the court hearing. He seemed disappointed.

'Just as I thought, nothing happened in the court. We filed the case, but Salim and Shabnam had a very good lawyer who responded by blocking our appeal to stay. They also countersued us for harassment.'

'Damn it. What's next?'

'Nothing. Just inaction. The next court hearing is set for the next month.'

'Next month? Man, when will our courts realize that justice delayed is justice denied?'

'I am trying to get some influential people to exert some pressure. And Dad is trying too. We have to get our deposit from them. We have to fight it out and hold our ground until then.'

We endured and persevered for the next seven days. Dad left early in the mornings before Salim and Shabnam got up. Abhishek would stay if I had an exam. If I didn't, he would also leave in the morning. Salim and Shabnam provoked an ugly confrontation every day, but Mom continued trying to contain any possible blowup. The nights were quiet in our room while noises and some loud parties in the living room disrupted any normalcy we tried to enjoy. Dad and Abhishek went from pillar to post to find somebody to help us. Abhishek had shown remarkable maturity in the last few days, staying and protecting Mom and Anamika and trying to find people to help. But soon it was clear that this was a well-planned operation and all the layers of bureaucratic chains were well oiled. From the security guards, who were surprisingly missing that night, to the chairman of our society to the council member of our area and, of course, the police, everybody knew that something very wrong had happened with our family, yet not a single person was willing to do anything about it. They supported the other side and told us to leave peacefully for our own safety.

It was about a week now that Salim and Shabnam had been staying in our house. We were having dinner sitting on the floor in the kitchen with Mom cooking on the floor. Dad was not home. The mood was pretty somber and everyone was lost in their thoughts.

'I haven't seen Shakuntala Aunty for the last few days.'

'Oh, Ankit. You don't know,' Anamika said.

'I don't know what?' I quizzed.

'Shabnam beat her with a broom and threw her out.'

'What?'

Anamika continued, 'It was horrifying to watch as Shabnam slapped her on the face, then repeatedly hit her with her hands and then picked up the broom and hit her again and again. She told her not to come back to the house ever again.'

It was painful to hear. 'These people are really evil,' I decried.

'Shh. Quiet. They will hear,' Mom warned.

'How is Dad doing?'

'He is okay.'

'When I saw him this morning, he looked sick. Did you notice that he had some red marks on his hands and neck? His face seemed swollen as well.'

Mom and Abhishek exchanged glances.

'It must be some rashes. He has been visiting some real dirty places in the slums,' Mom said.

'Just focus on your exams, Ankit,' Abhishek said.

'I am trying. When I am taking the exam, I am in a zone where I lose track of time. I'm not sure if it is a good or a bad thing. But I am trying.'

'Good, just don't fail,' Abhishek added.

'We have to hang on and get our deposit,' Mom said.

Seeing our Mom's steely determination, we were more and more determined not to get thrown out of our house.

Dad and Abhishek had tried everything, but nothing was working. The other side was very well connected and organized. Dad was out trying every strategy possible and would come home very late at night. Sometimes he would sleep at his friend's place. Abhishek reached out to everyone he could and tried everything, but the situation did not change. Watching Dad and Abhishek try so hard, I felt that I was not doing enough. I channeled all my anger and frustration into my exams. I treated each exam question like it was a demon in my path that had to be slayed. My exam preparation was not up to the mark without the proper books and the situation at home was only making it more difficult. Yet, I took the exams with unwavering determination.

It was the twelfth day when a harsher reality hit us; we were dealing with some really powerful people. We were sitting on the floor having dinner when Abhishek pulled out a newspaper clipping from his pocket. 'Look at this article I found about Salim and Shabnam.'

It seems that this guy was indeed a professional conman who took over people's houses, just as he had said. The newspaper article specifically mentioned Salim and Shabnam working as a couple. It mentioned that they were partners in crime, sometimes posing as a married couple. They had successfully evicted numerous families from their houses in a similar fashion and the article mentioned that they had orchestrated many operations of these kinds. In one instance, they had gotten an old helpless woman thrown out of her own house and had taken over that property. That lady, not surprisingly, had died from a car accident the next day. Our deepest fear about Salim and Shabnam were confirmed. We were indeed sharing space with ruthless criminals.

'These guys are very well connected. They have a comprehensive support network, including politicians to law enforcement and the mafia. It is unlikely that we will get our deposit back,' Abhishek said resignedly.

'We have to come up with a Plan B. Dad has found an alternate place to stay when we are evicted from here,' Mom said. Her optimism or at least her resolve was admirable.

'Yes. I looked at it as well. It is a small hut in one of the slums. It is close to the cowsheds.' Abhishek said.

'That's okay. I think anything is better than this. We can manage in a hut,' I said.

'I think we have to accept and prepare for the worst,' Mom said dejectedly.

'I agree. Staying here is torture,' Anamika chimed in.

'Shh. We can't let Salim and Shabnam hear us. This is just a backup plan. We will continue to stay here as long we can, maybe something positive will happen.' We were nearing the very end of our resistance.

'Nothing will happen. I prefer living near the cowshed. On the bright side, we will at least get the purest and freshest milk, right from the source,' I joked as everyone laughed. A little bit of humour went a long way on such days.

'In fact, when I wake up early to study, I will take a hot cup of water, put a tea bag in it and go milk the cows myself to get my cup of tea.' Everyone burst into laughter. It was good to see the family laugh after such a long time. Yet, under the streams of laughter, there was a new apprehension on how life was about to change in the slums after moving from this posh locality.

Finally, after more than two weeks of our captivity, through some back channel, they began to negotiate with my father. It was decided that they would give back some part of the deposit with interest that the company owed us, on the condition that we leave the house.

In the early afternoon, a truck came to take our stuff. It was mostly the heavy stuff like furniture and cupboards since most of the rest had been taken or burnt down by the goons. Dad had instructed the movers to dispose of all the large pieces of furniture, including the sofa, beds and mattresses. We were surprised by that. We packed up whatever little was left.

With us finally evicting from the house, Shabnam was elated. As we walked out of the living room, she came to chat with us. She seemed happy and her tone was uncharacteristically friendly. 'You know, I have been in this business of eviction for many years and I have not seen this kind of tenacity coming from anyone. Your family was tough. I had not expected that. Phew!'

We ignored her compliments just as we had ignored her many abuses, and we walked away from the house.

As we were about to leave in the quiet of the late night, we sat in the taxi with our souls broken. Abhishek was in the front seat with the cab driver and Mom, Anamika and I sat in the back seat. We looked back at the house where we had spent our entire childhood. We sat expressionless. We did not know if we felt happy that the ordeal was over and that we had won the fight, or sad that we were leaving our childhood home and memories behind. I guess we were too tired to feel any emotion at that moment. We just felt lifeless, unable to feel or say anything.

In the quiet of the moment, in the silence of the night, Mom recited the couplet from the Indian poet Mirza Ghalib:

Nikalna khuld se aadam ka sunte aaye hain lekin,
bade be-aabru hokar tere kooche se hum nikle

(We had only heard about how badly the Satan was banished from heaven's gate,
But I feel more disgraced as I am being removed from your quarters)

We all just looked at her and tried to smile.

5

REACH

'Where is the other room?' Anamika whispered in my ear as we entered our new home.

'Quiet. Dad will feel bad,' I replied, trying to suppress the question without answering.

We had mentally prepared ourselves to move to a small hut near the cowshed, but due to Abhishek's efforts, we were able to rent a one-room apartment in a building near the international airport. I was also confused about what a one-room apartment would be like, but I was happy that we would have a solid roof over our heads, especially for the rainy season.

We leased the apartment through a contact of Abhishek's friend. Since the arrangements had to be taken care of in a hurry, the apartment did not have any electricity. That night after our taxi reached the new place, I saw that it was a four-storey run-down building.

We were excited to see Dad. He had been at the new place trying to move in our things and set up the household for us. He was standing downstairs outside the building when we drove up. Dad started to take the luggage from the taxi and went upstairs. He did not stop to greet us. It seemed somewhat of an odd behavior since we were expecting a better welcome. There was no eye contact, just the quick shifting of our luggage. As we entered the apartment, he came downstairs to pay the taxi driver. He seemed kind of aloof.

There was no elevator, so we climbed up the stairs. As I

entered the door of our new rented apartment, it was dark. Dad had lit a few candles to provide some light. Entering slowly, we saw a small corridor that led into the kitchen. Before the kitchen, there was a bathroom on the left side and another room on the right. As we entered that room and looked around, I thought that it was quite a small one and maybe it was a conduit to another room. Anamika was walking in front of me. Walking further inside and looking around, it was obvious that there were no more rooms. There was neither a bedroom nor a living room, just this small room for the five of us to live in. I looked around. There was the bottom part of cabinet and by the window there was our large storage trunk which was covered with a sheet, so we could use it as a couch. Also, there was a small bench facing the cupboard. Dad had purchased some thin foldable mattresses which were stacked in one corner. He had also bought some food for dinner.

As we settled down not knowing where to sit, we sat down on the floor with candles between us. There was silence. Everyone was trying to find their bearings in the surrounding darkness. Mom started to unpack the dinner. Dad said he had already eaten and went to the kitchen. After we finished our meal, we started to spread the five thin mattresses on the floor to sleep on. As Abhishek and I were arranging the fifth mattress, we realized that there was not enough space in the room for it to fit. We were hitting the corners of the room. I looked at him and he looked at me. We hesitated a bit making sure not to mention anything that may highlight the apartment's shortcomings. We folded the fifth mattress along the wall and Abhishek said, 'We can just put down four small mattresses and you and I can share one.'

'Yes, that is a good idea,' I agreed.

Dad came from the kitchen and said, 'No need. I am sleeping in the kitchen.'

'No, it is okay. We have space in this room. Abhishek and I can share one mattress,' I said.

'I will sleep in the kitchen and that is final,' he said in a firm voice.

Mom looked at us and raised her fingers to indicate that we should let it go. Dad took the fifth mattress and put it in the kitchen and went to sleep.

As we were about to fall asleep, Mom got us kids in her typical huddle.

'That incident at our previous house and the verbal abuse from the police has affected your Dad very badly. We should give him some time to heal. Let's get some sleep.'

As I lay on the thin mattress, I could feel the hard tile floor below. But I felt a sense of comfort in the knowledge that there was no longer a threat from either Salim or Shabnam and that everyone, though uncomfortable, was safe and together again as a family. As I took a breath of gratitude, there was a sweet fragrance in the air.

'Where is that smell coming from? What could it be? It will be interesting to check out the neighbourhood tomorrow morning.'

When I went to the bathroom, I saw Dad sleeping in the small kitchen, which had space for just one mattress.

The next morning when we got up, I looked outside the window to trace the source of the sweet fragrance. Outside our building, there was a small area with chawls and a bit further there was the main road which led to the airport.

'There's a crematorium,' Abhishek said.

'What?' I said trying to hide my surprise. His answer explained the smell, which was coming from flowers and burnt incense.

Dad seemed to have left early in the morning and Mom joined us with the morning tea.

'Look, Mom. Roshan Uncle has still not left us and he will haunt us from there.' I tried indulging in some humour to defuse the unpleasant reality of having the crematorium in front of our new home.

'Ankit, don't be disrespectful,' Mom scolded me.

'I am joking. At least the airport is close by and the bus stop is five minutes away. With one change of bus, I think it will take about 45 minutes to reach my college,' I said trying to change the topic.

'How is Dad doing?'

'He is okay. I spoke to him this morning before he left. He needs some time to recover.'

'Yup.'

'The first thing I would like us to do is to return the money that Shakuntala loaned us. It was a nice gesture and we know she is not well off.'

'I have to go to college and catch up with my commerce courses.' Abhishek had not gone to his college for quite a long time and had missed most of the classes over the last few weeks.

'I can drop it off at her place,' I volunteered since my exams were over.

'I can come too. It would be good to see Shakuntala Aunty,' Anamika said from her bed.

'Okay,' my Mom agreed. It had been days since Anamika had been outside. Both she and Mom had been cooped up in the house for too many days.

So, after having breakfast, Anamika and I took the bus. We had a general idea where Shakuntala Aunty lived—close to our school. Next to the main road near the bus stop there was a small corridor which led to a narrow road surrounded by chawls on either side. At the entrance, we saw an elderly gentleman and told him we were looking for Shakuntala Aunty. He was more than happy to help us. 'Let me show you the way. I will walk with you.'

He called out to a young boy who was playing nearby, 'Hey Chandu. Go tell Shakuntala her employers have come to see her.'

The kid ran ahead shouting, 'Shakuntala's employers are here.'

People started coming out of their chawls to look at us. Everyone seemed friendly. Some were waving at us. As we navigated the narrow road, we took care not to hit our heads as some of the chawls on either side of the road almost met in the narrow lanes.

As we entered Shakuntala Aunty's chawl, we thanked the gentleman who helped us as he left. She was waiting outside and invited us in.

Once inside, she greeted us with a big smile and hugged Anamika. She caressed my sister's face, looking at her hands and neck. She caressed her face again.

'She is fine, Aunty. Nothing happened. She is not hurt,' I smiled reassuringly trying to allay her fears that Anamika might have suffered some injury.

'I don't know how your family was able to spend two weeks with that lady. She was pure evil...I have never seen such a horrible person in my life.'

'We are just glad it's over now,' I said trying not to open the fresh wounds.

'But we all felt bad about what happened to you, what you had to go through with Shabnam because of us. We are really sorry.'

'What are you saying Ankit? We were all in this together,' Shakuntala Aunty replied.

'Although I was not there, I was getting the news of your family from the domestic workers in your neighbourhood.'

'Now we have moved to an apartment near the airport. You should come and visit us.' I could not help but notice that her room was actually bigger than ours.

'I'll get you something to eat.'

Shakuntala Aunty opened a steel tiffin box and gave us some laddoos.

'How were your engineering exams?'

'I took them. I took all of them.' At this time, that was the only positive thing I could say. I had been so focused on making sure that I reached the exam hall safe and sound that I had not thought much about how I did in the exams.

'I hope you did well. It's your parents' dream. I remember

your Mom telling me how proud she was that you were going to be an engineer. How is she doing?'

'She is okay. She is working on getting settled.'

'And your Dad?'

'Okay.' I did not delve into the details that he was not doing well.

We returned the money to her and she gave us a steel tiffin box with sweets to take home. She hugged Anamika, knowing that she might not see her for a very long time.

As we walked along the tight lanes we saw the residents' friendly faces and felt their warmth. I thought about how people with fewer means can be so good at heart while rich people can be the most corrupt.

For the next couple of months, our lives started getting back to normal. We bought clothes, utensils, books and other educational material and household items. While Dad took care of the financial aspects, Abhishek and Mom took the initiative of doing most of the household chores.

Dad had become very reclusive and reticent. He would often stare blankly. When nobody was in the room, he would sit by himself deep in thoughts, staring out the window watching people pass on the street. If any of us were there, he would move to the kitchen window and look outside. If somebody was in the kitchen, he would walk outside and look around. It seemed that he was keeping a watch on who came and went, completely lost in his own thoughts. There was a sense of insecurity around him, which we had never felt before. If he noticed someone suspicious entering the building, he would get all worked up trying to track the person.

He was very pensive. Before the incident he spoke to us on a few occasions, but now his talks just involved instructing Mom to take care of the kids.

'Vijaya, the kids have woken up. Bring them tea.'

'Abhishek is home. Bring him a glass of water.'

'Vijaya, cut some fresh fruits for the kids.' He was big on his kids eating fruit. Every day, Dad took long walks and used to bring the freshest fruits from the market and milk from the cowshed. Beyond that, there was not much communication between us. The number of cigarettes increased.

I could feel he was troubled by negative thoughts, which were torturing him. I wanted to hold his hand and give him a hug and tell him it was going to be all right and that the good days would return. But I was hesitant to do so. All I thought about was working hard in my studies and making him proud. As kids, we did not know how to reduce his sense of dejection. None of us spoke of the incident with Shabnam and Salim, neither with him, nor among ourselves or with any friends. It was best to forget it and move on.

One day, when Abhishek and I were walking to the bus stop, I decided to broach the topic. We had not spoken about that night even once. It was a nightmare which we wanted to erase from our memory.

'I hope Dad is okay. It seems like something is eating him up from inside. He is quiet, but seems very troubled.'

'Yes, it seems so.'

'I was hoping he would recover with time, but he seems very troubled.'

'I know it is tough to watch.' He thought for a while before speaking. His hesitation added to my doubts.

'Those marks that I saw on Dad's hands and neck when Salim was at our house were not skin rashes, right?'

Abhishek thought for a while and considered whether he should tell me or not.

'C'mon, tell me. I can handle it. My exams are over now. He was beaten up, right?'

'Not once but many times during those 15 days, by many people. It was just so random and unexpected. He would be walking on the street and a group of people would come from behind and punch him and kick him until he would fall to the ground and then they'd leave him lying on the ground there. Sometimes, when he asked for help from other people, they would ignore his requests as they would turn out to be Salim's guys. And then they too would beat him up.'

I felt a surge of pain and anger rise in my body.

'I think it was not just the physical torture but also the mental abuse. Salim was an expert manipulator. Do you remember, in the initial days, when we were confident that we could get the court judgement and get them removed from the house with the help of law?'

'Yes. We thought that it was an open and shut case. Someone illegally enters your house and the court in all fairness should have passed the order to remove them.'

'Yes, Dad was hopeful and tried really hard. Our lawyer was sure that the judge would grant us sole custody of the apartment.'

'Law was clearly on our side.'

'But not that judge. As Dad was frantically running around with the lawyers, Salim met him in court on the day when we were expecting the final hearing. He told Dad to stand hidden in some corner and watch what was about to unfold.'

'Hmm,' I said.

'Right in front of Dad, Salim gave a pile of cash to the judge who was presiding over our case. And the judge accepted it happily. It broke Dad's heart to see this level of corruption in the country he had fought for when he served in the Army. I think Salim broke his conviction, his faith in the judiciary and his confidence.'

'That's awful.'

'Yup. The best of soldiers break under torture. Now it is up to us to give him his life back by succeeding in our chosen careers.'

'Yes, we will.'

'When are your results coming out?'

'Tomorrow. I hope that I pass.'

'I hope so too,' Abhishek said. The results of the exams were now even more significant after our recent conversation, and I felt the pressure.

'This is the first engineering exam. They tend to grade it tough so that they can weed out as many students as possible. I just hope I can get a passing grade. I took the exam in such a weird state of mind that I really don't recollect what I wrote. I know that I was determined, and I answered each question as if my life depended on it, but I really don't remember how I answered the questions. Let's see.'

'You will do fine,' Abhishek tried to reassure me.

The next day I went to the college to check my grades on the sheet of paper posted on the bulletin board. During the bus ride there, I silently prayed, *God, please don't let me flunk any subject and lose a year.*

Those exams had gone by in a flash, and as much as I was trying to recall I could not remember anything. My mind had been so focused on the events happening at home, the terror of Salim and Shabnam, that I was unable to recollect my experience in the examination hall.

I was especially concerned about the engineering drawing exam which I had taken under severe emotional distress. I thought about how I had jumped the walls to reach on time. A smile broke out when I thought about the moment I had returned after appearing for the exam and how I had stared down at Salim, putting my mini drafter over my shoulder like it was a gun.

Today John Rambo needs to pass his engineering exams, I thought.

The results were posted on the bulletin board on the second floor of the college building. As I climbed the stairs, I could hear my heart pounding. I moved through the crowd of students and looked at the list for my class. There was a row with the names of the students and one with the grades they had scored in each subject. When I found my name, I moved my fingers horizontally to see my score in each subject. My only wish was to see a number greater than 40. A sense of relief flowed through my mind as I saw all the scores were higher than what I had hoped for. I again reviewed the numbers making sure I was looking correctly under my own name. Each of them was above 40.

I passed. Thank you, God. I was filled with gratitude. I gave a huge sigh of relief as if a big weight had been lifted off my chest. I moved away from the crowd and stood with my back and head rested against a nearby wall. I breathed deeply.

Thank you, God. I was content to not add to my family's sadness. I could actually share a moment of happiness with them now.

'Congrats, Ankit,' one of my friends said shaking my hand.

'Thanks, man,' I said in a reflex as I shook his hand.

But wait, why did my friend congratulate me for passing? Does he know the backstory? That's impossible. Neither had I told anybody about our struggles, nor had I ever brought any friends home. This was to keep our financial distress private. Within our family, we barely discussed the events around our eviction. How could he possibly know?

'I am happy to just pass. It is a good feeling to move to the next level, isn't it?' I pressed on to see how much my friend knew.

'What pass? Don't be modest. You have got one of the top ranks in the college.'

'What?'

'You are among the top five scorers in the entire college. All the engineering streams have the same exam for the first year and you are among the top five students across all the engineering streams of our college. Congrats, buddy.'

'Hmm.' I was in a state of disbelief.

'Your name is on the merit list. There,' he said, as he pointed to another bulletin board.

I could not believe what he was saying. So I went and looked at the merit list. There I could see my name among the top five scorers in the entire college. I wanted to be happy at this achievement, but

I wasn't feeling so. It was good that I was able to get such high scores and it was great given the circumstances under which I took the exam. As bubbles of happiness started erupting inside me, they were quickly weighed down by other emotions. There was the cost that my family had paid, especially my Dad, so that I could take my exam. This is not an accomplishment in itself, but a step in the right direction. The goal of having a career was still far away, but one thing was for sure—I belonged in the field of engineering.

I went home and shared the news. Everyone was relieved. Dad just said 'good' and went to sit in the kitchen. Mom was extremely happy and wanted to celebrate the occasion.

'To celebrate this achievement, I am going shopping and getting new clothes for everyone.'

'Yeah,' Anamika shouted.

About once a year, Mom shopped for our clothes. She would take the local train and go to South Mumbai, near downtown. We did not go along to save on the cost of the train ticket. There was 'Fashion Street', lined with stalls from where vendors sold all kinds of clothes. Mom would buy two shirts each for Abhishek and me and maybe a pair of jeans for us every two years. The shirts cost ₹25 and if they were better quality they would cost ₹40. The fabric had some interesting prints and colours. From her choice, it was clear that Mom liked colourful printed patterns. Abhishek and I would share each other's shirts and jeans. As we grew bigger, Dad's shirts fit us, which gave us a bigger pool to share from. Mostly, each of us tried to stick to two or three shirts over one year. The rarity of this annual event made it precious and exciting. We would wait in the evening to see what bounty she brought home.

One day, when I was climbing the stairway to reach my classroom on the second floor, I overheard three female classmates talking about me.

'Hey, where is our class representative, Ankit? I haven't seen him for a few days,' one girl asked.

They were standing on the balcony of the second floor and I was a few steps below. I could hear them but they could not see me.

'I just saw him. He is not hard to find because he is always wearing the same jeans and T-shirt.'

'I don't know why he wears the same clothes every day. Maybe he just likes to,' they all giggled.

'Maybe it is just superstition. Maybe they bring him luck,' and they burst into laughter.

The words just pierced my ears and heart. My instant reaction was to turn back and walk away. As I turned around to walk back down the stairs and disappear, a voice inside spoke firmly, *You can't turn back, Ankit. You have to face your fair share of suffering.* So I walked up and greeted the girls and exchanged pleasantries as if I had heard nothing.

Even though I was there face to face with them, they were not able to control their laughter. One girl said, 'Sorry Ankit, don't mind our giggling, we had just shared a joke before you came.'

'It's okay, no worries.'

I knew that the joke was on me, but I saw no reason to say anything.

As I rode back home on the bus from college that evening, I tried to erase the incident and the feeling of humiliation from my memory. I wanted to fight it and make sure that it didn't define my college experience. I wasn't going to go back into my shell as I had done in junior college. My college experience had been rich and joyful and this one incident was not going to mar it. I decided to take this incident in stride and get more involved in college.

The following year I again stood in the class election and won comfortably to become the class representative for the second time. I also stood in the college student body elections and became the secretary, with the responsibility of organizing events. I participated in all the sporting events and was a member of the college soccer team.

We played in the inter-university tournament and went a long way. It was a big achievement for a young engineering college like ours. On the day of our last match, our coach told us that the school would pay for our meals at a good restaurant. So, four of us went ahead and ordered a lot of food. There were juices, appetizers, main courses that included pizza, noodles and ice cream. Each of us shared from each other's plates. It was like a feast. We were so hungry after playing soccer that we ate a lot. I hadn't had a generous meal in a restaurant for a while, and as I ate the food I couldn't help but recall the good old days.

Being poor in a rich country was bearable but being poor in an impoverished country was just plain tough. There were daily challenges every step of the way, but no one in my family shared their worries openly. We supported each other in the long battle to cope and rise above our present difficulties. So when it was time for Abhishek's exams, I would do all his chores and vice versa. I would help Anamika with her studies and when she was free she would help Mom with her kitchen chores. It was quiet in the house even when everyone was present. Dad would be in the kitchen looking out the window, Mom would be cooking and we would be quietly studying or thinking and suppressing our emotions.

The one-room apartment felt congested when everyone was home. I would find my mental retreat on the terrace. Our apartment was on the top floor of the building and from there we had access to the terrace one level above. Often, when I came home, Dad would move to the kitchen to give us some space. I escaped by going up to the terrace to clear my mind.

Looking at the open sky would be a liberating feeling, taking me away from the rigours of daily life. I loved to look at the changing colours, the shape of the clouds and the birds. Often there were pigeons flying around, some would stop by on the edge of the terrace and sing a friendly hello. If I was affable, they hung around a while. Sometimes, they would leave behind a feather as a gift. It was the most delicate thing in the world. I would admire the details of the feather and blow it softly from the palm of my hand and watch it dance with the wind. As it moved ecstatically with the wind, my eyes would follow its motion and it would bring a smile to my face.

Along with my morning and evening walks, I also started to study on the terrace. I would bring a mattress and a pillow outside and use the terrace entrance wall for back support. I would study and walk and soon the two processes became so intermingled that I would be walking and thinking about my course material, trying to focus. I often looked at the sky and wondered about my life and its meaning and the path I wanted to take for my career.

Some days I would listen to music on my Walkman. One of the things that had not been scavenged by Salim's gang was my small Sony Walkman. It was black and the size of a small rectangular box, and the headphones were a bent steel rod with round foam earbuds.

I loved Gloria Estefan's song 'Reach', which had been the anthem for the 1996 Summer Olympics.

I got a blank cassette and went to one of the audio shops and told them I wanted to record the song over the entire cassette. There were two 30-minute sides, A and B. I recorded the song on both sides. I would walk on the terrace under the open sky and listen to this song, over and over again. The lyrics were very inspiring to me.

If I could reach, higher
Just for one moment touch the sky
From that one moment in my life
I'm gonna be stronger
Know that I've tried my very best

I'd put my spirit to the test
If I could reach.

During the second and third year of engineering, the electronic engineering curriculum increasingly focused on core subjects. I was developing a strong interest in the field of microprocessor design. As our course work covered the evolution of the Intel microprocessor from its early stages to the Pentium processor, I found it fascinating how putting together a basic logic unit, like a transistor, in different ways could create something complex and useful. I thought that designing the microchips that were being used in personal computers was an amazing technological advancement. This field was a perfect intersection of my analytical skills and my desire to create something worthwhile. This is what had drawn me to the field in the first place; I remember when I had seen some cool electronic devices in my Dad's oil company. I could imagine its benefit for humankind, as Dad used to say, 'Whatever work you do, it should improve the life of the human race.' Even if it was small steps, I wanted to contribute to the progress of the human race and push the scope of development even further. The field of computer chips and design was a great avenue for me to make a contribution in.

I started to investigate this field and studied Intel's innovations and contributions. Microsoft was bringing out a new OS Windows 95 that was running on Intel's chips. It was changing the way people would interact with electronics through graphical user interfaces and it was achieving this revolution with the new operating system. I wanted to be part of this electronics revolution that was taking place. I was fascinated by the personal computer and Windows OS, and even more enchanted with the underlying microchip that was driving it. My current college course was not enough, since we had limited access to any PCs. It was only during lab classes when we could work on PCs, and that too by sharing it with four other students for 30 minutes only. I wanted to learn and do more in this field. I looked for opportunities in India, but there was not a single company working on chip design. To uplift my career, I had to get an advanced degree and there were no Master's or PhD programmes in engineering.

I began to read more books on this subject and I spent a lot of time walking and thinking about it on the terrace until it became an obsession.

All the great innovations were happening in the United States, especially in the Silicon Valley, which was aptly named, given the electronic chips were made of silicon. There was great research happening in computer engineering in American universities like Stanford, MIT and Berkeley.

It would be great if I could go to one of these universities and do research in this area. That is my dream.

That thought became a constant hum and a source of excitement during my walks on the terrace. How great it would be to do research with the smartest minds in the world! This dream was tempered by the reality of limited finances: how would I be able to study at these illustrious schools?

I had been adroitly avoiding the college field trips and picnics to nearby places because I was not able to afford it. So how could I even think of travelling to another country? But I kept thinking about it day in and day out. It was a dream that had kept me awake at night. With all my heart, it was the dream I wanted to fulfil, but how could I possibly achieve it?

Remember Ankit, dreams are beyond your grasp. That is what makes them worth fighting for. That is when you have to reach out for it.

Yes, yes, I had to rise above the stars by putting my spirit to the test.

I decided I would pursue my goal of doing research abroad. I knew my target and vision and now I had to find a way to achieve it. With my obsession for chip design and studying abroad, I slowly isolated myself socially and became less active in college. I reduced my participation in class and sports and spent a lot of time on our terrace. Even when I attended college, I would skip some classes so I could read journals and news articles in the cafeteria. There, I made friends with my classmates, Arun and Nihar.

They were both rebels and hated the Indian education system because it relied on cramming for exams and never taking the time to understand the material. They spent a lot of time in the cafeteria and less time in class. Our schedules often intersected. Arun was a jovial person who loved to eat. He was also very risk averse and always worried about the future and impending doom. Nihar had a lot of confidence. Their rejection of the education system in India moved them to prepare for studies abroad. They were both from well-off families and had a computer at home. Both Arun and Nihar were up to date with the happenings and innovations in the technical world. They were good friends and were open to sharing the information with me. With their help I found that I had to take the GRE entrance exam to qualify for a master's programme in the US. Universities evaluated the admissibility of applicants based on students' GRE scores and their grades in their engineering courses. A university would offer a scholarship if the student's scores were exceptional.

'So if I score very well on the GRE, I won't have to pay any fees?' I confirmed with Arun and Nihar.

'Yes. In fact, not only will they waive off your fees, they will also give you an additional monthly stipend for working in the lab,' Arun said.

'Wow! No college fees and then compensation for working in the research lab. That would be just great.'

I came home and went to the terrace again and listened to the lyrics of 'Reach'. This time I listened to the song with more enthusiasm, now that I knew what my dream was and was beginning to see a path forward.

In the next few days, I shared my aspirations with my family. I told them about how I could fulfil my dream of doing research in computer engineering without any additional expense if I scored high on the GRE exam and got a scholarship. Everybody was very supportive and encouraging.

'You can do whatever you set your mind to, Ankit,' Dad said. Usually very reticent, this time he chimed in with uncharacteristic optimism.

Abhishek had moved into the commerce field and now had his mind set on MBA from one of the top colleges in Bombay. It was clear to him that going outside the city would be difficult as paying for the college dorm would be expensive. Anamika had lost her effervescence and spontaneity. She too became serious with her studies and decided to take more control of the household operations, thereby granting Dad the space he needed to work things out.

Two years after the home invasion, Dad's company was finally ready to settle the employment case. It compensated a modest amount to us and admitted wrongful termination. I heard that the management had been aware of the disgraceful incident we had suffered and they felt bad. It was too little, too late. The case had gone on for almost a decade, but it felt like a lifetime. Dad was a changed person now and so were we.

The money and validation did not bring Dad any kind of joy. Several days after the case was settled, he summoned us into the room and said, 'My previous company has finally decided to settle the case.'

'They have partially accepted responsibility for the wrongful termination and are compensating me with some amount for the lost earnings.'

'That's good,' we said.

'They have provided monetary compensation only. What they cannot compensate is the time we had to endure the insult because of their poor judgement. After thinking a lot, I have decided not to invest this money in any more business ventures. I have seen one failure after another and I have wasted my life trying to succeed in business. Enough is enough.'

'No Dad, that is not true,' I said trying to prevent him from falling into the abyss of self-condemnation and dejection.

'Let me finish. The only investment I have succeeded in is my children. So, I have decided that I will put all this money, every last penny, into your education. I will provide you whatever you need for your education. Abhishek can do his MBA, Ankit, his masters abroad and Anamika, her engineering degree. It is a fixed amount and I think it will last until you all complete your education, if we use it discreetly. We will see what happens after that. A few years ago, Mom and I had decided that we would tolerate whatever suffering this city brought upon us so that you kids could have a future. We have endured a lot and you all have endured more than what you should have. You kids are my pride and joy. I will bet everything I have on your future.'

I felt very proud of our parents who had put their last penny on the line so that we could complete our education and fulfil our dreams.

'Also, I think with the extra money, we can move to a slightly bigger apartment.'

We were happy to leave the one-room apartment at last.

Dad had finally spoken openly to us after years of silence. The words he uttered gave me solace, that underneath the troubled thoughts, the basic goodness of his nature remained. I felt proud to have such wonderful parents. But I also felt the pressure. I had to get a scholarship from an American university now. The money was not enough to fund even one semester, but it would buy a ticket to the US. Also, I was aware that this money was not just for me. Abhishek and Anamika were entitled to pursue their education too, and I was not going to behave selfishly. I was thinking about getting a full scholarship and a stipend for my research. I could start sending money home. This motivated me even further to study hard for the GRE.

We moved to a bigger apartment that had a small living room, one bedroom and a kitchen. It had more sunlight and an open view, but was very close to the railway tracks. It was so close that we could see the local trains pass by every few minutes. Every time a train zoomed by, the apartment would shake and so would we. We would laugh it off when the chalky substance from the walls fell on our heads.

It was much better now that Dad did not have to sleep in the kitchen. Dad had intentionally taken an apartment on the top floor as he had noticed how I used the terrace for my studies. This accommodation was similar and provided the extra space that I needed. It was now all about studying and achieving my dream. I had only one goal and that was to get a scholarship at an American university by securing a very high score in the GRE. I planned and followed a very strict regimen for my preparation.

I would get up at 5.00 a.m. and take my mattress, books and Walkman to the terrace. There I studied till eight and then came downstairs for breakfast. At nine, I would go back to the terrace and study till two in the afternoon. To avoid the direct blaze of the sun, I put the mattress in the shade under the water tank that stood in the corner of the terrace. Being under the concrete structure full of gallons of water provided me some relief. The tank worked like an air conditioner on very hot and humid days. Then there was lunch at 2.00 p.m. after which I rested until four. Then I studied again till nine in the evening, after which I would take a break for dinner. I would then do one final hour of revision and planning for the next day. It was always difficult to push through from 10.00 p.m. to 11.00 p.m. I used that last hour to think about what I had studied that day, what I had to study the next day and how I could improve. I followed this 12–14 hour regimen on weekends, during summer breaks and on days when I did not have to attend college.

During all these months of waking up early to study, Dad never missed even one morning of getting up and making a cup of tea for me even if it meant him getting up at four. I would go quietly to the terrace and yet somehow, he would know and bring me tea within half an hour. He did not say anything other than 'tea'. The moment when that cup of tea moved from his hands to my shivering hands spoke volumes about his dedication. That cup of tea was like a panacea on those cold mornings with the cold breeze under the open sky.

On the days when I attended college, I would study in the library whenever I had a break and return home to study when I finished my classes. I would hang out with Arun and Nihar. Our friendship grew as we realized we shared goals. They generously shared information with me since they had access to the outside world. Other than my relationship with them, I barely spoke to anybody else during those days. I was just a shadow of who I had been in the first year of engineering. I was obsessed with the GRE and my only thought was how to get a score high enough to get a scholarship.

The GRE had three sections worth 800 points each: verbal, math and analytical. Six months into my preparation, I took a practice test. I scored almost full marks in math, but in the verbal and analytical I did not do well. I was missing 200 to 300 points in each section. I worked hard to understand each mistake that I had made. I retraced my steps, trying to understand my thought process. How had I arrived at the wrong answer? I made notes documenting the mistakes to ensure that I did not repeat them. I also gathered similar questions and made some of my own, trying to ensure that I did not make the same mistake again. The verbal section was mostly about memorizing 50 wordlists and remembering them. I took books from library to improve my vocabulary and started reading more newspapers, so I could understand how words were used in different contexts.

I also got a book that explained the origin of words. I wasn't too concerned about math because I was good at it and was scoring well on the practice tests. To improve on the analytical section, I got Mensa books and solved puzzles on a regular basis.

I got into a cycle of taking practice exams, correcting my previous mistakes and then scoring higher than I had on my previous test. When I was feeling confident, I would pick a date to take the exam. I was absolutely obsessed with GRE. I did not play sports, watch TV or talk much to anybody. On the weekends, I would see the kids playing cricket in the apartment compound. I was tempted to play with them for few hours but I resisted the urge because it might tire me and then I would miss studying as per my schedule.

It was all about improving my score and focusing on what I needed to do to score higher on the next practice test. I became angry at myself when I repeated the same mistake. Gradually, my score started to improve. On the last few practice tests, I scored above 2,300 out of 2,400; on some of the tests my score was 2,340, which I thought should definitely get the attention of some university. The GRE that looked like an insurmountable towering mountain not so long ago, now seemed surmountable.

A few weeks before the exam, my friends informed me that the format of the GRE had changed. Instead of the paper and pencil test, it would be a computerized version. That was not a good thing for my preparation as I did not have a computer at home. I continued practising with paper tests.

There was a big difference between paper and computerized exams. On paper tests, my approach had been to complete all the easy questions first, mark the difficult ones, then go back and attack the ones I had left blank. This allowed me time to manage my tests and maximize my score. However, in the new computerized format, there appeared only one question on the screen at a time and you could not go back to previous questions once you entered your answer. It was an adaptive scheme where the next question was based on how you answered the previous question. If you answered the previous question correctly, then the next question would be slightly more difficult and so on. It was a completely different format than paper tests.

I needed to practise some computerized tests to familiarize myself with the format. It was clear that doing more paper tests had limited benefit. Computer tests would take hours to complete so going to an Internet café would be very expensive. I told Mom about it and she discussed it with one of our neighbours who lived on the first floor. She was an old lady and they had a PC that was not being used since her son was not home. She had agreed, somewhat reluctantly, so I put the test on a floppy drive and I went to our neighbour's place. Aunty did not look too pleased to see me.

'Thank you, Aunty. Thank you for allowing me to use your computer.'

'Yes. I don't know anything about it. Only my son uses it.'

I put in the floppy drive and started to run the tests. Aunty was looking over my shoulder. As I started to focus, trying to understand the test, it was difficult to understand the flow of questions that were appearing. There were keys and symbols I was seeing for the very first time. I made mental notes to understand what the keys were and how to use them. Fifteen minutes into the test, I was still struggling. I took a deep breath. The computerized test was tougher than I had thought it would be.

C'mon, Ankit. Fight. Focus. I tried to concentrate.

'Are you done?'

'No, no. I am still studying.'

'Oh, okay. I thought you were done. Does it consume a lot of electricity, this PC?'

'I don't think so, Aunty. It should not,' I said trying to focus on the exam and launching another assault on this strange computerized enemy.

'It is very expensive. We don't let anybody else touch the computer, except our son.'

'Yes, Aunty. I understand. I will be careful.'

'Nobody will be able to repair it in India if it goes bad, you know.'

I moved my attention to the present conversation.

Now I was catching her drift. Aunty did not want me to use her computer. That was clear. I thought for a few seconds. I stood up, removed the floppy disc and left the test midway, thanking her.

I continued taking the paper tests and was happy that I was consistently hitting in the 2,300s out of 2,400. I was hoping that the computerized tests would not throw me a curveball. I didn't need any more surprises.

During the engineering finals over the last few years, I had acquired this habit of taking too much pressure on the days close to the exams and would not sleep. I excessively thought and planned for the next day's exam and this stress would trigger weird sneezing and itchy eyes.

We had gone to the doctor a few times to see why this cold came only during exams, but he had no idea. It was like a mystery illness that aspirin could not cure. On the evenings before some of my engineering exams, I would lie on the floor suffering bouts of sneezing with watery eyes while my sister rubbed Vicks on my forehead and feet, hoping to cure the sneezing. Many years later I would find out that this mysterious illness was just allergies triggered by dust, pollen and stress.

To avoid any further health issues before the most important exam of my life, I had decided not to study two days prior to the GRE. I closed my books and stopped my daily regimen. I was feeling pretty satisfied with my preparation on the paper tests. I was not sure about the computerized format, but I tried not to dwell on it. How different could it be? The evening before the exam, I went to the living room to hang out and watch TV with Mom and Anamika, as they were the only ones at home. I sat there watching TV as Mom started to peel some oranges for us. We were watching music videos and chatting about movies. Anamika told me about the latest movies that were going to be released. Initially, it seemed awkward. It had been so many years since I had actually sat in the living room and chatted with my family while watching TV. I had grown distant from my siblings, especially from Abhishek. He was working hard to achieve his goals, charting his own course in commerce. It was almost as if I had lived alone on the terrace and in my head.

But slowly I got into the groove as we chatted, laughed, exchanging stories and memories from our childhood.

Anamika said, 'Ankit, let me tell you something funny.'

'Sometimes when you go the bathroom, we can hear you say, "Come on".'

'Mom and I laugh about it, not knowing if there is something wrong with your stomach.'

'I don't say those words in the bathroom.' Yet, in the back of my mind I was now realizing that I was doing that to motivate myself during my GRE preparation. There was the ongoing internal dialogue, but I had never realized that it was coming out loud and that others could hear me outside the bathroom.

'Ask Mom,' she said.

Mom nodded in agreement. 'It's okay. No big deal.'

'I hope everything is fine with your stomach,' Anamika said.

'Yes. I just motivate myself to study.'

I joined in the laughter, as it was funny once the reality of what I had been doing hit me. It felt good to laugh.

'Talking about toilet humour, you have to share with us what happened between you and Abhishek when you both went into the bathroom at the same time.'

'Oh, no. Not that incident. I am not sharing that story. It is too embarrassing. I am not telling you,' I said.

'What incident?' Mom asked.

'Where is Abhishek? I haven't seen or talked to him in a while,' I asked wishing he was there with us.

'Abhishek, besides attending his classes in commerce, has taken a part-time job. He has not told us what it is, but it seems that he is putting in a lot of hours,' Mom said.

'He has not told me either. He is very tired when he returns late in the night. Both my brothers work so hard and I am so proud of you both. I wish I could be like you guys and not be in this protected shell that you have put around me,' Anamika said.

'Don't worry, sister. Your time will come too.'

'Ankit, you are my role model. I am sure you will do very well in the exams,' my sister said.

On the day of the exam, I was feeling great. I had slept well and had woken up very late. I was happy that I didn't have watery, itchy or tired eyes since I needed to be able to see well for the computerized exam. In the afternoon, I went to the examination centre where they assigned me a computer to take the GRE. As I started the computerized sections, it took me a while to get accustomed to the format. There was a clock on the side of the screen which added to the pressure I was feeling. I was not familiar with the format and was not sure if I was answering the question correctly. My time management was in disarray since I did not know how much time to spend on each question. I tried to stay focused. It was a very uncomfortable and unfamiliar feeling to take an exam on a computer. At the end of the exam, the score showed up. My heart sank. I had a total score of 2080 out of 2400. It was nowhere near the scores I was getting on the paper practice tests.

I was shaken up. It was a lower score than I had expected and, more importantly, it was not enough to get a scholarship. The feeling had not sunk in yet and I had to vacate the computer desk quickly.

As I was leaving, I saw my friend Nihar, who had also taken the exam at the same place. I could barely muster a smile when I saw him.

He said, 'Don't tell me that you scored 2,400 out of 2,400.'

'No man. I messed up. I could not figure out how to take the computerized test. I scored much lower—2080,' I sighed.

'That isn't bad,' Nihar said sympathetically.

'It is. I won't get a scholarship with that score,' I said as I hurried out of the centre.

The bus I took back home was almost empty. Besides the driver, there was just an elderly lady sitting on the front seat and there was the conductor. When I boarded the bus, I was in a state of shock. I sat down on the seat closest to the back door of the bus. The conductor came over to me and I bought a ticket. Over my shoulder, I could see the sun setting. The birds were flying in a flock returning to their homes. The view was similar to the one I saw while studying on the terrace. As I watched the sun go down, the realization hit me that this was the end of my dream. With a score of 2080, no college in the US was going to give me a scholarship. If I didn't get one, I couldn't afford the tuition fee since we didn't have enough money. The door for further education had been slammed shut. No longer would I be able to achieve my dream of working in chip design research. What would I tell my family? My parents had pinned their hopes on this. I wanted to succeed, but today I had failed.

As the sense of failure engulfed me, I felt a pain in my gut and my entire body was shivering. As I clenched my jaw to control this pain, tears started dripping down my cheeks.

O God, I had worked so hard. I could not have worked any harder. I swear, I swear. I could not have worked any harder. I spent studying for the GRE every waking hour for months.

I remembered the long hours, from dawn to dusk, studying for months. I remembered waking up early in the morning, the afternoon hot sun bearing down as I sat under the water tank and the late nights when I would push through with the last ounce of energy I could muster.

I clenched my hands over the rails of the bus seat in front of me and put my head down over my hands and let out a loud cry of pain.

I was sobbing very loudly.

What more could I have done? I don't mind a fight. But this was not a fair fight. That is not fair, God. Changing to a computerized format when I didn't have a computer to practice on was not fair.

I kept sobbing, thinking how unfair life had been. *You have not been fair to me, God.*

I thought about my childhood, when Dad lost his job and the painful experiences all of us had to endure. I remembered watching my entire family stoically endure suffering and humiliation. Yet we all fought with quiet dignity and hard work. We never hurt anybody and never cheated or took a shortcut. Why was this happening to us? Why was my dream being shattered? I had tried to be strong for so long, but today the floodgates broke open. I let it all out. I was wailing loudly.

As I wiped my tears with my wet hands, I noticed that the lady at the front seat and the conductor were sympathetically looking towards me, wondering what had happened. But I continued crying and howling in excruciating sorrow. I had never cried like this before, I had never complained about life. But this day I was very angry at God for giving me such a difficult life. I was holding God responsible for shattering the dreams I had worked so hard to achieve.

I cried and sobbed continuously for 45 minutes, during the entire bus ride. I couldn't help myself. The tears flowed uncontrollably. When I got off the bus, I sat at the bus stop and cried some more. All the painful memories were surfacing. And I was thinking of all my hard work over the last few years that had just been washed away. I had promised I would not disappoint Dad and now I had.

I spent another hour at the bus stop to gather myself before going home. I had to be strong in front of my family. It was getting late and it was already dark. I slowly walked home.

Anamika and Dad were sitting on a bench under a tree outside the building anxiously waiting for me. I took a deep breath. They noticed my heavy and glassy eyes.

'I did not score well. I only got 2,080 out of 2,400.' I said with a grimace. By now everybody in my family knew what score was needed to get a scholarship. This was definitely not high enough.

'I will pursue my dream. I will go to the US for further studies,' I said. They put their arms on my heavy shoulders and we walked upstairs.

'I don't know how I am going to do it, but I am going to do it,' I declared.

6

PURSUIT

'*The mountain just became taller,* I thought to myself as I looked at the distant hills from the terrace.

Out of habit, I woke up early the next morning. Uneasy and not able to stay in bed any longer, I got up and retreated to the terrace. As I strolled around the terrace with the cool breeze, the light of the dawn reminded me that after sunset comes sunrise—a new day was about to begin.

The GRE results from the previous day were an absolute shocker for me and the path for higher studies had just become narrower. The fog looked denser now than it had before. Alternate options started to find their way into my mind. For the last two years, higher education and the GRE were all I had thought about. Should I start to think about focusing on the campus interviews and get a job? They are offering good high paying jobs in Mumbai and I will get to live with my family. I blocked those thoughts. I needed to stick to the path I had set out for myself. I had no backup plan. As I looked at the spot under the water tank where I had spent months studying, I had to now work harder to ensure that those hours do not amount to a complete waste. Now was the time to focus all my energy and push even harder to get through and achieve my goals. I started pacing around, contemplating the next plan of action.

With my low GRE score, getting a scholarship in a top-ranked university was improbable. Without a scholarship, there would be no chance to go abroad since the tuition was way too high. Currently, I did not think we had money enough to buy a plane ticket. The best way forward was to apply to a lower-ranked university that could give me a scholarship and after a few semesters I could transfer to a more prestigious one. Yes, that is a good plan to pursue. I now needed to focus on writing a good application.

As I was walking lost in my thoughts of charting the detour, I saw Dad at the entrance of the terrace with a cup of tea, just as he had been bringing me for years now. A smile broke out on my face as I felt the warmth of his unwavering commitment.

I said, 'Good morning, ah, tea,' as he handed me the warm cup and I took a small sip.

'Good morning,' he acknowledged with a smile. He wanted to say something but held back and started to walk away.

With no more study materials to keep me company, I suddenly felt lonely standing all by myself on the big terrace. I felt the need to talk to someone.

After taking a few steps, Dad turned around and came back.

'Ankit, I know that the GRE results were hard on you. I also know that not having a computer at home affected your chances. I really wish I could have bought a computer for you but…'

'It's okay, Dad.'

'But what I can do now is pay for the consultation services that you had spoken about, the one that helps with US university admissions.' There was a consulting firm that helped students navigate universities in the US and complete the application process. It was an expensive service with a good reputation. I was happy to get some help with the process since I did not have much knowledge about American universities and I did not want to mess up again.

'Thanks Dad. That would be great.'

'Also it would be wise to apply to a few more colleges to increase your chances.'

'Thanks.' I noted that each college application would cost

more than my family's monthly budget.

'I believe in you. Stay on track. Don't get derailed by this setback. Focus on your goals and don't give up,' he said as he left. I continued pacing the terrace thinking about coming up with the best application so that I could receive a scholarship to a very good American university.

During the next few weeks, I worked with the consulting company and completed my university application. The first thing the agency asked about was my goal. I told them in no uncertain terms that I didn't have enough money for college tuition. So, if I didn't get a scholarship, I wasn't going to the US. It was that simple. I said with conviction, 'Let's apply with that primary goal in mind.'

We applied to about eight lower-ranked universities which generally provided scholarships. The five highest ranked universities were now out of reach. So, I went ahead with the four universities that were ranked among the top 15, just in case. With a powerful statement of purpose, good recommendations from my professors and transcripts of my grades from the first year engineering course, my application would look good. I wanted it to look more than good, so I highlighted my involvement as a council member of the student body and my athletic abilities as displayed in the school soccer team. This painted a well-rounded picture of who I was. Also, I completed an internship at the Nuclear Reactor called BARC in the outskirts of Mumbai, where I developed a fault tolerant system for nuclear reactor shutdown logic. Everything looked alright except for the GRE score. As I mailed in the packages, I prayed that the reply would be affirmative and include a scholarship. Since everything was done through the traditional mail system, it would take months for the application to reach the universities, for the universities to process the application and then reply, leaving a nice period of lull and anxiety.

I spent time helping Anamika with her class XII board

examinations. She wanted to be an engineer like me. As I helped her prepare, I couldn't help but notice the similarities. It was her turn to enter the fire pit where she needed to burn her feet as she walked towards her goal. The goals seemed far beyond one's capacity. She too would have to try as hard as she could. Instead of early mornings, she chose to study till late in the night until 2.00 am., trying to push her physical limits and disrupting her mental peace in the struggle to achieve what seemed beyond her grasp. She was constantly trying to improve her capacity and push her limits. When her best was not good enough, there were moments of frustration. And the more frustrated she got, the harder she worked and the higher she set her goals. The vicious cycle of setting higher expectations of oneself leads to constant discomfort and angst and Anamika was experiencing what I had been experiencing for years.

One day, around noon, Abhishek and I were sitting in the living room reading the newspaper when the doorbell rang. As I opened the door, I saw Anamika with a new haircut. She had cut her long hair and now sported a very short hairstyle.

As she entered the apartment and saw the look of surprise on our faces, she tried to explain her decision.

'I wanted to cut it really short since my long hair was giving me headaches.'

Our faces revealed our reaction. This was our little sister who loved to dress up, dance and watch beauty pageants.

'C'mon guys, my hair was giving me headaches and pimples on my forehead. That's why I got the haircut, trust me. Don't look so shocked.'

'Really?' I asked, not convinced with her reasoning. Her explanation was not doing much to hide our surprise and disappointment.

'I just wanted to focus single-mindedly on my exams.' Anamika was a good looking girl, but now she wanted to deglamourize herself so she could fully commit to her studies.

She then put her hands on our shoulders and pointed to the reflection of our faces in the front window.

'Look, we are like three brothers now.'

As I looked at the reflection, I could see the same grimace and disappointment on Abhishek's face as mine. Our little sister had indeed become as good a liar as we were.

Her hard work was rewarded as she scored well in class XII exams and had the chance to get into an engineering college. She too had to go through a centralized selection process of choosing a college based on her grades. This time, instead of Dad accompanying her as he did with me, I went with her. Standing in line waiting for a merit seat and fearing it to be disappearing, I saw her experience the same anxiety that I had felt a few years before. I asked what field of engineering she was interested in. She replied, 'Anything is fine, brother, as long as it does not cost too much. I just want to be an engineer.'

As her turn came and both of us went to the counter to pick a seat, the official started telling us the names of the colleges and the fields of engineering that were available. The colleges he mentioned were not very good and quite far from home. It would be very difficult for Anamika to travel two hours each way every day. I noticed that the official was pausing, and his expression revealed that he was hiding something. Looking at him, I instinctively felt that he was concealing something. I had to act. On an impulse I put my head through the small window of his counter, so I could peek into the computer system in front of him.

'What are you doing?' He was taken aback as my head moved close to his.

I ignored him and continued to look at the screen. I kept my focus on the screen as he tried to push my head away.

'Look, look. There is a seat left in the high-ranking college in chemical engineering that we are eligible for,' I said as I pointed to his computer screen.

'Ahh. But there are other seats you may be interested in.'

'Are you joking or are you trying to hide something from us? We want that seat.'

'I cannot give that to you,' he said. He most likely wanted to save that seat for someone else, someone at a lower rank than us and whose turn had not come up yet.

'Why? We are eligible for it. We want it.'

'Sorry. I cannot give it to you.'

'What do you mean? It is not up to you. Call a supervisor,' I shot back.

A big commotion ensued as more officials gathered around. All the other students and their parents looked on as the admission process came to a standstill. There were a lot of back and forth arguments as I was adamant to get that seat. My sister was standing to the side, embarrassed by the turn of events and not part of the argument which was quickly becoming quite ugly. High ranking supervisors came and looked at the screen. I was adamant and I was not prepared to give in even one inch. That seat was available and I wanted it. Compromise was not an option.

They finally relented and gave us that coveted seat. The argument came to an abrupt halt as the official handed us the receipt and left haughtily. As I took the receipt, I raised both my hands towards the sky and closed my eyes in exhilaration.

'Yes, jhakaas!' As I exhaled and opened my eyes, I saw my sister staring blankly at me with a deer in the headlights look. She was surprised but also critical of the aggressive posture that I had taken. She had not seen me exhibit such pugnacity like that before. This was the first time she had witnessed my ability to be aggressive and confrontational.

I smiled hugging her and said, 'I am sorry. Sometimes you have to fight for what is rightfully yours. Not sometimes, but all the time.' As I put my hands around her shoulders, I was still beaming with joy at our victory.

'You are going to be a chemical engineer. And you are going

to graduate from the best chemical engineering college in all of India. Congratulations!'

'Okay,' she said.

'Mom and Dad will be so proud of you.' I was very happy that day knowing very well what a great path and career my sister was about to embark on.

A few months later, I started to receive admission offers from the universities I had applied to. I knew from the large-sized envelope itself that it was from the US because it was unlike anything I had seen before. It started with admissions from the low-ranked universities. As I nervously opened the envelope, I read the line that said 'admitted'. My eyes frantically searched for a mention of a scholarship, but there was none. I read it again but still could not find any allusion to one. Every afternoon I waited for the postal worker who arrived dressed in light brown clothes on his bicycle. Dad would be looking outside the window and would inform me when the mail had arrived. As I opened the admission package that contained a letter and a university brochure, my eyes would first search for the line saying 'accepted' and then for the word 'scholarship', which I hoped would appear towards the bottom of the letter of admission. I did not pay attention to the brochure, although I did notice the beautiful landscape and new university buildings on the cover. I was accepted to most of the lower-ranked universities I had applied to, but none of them offered me a scholarship. I was rejected by three of the higher ranked universities, but was accepted at one of the top 10. Texas A&M, which was located in College Station, Texas, accepted me but did not offer a scholarship. There were very few university replies outstanding and my hopes began to wane.

I decided I needed to directly contact the university and ask for a scholarship. The universities that accepted me also included a Form I-20, the certificate of eligibility for non-immigrant student status. All these acceptances were useless to me without a scholarship, since without it I would not be granted a visa to go to the US. To get the visa, my parents would need to show their financial assets to prove that they had the resources to pay my tuition fees. I just needed one scholarship to obviate the need to present our financial assets at the visa interview.

I decided to correspond with the university professors and deans to ask for an assistantship. In the late 1990s, there was this new reliable and efficient way to communicate via the Internet. It was a wonder how we could reach each other across the globe in such a short time. Sometimes an answer would come within a few hours or the very next day in some cases. Emailing would be the best way to communicate with the engineering professors in the US. I asked my friend Nihar to create an email account for me. 'Hotmail or Yahoo?' he asked me. I didn't know either, but I chose Yahoo since it had a nice ring. The next day he gave me a piece of paper with my ID and password. The former was confusing with underscores and numbers, including part of my first and last names.

'What weird email ID is this, Nihar? Couldn't you get a simpler one?'

'Yahoo recommended this one.'

'Recommended? Why couldn't Yahoo give me a simple ID, one that I could remember?' We knew very little about Yahoo or email at that time.

'Yahoo itself has a crazy name. Why do you think they will give you a simple one? Anyways, it's done, man.'

'Forget about other people, I hope I can remember this ID myself.' We laughed about it.

My email correspondence did not produce any scholarships. The professors replied that I first had to come to the university to talk to them and then the matter of a scholarship could be addressed. I wish they could have understood that I couldn't reach that stage without a scholarship, since I would be rejected at the visa interview for my lack of financial viability.

Although several universities accepted me, not even one

offered a scholarship. With no financial documents to present at the visa interview, the path to advanced overseas studies became even more remote. There was another path right in front of me which I had failed to consider.

More and more software companies were coming to our college campus. It was 1999 and Indian software companies were growing steadily fueled by the pending Y2K problem, also known as the millennium bug. This bug, also known as the Year 2000 bug, referred to a problem in the coding of computerized systems. It was projected to create havoc in computers and computer networks around the world at the beginning of 2000. There were Indian software companies contracted to assist American and international clients with their computer digitalization and software tasks. The international projects were ballooning as computers were becoming more prevalent. As the IT companies started being paid in US dollars, the employment packages that Indian companies offered were very generous. If I took one of those high paying jobs at a local IT firm, I could very quickly turn around my family's financial situation.

With Abhishek also working, we could buy a bigger house and lead a comfortable upper middle-class lifestyle. I would get to be close to my family and could become a project leader or manager in a few years drawing a very handsome salary. With Anamika working in a couple of years, we would have two engineers and one MBA graduate earning in our household. There were ample opportunities in the emerging and changing India to capitalize on and become affluent. This was an easy and attainable path. It was a sure promise of a good life with no mental torture required along the way.

I was also feeling guilty about the expenses my parents were incurring as they were helping me achieve my dream. It was taking money away from Anamika's and Abhishek's careers. So, I floated the idea of staying in India and working at a local IT firm to Dad when he brought me tea on the terrace the next morning.

'Dad, I have received replies from all the universities I applied to. I was accepted into one of the highest-ranking universities and all the other acceptances came from lower ranking schools. However, none offered a scholarship.'

'It's okay.'

'I have no chance to get a US visa without scholarship because we need to show that we have enough money to pay for my tuition and other expenses.'

'How much money do you need?'

'I think around $25,000 to $30,000,' I said adding that it was just the bare minimum. I did not mention that I also had to show other assets as well, including Dad's income. I wanted to keep the conversation simple and not concern Dad any further.

'Mmmm. I know. That is a huge amount in rupees.'

'Yes, it is. I am thinking of putting off the idea of going abroad. A lot of good software companies are coming to my college campus and they are offering very good pay. Maybe I can work for one of those companies.' At the back of my mind I was sincerely hoping he would reject the idea. The campus jobs were limited to software development and my heart was set on doing chip design.

'No. Don't pursue money, pursue your passion, Ankit,' he said. I was relieved when I heard those words.

'I know. It is difficult. It is the nature of things. When I was 18 years old, I left the luxury of my family home in Dehradun to pursue something bigger in life. If someone had told me then that I would have a family where my son would be going to the US and working to change the world, I would have jumped at the chance. Don't back off from your pursuit if you have hit a hurdle.'

'Hmm,' I said as I took a deep breath acknowledging his advice.

'Look, I have family and friends in my hometown in North India. We are a tight-knit family and I have helped many of them in their times of need. Two of my brothers are in banking and they can help arrange a bank loan. Also, many of the young men who I helped a decade ago when I was in the oil company are now doing well. They or their families can surely lend us some money.'

'Yes, that's true. We are not asking for a lot. I mean they just have to deposit it in our account for a few months. We can return it after we present the bank statement at the visa office. I think this is a chance worth taking.'

'See, I told you it was possible. We can make it happen. Once you finish your final engineering exams, both of us will take the train to Dehradun. Remember that easy things are easy to do and tough things are tough to do. Only the brave try the tough things and that is what defines them.'

'Yes. Let's do it,' I said excitedly, his optimism was infectious, and I felt it echo through my body and mind.

After I finished my final engineering exam, we took the train and went to Dad's hometown in Dehradun. First, we tried getting a bank loan with the help of Dad's brothers. Two of them were employed in a bank but their influence was ineffectual. Since Dad did not have any current income or any assets like a house or land, we had no collateral. His brothers could not do anything as they didn't have the authority to bend the rules. He then approached other close family members and childhood friends for a short-term loan, but none of them could help. Many of them did not have that kind of money and those who did were unwilling to take the risk. Everyone had their own family and kids to take care of.

Suresh, the husband of Aunt Bindo, Mom's best friend, extended whatever help he could. He was a businessman and had a small-scale factory. He and his wife had known Mom for many years and had stayed in our house as well. Suresh was a good man. He told us that he couldn't offer us any cash, but would get his accountant to create a document on stamp paper. This document would show that his factory was offering collateral for the fees. At that moment, Dad and I knew that this was not solid financing and an official at the US Consulate would easily see through it. We were grasping at straws and decided to accept the document as a last-ditch effort. What we needed for the interview was actual cash to provide proof of our financial viability. What we needed was a big loan for a short period of time.

We knocked on door after door but none of them opened for us. It was painful for me to watch Dad during those visits. He was like an old, retired boxer trying to get back in the ring. Before each visit, he would take a deep breath and pump himself up. We would be welcomed warmly and offered something to eat, while Dad would make the same pitch with the same conviction every day. He would tell each of them how amazing it was for someone to go abroad to study and become a bright star for others in the family to follow. I would sit quietly and listen. For the last three years, I had spent most of my time on the terrace with minimal social contact. My social skills were very limited as my mind was singularly focused on my education. I was literally living inside my head, so during these visits I remained silent except the hopeful 'Hello' and disappointed 'Bye'.

Dad, in contrast, displayed his enthusiasm and commitment as he talked about his early days trying to highlight his glorious past. From the conversation it was clear that he enjoyed some kind of a legendary status in his hometown. However, that was then and this was now; his current standing with no job and source of income was in doubt. He recounted how he had driven for three days from Mumbai to Dehradun because his father had told him that the only car in the whole family should be at his youngest son's wedding.

There was a story that took place in the 1980s, when he had come home to Dehradun for a summer visit and found his mother extremely sick with cancer. He had immediately taken her to Mumbai for treatment. There was no time to reserve a seat, so he sat on the floor of the train holding his sick mother in his lap for the entire 36-hour train journey. He then successfully had her admitted in the best hospital in Mumbai. There she was treated for several months but could not survive the cancer.

Dad assured everyone that he would return whatever money he borrowed. His word was his bond. He reminded everyone how he had helped other family members in their careers, and now that so many had successful careers it was their turn to reciprocate. For more than one month, we went to every household we could. But no one stepped up.

The train journey back home was very quiet. Dad was disappointed. He never made eye contact with me as he wanted to hide his embarrassment. I could see from his expression that he was in the same place as before when his thoughts tormented him. His quiet exterior did not fool me. During the 30-hour train ride, we did not speak much as we both were lost in our thoughts. I wanted to give him some space and spare him any embarrassment.

Unlike that one, train rides in India had always been fun. When we were kids, we would travel by the same train during our summer vacations. The highlight was the snacks and sweets sold at different train stations. Every state in India has its own unique culture and every station its own unique snacks. When the train would stop at any given station, we would buy the snacks famous in that region. One place was famous for one kind of sweet like petha from Agra, another would be famous for its sweet milk, while other was known for a specific hot or cold dish. You could get a taste of it at the stalls of the railway station. Though we did not speak, Dad still continued that tradition and purchased the snacks I had always enjoyed. On that trip, I found a snack placed next to me when I woke up. This was all done in silence.

When the train finally reached Mumbai, we got off the train with our luggage. Dad paused and looked at me. His lowered eyes conveyed his despondence. He finally broke his silence and said in a sad voice, 'Ankit, I spent my whole life trying to help people. I have given the most productive years of my life protecting the borders of this country. There must be around 50 families I have helped in my lifetime. And that is at the very least. I have made the careers of so many misguided youths. And now, when my son needs help, nobody comes forward.'

I listened without saying a word. I did not want to utter anything. I wanted him to express his feelings instead of bottling them inside.

'Not a single person. And I can't do anything about it. At this moment, I feel so helpless as a parent. I can't do anything for you, son.'

He then hurriedly emptied his pockets out of disgust and said, 'You wanted 30,000 dollars, but I have only 40 rupees in my pocket. That is all I have for you. I am so sorry, my son.'

'It's okay, Dad. It really is,' I said as I gestured him to put the money back in his pocket. I put my hands around his shoulders.

'Please don't worry about it, okay?' I did not want him to go to the dark recesses of his mind.

'Please don't think too much about this. It's going to be okay,' I added trying to calm him. But in my rational mind I knew that everything was not going to be okay. This was a major setback as my visa interview was only a few weeks away and I didn't have the most basic requirement to get the visa.

I decided to go to the interview at the US Consulate anyway. Aside from the financial document, I had everything else in place. I arranged all the documents in the required order—the Form I-20 from the top university in Texas and my passport. Since none of the universities had offered a scholarship, it made sense for me to take the acceptance letter from the highest ranked university as my strategy to fill the void created by the missing financial documents. I attached it to my educational certificates. I had hoped to convince the official at the US Consulate that even though I did not have the money, I was meritorious enough and deserved the opportunity to further my education in the US.

The evening before the interview, I showed the documents

to my friend Arun so that he could double check everything, since he had already had his interview and received his visa. As Arun perused the documents, everything looked in order until he reached the financial section. In that part, I just had that one document with the stamped paper showing my mother's friend who had put his factory up as collateral. He looked at it and read it in bewilderment. We both were smart enough to know that this was not enough for the visa.

'Sorry. I am not going to show that,' I said as I removed the document and put it at the back of the folder.

'Okay,' Arun said.

As he moved on to the next document in the folder, he realized that there were no more financial documents. He paused and then checked the remaining documents.

'I guess it seems alright,' he said, a bit hesitant to acknowledge the elephant in the room. There was a moment of silence when he considered what to say next. He collected himself.

'I think the application actually looks good. You are showing that you were accepted at a top tier university and your certificates are great. I think you might get the visa tomorrow.'

'Arun, you are the most pessimistic person I know. But thanks for trying to be optimistic for me at this moment. You are a good friend.'

Arun acknowledged that he empathized with my dire situation.

'You know, it was completely out of character for me to be optimistic,' he said laughingly.

'It is always easier to be optimistic than pessimistic. To look at the bright side…that was not that difficult, was it?' I said smiling.

'It was tough for me. Hopefully things will work out for you.'

'Arun, I can only play the hand I'm dealt, right? I will just give it my best shot.'

'Yup, good luck man.'

'Thanks, I'll need it.'

∽

The next morning, I got up at 4.30 and went to the US Consulate for my visa interview. I made sure that Dad did not come with me. He wanted to accompany me, but I lied to him saying that my friends were going with me. In reality, I knew that I would be rejected that day and I did not want him to suffer through further dejection. He had been knocked around and bruised enough from our previous trip together. I had to take this punch of rejection all by myself.

The agenda of the day was a 45-minute train ride to the US Consulate which was located in South Mumbai.

So, I took the local train early in the morning. The compartment was almost empty. I sat in the window seat and looked outside. There was an eerie quietness in the train. The sun had not come up yet and I was consumed with nervous thoughts of how the day was going to play out.

Today could be the end of the journey for me.

The US Consulate is very strict about procedures. When the official sees that I don't have the necessary financial documents, I will be summarily rejected. No more university and no more research. The US visa stamp looked like a fleeting thing as I felt the breeze blow from the open window of the moving train.

C'mon Ankit. Stay positive. Keep fighting. Yet as I sat there, more scary thoughts flooded my mind. What if they insult me while rejecting me at the consulate? What if guards throw me out in front of all the students, just like at the cricket trial at junior college five years ago? They might shout at me, 'Did you not read which documents were required? Do you think you are so special that you are applying to an American university without having the money to pay?' They could hurl abuses at me, tossing me out of the building. If they were going to reject me, I hoped that they would do it politely. Somehow, I imagined there would be a kind and understanding American lady at my interview in whom I could confide and explain my situation. My family's financial standing should not be an obstacle for me to reach my goals. I had worked very hard and I deserved to be admitted to a graduate programme in the US. My goal of studying and contributing to human development through engineering was noble and there was no need for money to undermine my vision. But then my more rational self knew that I would be rejected for no other reason than my inability to pay.

As the train jerked into motion, I felt like I was being taken to my execution. All I needed was a quick polite 'no' from the consulate official. I was praying. I was just glad that Dad was not with me and I was by myself. I clenched my teeth and told myself to be strong for what was about to happen. It felt like the moving train was going to be stonewalled and that I was heading into a train wreck. I just had to brace myself for the impact of the oncoming onslaught. I had to be strong to face my destiny. This was a test and I was struggling against the power of my executioner.

Most of the people waiting in line outside the consulate at this time of the year were students. They were very excited and were seen discussing their future plans, standing in a group. They seemed very happy and were joking around. For them, today was the day when the doors of opportunity would throw wide open. I was standing gloomily alone. Those same doors were slamming shut for me.

'Which university are you going to?' somebody nearby asked me.

'Texas A&M in College Station.'

'That's a good university. You must have gotten some good grades to get in there.'

'Yes,' I said thinking that it was a good university that I would not be going to.

'Oh, Texas. Everything is big in Texas.'

I did not know what that phrase meant, but I acknowledged it nevertheless.

'Yes. It is, yes.'

I realized that neither did I know much about Texas, nor about the US, for that matter. I had been so focused on fighting through my financial mess that I had not read about the country, the state or the place I was going to. I made a mental note that if I got the visa, I would go to an Internet café and read about the US, Texas and College Station, and try to investigate what was so 'big in Texas'.

After a few hours of waiting in line, we got the tokens and went inside. Looking at the counters as other students were being interviewed, I anxiously awaited my turn. From where I was sitting, I could see the students but not the interviewers. I guess my search for the kind elderly female employee was useless as we could neither choose whose window we got called to, nor could we see the interviewers before they called us. I looked at the students as they finished the interviews. You could tell from their expressions if they had been given their visa or not.

For the next few hours, I kept looking at the students and making notes. It seemed like 25 per cent of the students were being denied their visas. The chances were looking slimmer by the second and I was picturing a short interview followed by an abrupt rejection. I did not plan to plead my case unless there was a kind person on the other side of the counter. Or maybe I should plead since this was the only time I would ever get to fulfil my dreams of studying abroad. My thoughts were all over the place, like a ping pong match. It was agony waiting and thinking of different ways I'd get punched in the face. It had now been a few hours since I had entered the waiting area and it was close to lunchtime. I had not eaten since 5.00 a.m. I had hoped to have my interview before lunch. The agony of the wait with my mind going crazy was too much to bear on an empty stomach.

A few minutes before noon, they called a set of six numbers one after the other and asked the holders of these numbers to report to the same window. My token number was among these numbers. Perplexed why we were called to same window, the six of us got up. *Mass rejection*, my restless mind piped up. As we went to the window, the employee on the other side handed back our passports and a letter without saying one word. As we moved quickly through the line to collect the documents, I received mine and casually looked at them. I could not believe what I saw—my visa application had been approved. My mind went, 'Wait. What?' But I did not want to ask any questions. Still befuddled, I took my approval and walked outside. The five other students followed me out and they too looked confused but happy at the same time.

'Why were we not interviewed?' asked one of the five.

'I don't know man. It is very confusing. I was expecting some questions at the very least.'

'Wait. Which university are you going to?' one person took the lead to make sense of the situation.

'MIT.'

'Ohio State.'

'VTech.'

'UC Berkeley.'

'Texas A&M,' I said.

'Ah, okay. It makes sense now. It seems they have given approval to all the students from top-ranking universities without any interview,' somebody ventured an explanation.

'Hmm. That makes sense,' others agreed.

I could not believe it. I had my hands over my head. I had to pinch myself to believe that it was true. I could now graduate from a top US university. I called home from a phone booth on the road and told my parents. I guess they had been expecting a rejection and they were ready to sympathize with me, but they were surprised and extremely happy. The person in charge of the phone booth was blind. As I finished the call, I put two one-rupee coins in his outstretched hands, tapping it to indicate I was paying extra as I was exhilarated. Instead of taking the train, I decided to take the bus because I wanted to stop by the famous temple, Siddhivinayak.

I entered the temple still not believing what had just happened. I sat on the steps facing the idol. For one hour, I sat with my hands clasped over my face and head bowed in gratitude. I thanked God. In my life, the only successes I had experienced were the ones I had worked extremely hard for. Luck was always for the other team, the rival team that was always laughing and kicking us around as our family tried to survive with grace. And today, when I needed it the most, for a brief moment, it had come over and visited my corner. I was so filled with gratitude that day. I apologized to God for my outburst after my poor GRE results during the bus ride. I assured Him that I still believed that higher intelligence was there to guide me. It was the happiest I had felt in a very long time.

I came back home. Everybody was overjoyed. We shared our excitement and celebrated, eating my favourite jalebis and samosas. There were smiles all around, but the most cherished one for me was that of my Dad. When I told him that his efforts in Dehradun were not in vain and 'that the financial document from Suresh Uncle was why I got the visa today,' he seemed pleased.

The celebration continued till the next morning. I walked to the terrace with my passport in hand and shared the news with my companions of the last few years—the mattress, the water tank, the pigeons, the mountains, the rising sun and the clouds. I opened the passport and showed the stamped visa to everything around me. A pigeon feather joined in the mirth and we danced together, round and round with the passport in my hand. I felt like flying with the feather. Yes, I was going to fly soon. Then the thought hit me: I did not have the money to buy the plane ticket or the money to pay for the first semester. If I didn't deposit the fee at the beginning of the semester, the university would deny me a place and I'd have to come back to India.

There was not much left in Dad's savings account. He had

remained true to his word and used all the money he got from the company's settlement for his kids' education. Abhishek had moved into commerce and was pursuing his MBA. I knew I could not let Dad pay for the airplane ticket since that would seriously limit and affect the education possibilities for my brother and sister. So I decided to pursue a scholarship from some charitable funds. During the next few days, I put together a plan to appeal for all the scholarships that were available to students going abroad. I had a few months left before the first semester started to raise enough money to buy a plane ticket.

Over the next weeks, I took the local train to go to South Mumbai, the financial hub of the city. Most of the charitable funds were operated by the big industrial houses and they were located in the southern part of the city near their headquarters. I visited all of them and tried every possibility. I collected information from various sources, filled out applications, interviewed with a variety of charitable funds and explained why I deserved a scholarship. I showed them my certificates including the one showing that I was a school topper and the document showing the high-ranking university I was going to attend. I explained to them the field of chip design that I wanted to pursue and I shared the fact that my Dad had been in the Army and had served the country, hoping that this last bit of information would elicit someone's sympathy.

I would take the train at the peak hours in the morning. I could have waited to take a less crowded train, but I wanted to be the first in line when the offices of the charitable trusts opened.

Riding in the Mumbai local train was a character-building experience in itself. It was not for the faint of heart. The train's compartments would be full beyond capacity. The train had separate compartment for women, the handicapped and first class. The real action took place in the men's second compartment. The train would stop for about 30 seconds at each station. It would already be full and only a few people would deboard at any of the stops. But, more would enter with majority of the passengers going to their offices in South Mumbai. These offices were located in the downtown area which was the last station, about 15 stops after I got on. If you wanted to board the already full train, the key was to strategically position yourself. You had to judge which of the compartments was the 'least' busy and where that compartment would be when the train stopped. You had to make sure not to be standing at the door otherwise you could be trounced by the herd of people rushing out. You had to position yourself at the corner of the door such that when one herd left, you could step aside and then get on when the next herd of people boarded. If you were behind the mass of people entering, you would not have any space left to get in. So, you would miss the train or you would be left hanging outside gripping a rail outside the train. The force of the people pushing you as you held on, while half of your body was hanging outside feeling the gusts of air, was somewhat terrifying. If you were lucky enough to position yourself inside and reach the middle of the compartment, you would not be able to see anything as darkness descended with the rush of people all around. There was a steel bar above to hold on to, but if it was not directly above your head you couldn't stretch far enough to reach it. If you did so, you would be moving into someone else's coveted space. You had to rely on your balancing skills as the train would move steadily along. It was difficult to stay balanced as moving your feet further apart might mean you were stepping on someone. It was a challenge of choreography. Though hardly graceful, it worked somehow. It was best not to breathe during the three-to-five-minute ride between stations.

In the darkness, you would be so disoriented you wouldn't know which station and on which side of the platform your train was about to stop. So, you had to ask a fellow struggler which station was coming up next and on what side it would be on.

Despite the absence of good infrastructure and the daily struggle of jockeying for position, there was never any conflict among fellow travellers. The train compartment was a microcosm of India, people struggling to survive. The reality of train travel highlighted the ineptitude of a corrupt bureaucracy. People were doing what they could to make ends meet and provide for their families. The passengers' faces revealed their quiet determination to do what was necessary to move up in the world. Upward mobility was an achievable dream for some, yet all showed a stoicism that characterized the spirit of Mumbai. I felt a kinship with my fellow travellers as we were all hustling for a better life.

By the time I exited the compartment, my clothes would be in disarray. I would emerge with an untucked shirt, the belt of my pants would shift away from the centre and my shoelaces would be undone. Not only would I be visibly disheveled, but I would have taken on someone else's body odour.

One afternoon upon returning to my home station, I had descended the train and I was trying to tie my shoelaces when I saw someone on the same platform, at a distance, wearing the same formal trousers I used to wear with the shirt looking familiar as well. The person's back was towards me and he was carrying a kind of a formal backpack. He had some documents in his hand and was showing them to the passengers descending from the first-class compartment of the train. He approached them, trying to talk as he pointed to some kind of brochure. Some people listened and some kept on walking, not paying any attention. Some passengers already frustrated with the train ride would just wave him away. As I looked closely, I saw that it was Abhishek.

I hid behind the pole to see what he was doing. It seemed like he was selling some kind of insurance policy to the passengers. He had only told us that he had a part-time job in a bank but nothing beyond that. As the next train pulled into the station, Abhishek once again approached the descending passengers, most of whom rejected him outright with disgust. Abhishek would then move to the next person hoping to make a sale, but very few seemed interested in what he was selling. Many would vent the frustration of their experience of the difficult train ride on him.

As the train left the station, Abhishek would try to brush off the rejections and pump himself up for the next group.

As I watched my brother being treated like a street hawker, I wanted to go over to him and put my arm around his shoulder and tell him everything was going to be all right. But I held back. He had not told us what he was doing because he was ashamed. I gave him the space to fight his battle, so I left quietly.

After many weeks of sustained effort, my hard work bore fruits as one of the charitable funds from the Tata business family decided to give me a loan of ₹25,000 for four years. That amount would cover most of the cost of the airline ticket. Getting rest of the money from Dad, I was able to immediately book my ticket to Houston. I knew that I was booking the flight quite late since the trip was just one month away, but I didn't have a choice. I had to wait until I had the scholarship money in hand. With one more hurdle crossed, there still remained the biggest one—the tuition fees. I needed to deposit them within a couple of weeks of my arrival in the US. If I didn't complete this transaction, I would be sent back to India.

As the flight neared, I intensified my search for a scholarship and extended my quest to other parts of the city. It was tough walking from place to place around the city. I ate a vada pav. It was very tasty and cost about ₹1.25. Some days I drank sugar cane juice from a street vendor or a fruit shake of ₹2.50, which was definitely not made using fruit but some flavored syrup; nevertheless, they tasted good, especially in India's summer heat. I also visited the American study agency which provided students preparing to go overseas with information and maps. We were allowed to use the Internet on their computers for a short time, so I had the chance to read about the US, Texas and College Station. I looked at my college website and started sending emails to professors in an effort to secure an assistantship.

I also enrolled in a computer class which taught basic C programming and Microsoft Word, Excel and other skills. I was hoping that if I could learn a diverse set of computer skills, I would be able to increase my chances of getting an assistantship and getting my fees waived. So, during the day I searched for an assistantship and in the evening I attended computer classes. I sat in the class for one extra hour trying to learn as much as I could. As I sat alone, a computer teacher helped me. Over the weeks, I developed a good rapport with him as I comfortably confided in him about my fears. I told him that I was going to the US for a masters in Engineering, but that I did not have the money to cover the tuition fees and I didn't know what to expect when I arrived there. If I didn't have the money, I didn't know whether they would send me back or if I would have time to raise the tuition fees since I was already studying. He was sympathetic. I told him that only a few weeks remained and the chance of getting a scholarship either from India or from an American university was quickly diminishing. I explained that my efforts were not bearing fruit and doors were staying firmly closed. I also shared with him that I had to find somebody to give me a loan.

One evening, he told me out of the blue that he had found a way to help me. He said he spoke to his sister in New Jersey and she was willing to loan me the money. Although the interest rate was exceedingly high at more than 10 per cent, I happily accepted the offer. I was elated and thanked him. I assured him that I would pay her back as soon as I completed my degree and got a job. It would take two and a half years maximum. I expected to get an assistantship during the first year and, in that case, I could start repaying her in a few months.

Getting the loan was an amazing news, so I decided to take a break from my daily pursuit of a scholarship. The local train trips and my visits to numerous offices every day had become very tiring and now I had less than two weeks before I took my flight to the US. I wanted to spend some quality time with my family. Mom started to teach me some basic cooking skills like making tea and preparing simple food as Maggi noodles. She also taught me how to make kidneys beans and put together a plan to teach me how to prepare other dishes too.

I completed my evening computer course, but I continued to spend time walking around the area hoping to run into my former teacher to discuss the loan. I was trying to figure out whether it would be better to get the cash here before I left or to wait until I reached the US. I didn't see the teacher in the first few days because he had left work early. Finally, we met up but then he had to excuse himself due to a prior engagement. On other days, I saw him sneak away from me, trying to avoid any direct contact. Soon, only a week remained for my departure and thus I needed to talk to him. I went early in the morning and waited for him to arrive. As he opened the door to the school, I entered the building with him. He had a look of surprise and shame on his face and was avoiding any eye contact.

'Look Ankit, my relatives have backed out from giving the loan.'

I was devastated. I was counting on this loan. It was my only option. I couldn't pay my tuition fees without it. I wanted to be angry and shout at the teacher. I wanted to know why he hadn't told me this earlier. I wanted to know why he had volunteered to help me and what made him back out at the last minute. I had lost valuable time counting on him. I didn't know what to say. I was very angry but aware of Mom's teachings to suppress my initial impulse. All I could say, enduring my pain, was, 'Why?' I then walked out as he stumbled to find words of consolation. I had no time for his sympathy or excuses as I barely had time to find another option before my flight.

The following morning, I returned to my daily routine: I took the train to South Mumbai hoping to get a scholarship. I was praying for some miracle to happen. Something would click, somebody would help me. I had only three days left before my departure to the US. My parents as well as Abhishek and Anamika were all worried about what was going to happen. Everyone shared my feelings of agony perhaps for slightly different reasons as sending a kid to a foreign country with no money was a scary thought for my family. In the evening when I came back from the daily grind of my search, I was exhausted and gloomy.

'You know, Mr Patel, who is Dhruv's uncle, lives in Houston. Maybe he can help. I have his number,' Dad said cautiously.

'It has been almost seven years since we last spoke to him. I don't know if he will remember us.' I said.

'We can call him up. At least he can pick you up at Houston airport.'

'I can ask the student association to do that. You think we can ask him for a loan?'

'I don't know. He is a good person. Maybe he will help.'

'Let's try. We have explored every other option, but without success. Why not this? I have visited some out of the way places, I have had to walk through the slums and I have had to endure obstacles and rejections at every turn to get a scholarship. This is just a phone call anyway. It's worth a shot.'

'Ok. Let's do it. And let's give him your flight information'

Dad walked for 15 minutes to the phone booth to make the international call. I waited outside the booth, feeling anxious and worried.

Dad spoke for about five minutes before he came out of the phone booth with a look of confusion and uncertainty. I asked, 'Did he agree to give me a loan?'

'I don't know. He was happy to hear from me. I told him about you and your graduation plans from Texas A&M and he said he would pick you at the airport. I had done the same for him when he came to India, so I gave him your flight information.'

'What about the loan?'

'I told him that you may need some financial help as well and he paused and said, "Pramod bhai, I will take care of it."'

'"I will take care of it." What does that mean specifically?'

'I don't know. It has been many years since I spoke to him.

I don't know if he remembers me. At least he is picking you up at the airport,' Dad struggled to explain.

As we walked back home in the darkness of the night, my mind was flushed with confusion as I tried to decipher Mr Patel's phrase, "take care of it". I wanted to ask more questions, but I held myself back to make sure I didn't pile any additional pressure on Dad. I had already been duped by the teacher a few days earlier and I was scarred by that experience. Over the last couple of months, I had been rejected so many times for scholarship that my trust in humanity had waned. I could not believe in this latest possibility of financing. But I kept silent. The next morning, I was back among the crowds on the local trains as I continued my quest for scholarship.

My flight was late at night and on that morning, I was in South Mumbai searching for scholarship again—a last ditch effort. I hoped that if I could secure financing, the money could be sent to the US. The rupee to US dollar exchange rate was high; any large amount in rupees would not have made up the fees. In my pursuit for financial assistance, I had little time to prepare to leave and say proper goodbye to my family. Mom had been packing my bags for a week, and often I would notice her moist eyes, but I did my best to ignore them as I wanted to keep my focus on my goals and not be distracted. Anamika was emotional and Abhishek was stoic. He made sure that Mom packed the best of our shared clothes for me, including the best pair of jeans, the best trousers and the best shirts.

It was around 10.00 p.m., the night of my departure. My flight was scheduled to leave around 2.00 a.m. We finished dinner and Abhishek had bought my favourite ice-cream. My bags were packed, I was dressed, and we were about to leave for the airport. I was sitting in the living room on a small stool with my family around. Everyone was quiet and the mood was sombre.

As I was tying my shoelaces, I looked at the shoes and noticed how worn the soles had become as a result of the constant walking.

I kept inspecting my shoes as if they were a diary telling me stories about my trips to the city. The shoes also reminded me of my failures to get the required financing. My mind drifted into a mode of self-examination and self-loathing.

Could I have done anything more? I agonized internally. I was so stupid to have believed in the computer teacher. I'd lost critical time waiting for him to come through with the money. Maybe the trust fund I tried this morning will agree to give me the money. They have my email address. When will I have to deposit the tuition fees? I think I'll have two to three weeks before classes begin. Will they throw me out of the school if I don't pay at time? What about a return ticket in that case? Will they pay for that or will I be left wandering alone in the streets of a foreign country? Oh dear! How will I get back to India if they kick me out of the university?

Suddenly I felt a tug on my shoulder. Dad bent down and raised my shoulders, so I was face to face with him. He started sobbing on my shoulders. He held me tightly with his hands around me and kept crying.

My thoughts about my future came to a standstill. I was suddenly hit with the reality that I was going to be leaving my family. My parents and siblings had been with me for 21 years. Together we had been through thick and thin and stuck through all of life's adversities. We fought every hardship with dignity as we clung to our values, always together with heads held high. If one of us faced a mountain, we climbed it together. We had been there for each other through life's ups and downs. I had never travelled alone without family or friends. The longest I had been away from my mother in my entire life was for 15 days. My family had always been at my side. The only certain thing in this uncertain world I could count on was the steadfast love and support of my family. Now the presence of that would go away. A sudden emptiness filled my heart and doubts crept in.

Seeing my father crying in my arms, I questioned my mission.

I could have an engineering career and an easy life in India, all with the comfort of staying by family's side. Why am I subjecting my family and myself to pain and suffering in the real world to achieve an imaginary goal? Was all of this worth it?

I clenched my teeth and bit my lip.

Don't be weak, Ankit. You have to do it. You have to achieve your dream of having a life of value. You have not come so far to turn your back now. You are going to make this happen and nothing is going to change that. Stay on the path, Ankit.

I recited the lines of my favourite poem, 'Agnipath'. I have to let go of my comfortable shell to cross the ocean. I have to pull my anchor out of the calm waters and head into the stormy rough ocean of the unknown. There was a steely focus in my eyes as I continued staring at my shoes. I still had a lot of miles to walk and Texas wasn't big enough for that.

But Dad continued crying on my shoulders relentlessly. I could feel his sobs run through my entire body. I could feel the moistness of his tears on my shoulders. From this point of the journey it was me alone. I was going to miss my family and I felt an aching pain in my heart for what was going to be an ever-present vacuum. I wanted to cry as well. I tried holding back my tears as I kept staring at my shoes to avoid looking at Dad. I wanted to be strong and focused and not weak in the eye of a storm that was about to engulf me in the distant shores.

But I was going to miss Mom, Dad, Abhishek and Anamika a lot. It was going to hurt so much. As I closed my eyes, as much as I tried to resist crying, there was a mutinous tear that sneaked out of my eyes and rolled down my cheek.

'I will not give up, Dad,' I whispered in his ear. 'I will walk the distance with fear, but I will not change my path.' I reminded my sobbing Dad of his own words from that Diwali night as I quickly wiped the single tear away.

As I entered the airport, my family came to see me off. I waved them a goodbye. As I passed through ticketing, luggage drop off and customs, from the corner of my eye I could see my family walk along with me from outside the airport looking in from different glass windows. They wanted to get one last glimpse. I did not look back. I didn't want to see Mom crying on my brother's shoulder. I needed to be strong.

I took the flight. I did not have credit cards. I took small change for phone calls which would exchange for five dollars or so.

With that, I arrived in the United States of America with empty pockets. All I had was a passport with visa and the steely grit to scale any mountain that lay in the path of my destiny.

7

LAND OF OPPORTUNITIES

'What is the purpose of your visit to the United States?' The officer in a blue shirt sitting at Houston airport's immigration desk inquired as I approached him. 'Hello. I am here to do my masters in computer engineering at Texas A&M, in College Station.'

'Hmm. Can you...' I interrupted him before he could question any further.

'The reason I am here is to further my education so I can make a genuine contribution to the field of electronics and chip design,' I said confidently.

I said those words to convey my conviction. I felt good about standing there and knowing that I was going to make a difference. It was the simple truth. Underneath all the challenges that I had faced, and was about to face, that was the simple truth. I just wanted to study and make a contribution to society.

I kept staring into his eyes, hoping that he would see the same truth. I also hoped it would dissuade him from asking further questions, especially about how I was going to pay for my college tuition. I had no satisfying answer for that. There was no way I was going to tell him, 'My Uncle said on the phone that he was going to take care of it.'

'Can I see your visa documents?' he asked.

'Sure, Sir,' I said. 'Here is my passport and college admission documents.'

He started looking through the pages of my crisp new

passport. As he glanced at each page, I held my breath and then silently sighed. I made sure not to breathe loudly or quickly since that would convey anxiety and raise doubts.

As I waited for my documents to be reviewed, I tried to stay mentally sharp for any further questions. I could feel the fatigue from the long flight creep into my body. I looked at his watch and saw that it was late evening. It had been around 28 hours since I left my home in India. I had barely slept on the plane.

Most of my time on the plane was spent just staring at the back of the seat in front of me and thinking about what lay ahead. I was sitting in the middle seat halfway back in economy class. It was not comfortable and I felt cramped with little room to move or stretch my legs. The view outside the window was blocked partially by my neighbour and partly by the wing of the airplane. Although this was the first flight of my life, I found myself missing the comforts of cross-country train rides, including the open windows. I remembered the sights of the landscapes and taste of the food on the train trips we had enjoyed as a family. I tried to block the thoughts of my past and my family, so I could focus my energy on the future.

I was chalking out plans, alternatives and multiple 'what if' strategies. I was coming up with multiple options for multiple possible streams. I had to be prepared for whatever wrench might be thrown into my plans. It was like writing a computer programme in my head with programming constructs.

What if Vrajesh Uncle does not come to pick you up? You will have to look for someone going to College Station. What if there is no one going. You will have to spend a night at the airport and call the Indian student association to pick you up the following morning. Through email exchanges, I had already arranged to stay with some of the students for the initial few days.

Make the call using the collect call system from the telephone at the airport and stay there until they pick you up. Mom had packed food which would last a few days, so you would be good for a couple of days. Also, make notes on what you need to do to get the assistantship. That was the key challenge.

I laid out a detailed strategy to secure a scholarship. I knew which departments to approach first. What if I don't get a scholarship and can't pay the fees? I will talk to the department head and ask for more time to raise the money so I could stay. I could work somewhere else, actually anywhere else so I could make money to pay for my tuition. The masters programme was for two years so I needed the fee for four semesters. That would be a lot of money to earn in a short period. A lot of my current options were dead ends leading to my return home. It was frightening to chart such a course. I kept pushing myself to think hard to come up with alternate possibilities. My lack of knowledge of this new country and its laws and rules made planning the unknown seem like walking in dense fog.

I was imagining a maze. My goal was on the outside of the maze and I was running through it figuring and chasing the path to reach the way out. But every path I was following reached a dead end. As I tried to pivot to an alternative path, I was moving further and further away from my goal. I could not find a way to reach it. The scary thought was that there was no way back for me. I did not have any money with me, so I could not buy an airplane ticket to fly back home. Twisting and turning in the cramped seat and in the pressurized chamber, I felt scared and stranded with no path ahead and no path behind.

I resolved to remain focused, push forward and plow through until I reached my goal. I decided whatever challenges were about to unfold in front of me in this new country, I would fight each battle with determination and conviction. I would not retreat.

So, as I stood at the immigration desk holding my gaze, I could feel the muscles underneath my eyes hurting. I finally heard the words like raindrops on parched land,

'Welcome to the United States of America, Sir.' He stamped '13 Aug 1999' on my passport.

'Thank you very much,' I replied. I closed my eyes and exhaled deeply. Hurdle number one crossed.

I noticed how brightly lit and clean the airport was. All the floors and glass doors of the shops were glistening from the lights above. The airport reminded me of the lobby of a swank five-star hotel and the glass doors of the shops that lined the perimetre of the space. The floors were swept so clean that the light reflected off it.

Some of the passersby had cowboy hats on, pants with silver belt buckles and cowboy boots with spurs on the back. Several men had long moustaches just like my father had sported during his Army days. The cowboy boots reminded me of the western movies I had seen. I thought of Clint Eastwood and the movies I had seen him in. I thought, *Vrajesh Uncle, go ahead, make my day*. I smiled at the thought but brought my attention to the task at hand, scampering to the baggage claim where I collected my two big bags. Mom had tied a special yellow cloth on their handles to make sure I would be able to identify them. I loaded the bags onto a trolley and looked around. There were people coming in, meeting and hugging their friends and family members. I looked around and there was no sign of Uncle or Aunty.

I walked and circled the baggage claim area. I looked through the glass doors and saw numerous parked cars. I noticed the automatic door and how it opened by itself when you stood close to it. What a cool and useful design that was. I looked at the door sensor and tried to move closer to see when it opened. It made so much sense to have automatic doors at an airport where people carrying their luggage did not have a free hand to push the door open. I played around with the door and began considering whether to stay at the airport or go through these doors and look for Uncle. I waited and walked around the airport for 30 minutes, but no sign. I began to get nervous. My mind started screaming Plan B, Plan B. I hesitantly walked around the baggage area hoping to see anyone who looked like a student, hoping to find someone going to College Station. I wanted to hitch a ride with them, with anyone, but I couldn't find anyone to accompany me to the university. After another 15 minutes, I walked back and sat on a seat in the baggage claim area.

Most of the people on my flight had now left, picked up by their family and friends. Many were exchanging hugs and kisses with their families, which made me feel more homesick. There were very few people standing around since most of the passengers from my flight had already left. The quietness was creepy. In Mumbai, there are only a few quiet places. Noise is everywhere, be it people, car horns, birds or just a general hum to the city. It provided a sense of security at a visceral level. Here the quietness and loneliness at the airport made me uneasy and afraid. *Plan C, Plan C.* My heart was racing at the thought of spending one or more nights at the airport. My anxiety reached extreme levels.

I looked at the seat next to the baggage claim carousel. This was the wall of the maze that I had hit and it was blocking my path. Knowing Mom, I knew she would have packed ample food for me, so I figured I'd be good to spend a few days at the airport if I had to. I moved my head from side to side and stretched my aching body.

I imagined Aunty not coming and that I would be spending time just waiting. I pictured the seat as an opponent in a boxing ring and I snapped my hands a few times as I gazed hard at the chair. *Fight on,* I told myself as my body slumped into the chair. I tried to get comfortable in the seat where I was planning to spend an unforeseeable amount of time. At least these seats were more comfortable than my seat on the plane.

As I sat down, I put my hand over my tired eyes, pressing them against my temples to relieve myself of a throbbing headache. I kept looking at the sliding doors and admired their design. After a few minutes of waiting, I saw Alka Aunty walking hastily through the sliding doors towards me. *Oh, thank God.* I felt a sigh of relief.

Alka Aunty had a spring in her step. She was a thin lady in her mid-30s around 5'2", dark skinned with long curly black hair and big eyes. She was wearing trousers and a T-shirt with a scarf around her neck. 'Ankit, so sorry we are late. Your uncle had a diabetic attack, so we had to rush to get his medicine,' she said as she hugged me.

'Is he okay now?'

'Yes, he is waiting in the car. He still wanted to come to pick you up. Hope you had a good flight.'

'No problem, Aunty. Thank you for picking me up.' I was relieved to see her and to finally leave the airport. While walking through the doors, I looked back at my newly made friends for one final time—the seat and the sliding doors.

So long, my friends.

Alka Aunty escorted me to the waiting Volvo hatchback outside the terminal where Vrajesh Uncle was standing outside the car. He wore leather shoes, the slip-on kind. He was tall, with an air of self-confidence and had a distinct style. He was wearing white trousers and a bright colored shirt with the two top buttons undone. I felt the firmness of his handshake as he said, 'Welcome, my boy. How are your Mom and Dad?'

'Good. They send their best wishes to you.'

He was chewing gum, which I presume was to increase his sugar level. He helped me load the bags into the big trunk of the hatchback. Alka Aunty settled into the driver's seat and I sat in the back.

'How are your Mom and Dad really doing? I was so very happy to hear Pramod Bhai's voice after almost a decade. It was like finding a lost friend,' Vrajesh Uncle said fondly.

'You know your Dad is one of the most generous people I have met in my entire life. He was kind to me and my family. Whenever we were at your home, there were always some other guests staying over.'

'Yes. In those days there were people staying who even we did not know. Once Dad was coming back from Delhi, he brought home complete strangers. It was a family of four whom he had met on the train and since they had nowhere to go in Mumbai, they stayed at our place for a week,' I said evoking laughter from both of them.

'Your Mom supported him ably. She was in the kitchen constantly cooking meals to ensure that everyone ate well.'

During the remaining drive to their home, I could barely keep my eyes open. I was so tired. I barely remembered reaching their house, eating dinner, climbing a flight of stairs and crashing into a very comfortable bed.

The next thing I remember is waking to a doorbell. I opened my eyes. I was lying in a single bed with another bed on the other side of the room. It was warm and bright outside. There was a picture of Viraj, their son, and medals hanging on the wall. It was almost noon, according to the clock on the side table. My first thought was of my family. I missed Dad's cup of tea and his warmth as he would hand the cup to me on those chilly mornings. I missed Mom's care. She would never let us sleep till noon. She would tickle our toes continuously until we gave up and got out of bed. I wondered what Abhishek and Anamika were doing right now. It would be nice to talk to them on the phone. But then I did not want to waste Vrajesh Uncle's money on an international call.

The mattress and the duvet were so cozy and comfortable, and the pillow soft and fluffy. Back in India, the pillows were so firm that one could do some serious damage in a pillow fight.

I lay in bed for a while looking at the ceiling, waiting for the next challenge. I was happy that there was a computer with a modem in the room. I had to use the Internet for doing some research for assistantship. Vrajesh Uncle had not talked about providing the tuition fees yet. I thought there was no use in bringing up the topic. There were only two possibilities—he wanted to pay or he didn't want to pay. In both these options, my asking would not help. If he wanted to pay, I would not have to ask, he would offer it himself. If he did not want to pay, asking him was useless for there was no way I could force him. He was nice enough to pick me up and I should appreciate that.

I got out of bed and walked downstairs. I saw many beautiful showpieces in the house. There was a samurai sword hanging across the wall and family pictures hanging nearby. One showed Vrajesh Uncle receiving an award from the then president of India for his work as the president of the Indian Association in Houston.

The house was big. We, as city apartment dwellers, would call it a bungalow. Next to the room under the staircase was the kitchen. The kitchen was not a separate room, and on the other side of the kitchen was another space from where the sound of the family's laughter was coming. As I saw Uncle and Aunty, I greeted them with a good morning.

'Hey, Ankit. Come join us. Since you are here, we have ordered pizza today,' Uncle said gesturing me towards the two open pizza boxes.

'We love pizza. I am Zarna. How are you?' She was a 16-year-old girl with braces and her hair was tied in a ponytail. She was wearing a T-shirt and pyajama bottoms.

'This is my son Viraj,' Aunty said pointing to her son sitting in the corner playing video games. Viraj was about 14 years old. He wore long shorts and a T-shirt, both of which were a couple of sizes bigger than his actual size. He had used hair gel to style his hair into spikes.

'Hey,' he said with a rapper's attitude and an unnaturally deep voice.

'Ankit, we informed your mom that you have arrived safely,' Aunty told me.

'Ankit, when does college start?' Uncle asked.

'The first week of September.'

'You have some time. You should spend a couple of weeks with us getting used to America and learning the ways of this country.'

'Yes, Ankit. You should,' Aunty agreed.

'I would love to, but I have to leave in a couple of days because I have to look for an assistantship which will help me pay my fees,' I paused intentionally. If there was a time when Uncle was going to make an offer, this was it. I waited, holding my breath until I could hold it no longer.

He should have said, 'Don't worry. I will take care of your tuition fees. Just relax and embrace the experience of the new country.'

But after a long pause he said, 'Okay, as you wish. We will leave in a couple of days. We will stop over in Crockett on the way. I will show you my gas station.'

'He means petrol pump,' Aunty clarified.

'But it is more than a petrol pump. It is also a convenience store,' Uncle added.

'I came to the US in the 1970s, struggled for many years working day and night shifts in motels in the 1980s, and then I got married and bought the gas station. It is tough work, you know, you have to work day and night and even on weekends since it is open 24/7. Now due to my health, your aunty and Zarna work there.'

'That's great,' I managed to say with my mind still fixated on the previous topic. It seemed that he was not willing to give me any financial help, which made sense since he had two kids who would be ready for college soon.

I gobbled up a few slices of the pizza, which I found to be too cheesy. In India, the cheese was sprinkled lightly on the pizza, like a dressing similar to a supporting actor in a movie. On this pizza, the cheese was the main actor. It pulled and stretched, playing a major role in each bite.

After the meal, Uncle suggested, 'Hey Viraj, why don't you take Ankit outside and play something? You'll get some much-needed exercise. Playing video games all day does not give your body a chance to move,' he chided his son.

'Okay. We can play football,' he reluctantly agreed.

I was happy to go outside and play football. It had been a while since I had tried out my dribbling and kicking skills.'

As Viraj and I went to the garage, he picked up an oval shaped leather thing and started to walk through the open garage door.

'What is that?' I asked.

'This is a football.'

'A football is round.'

'No. This is a football. It is an American football. I think you mean soccer.'

'Trust me. I represented my college at football tournaments. It is called football. I have T-shirts and trophies stating football. The football I kicked was round.'

'It is different here. You hold it like this,' he said gripping his hand around the threads, 'and throw it like this' and got the ball to rotate with a swiping motion of his right hand.

'Well, if you throw it, why don't you call it throw ball? Football should be played with a foot, no?'

'Well, it is different,' he smiled and gestured me to move further away.

Then he threw the ball and I tried to catch it like a cricket ball over my shoulders. 'Ouch!' I felt the edge of the oval ball in my palm. I threw it back imitating his actions but the ball rotated many times.

'You got to spin it to get the spiral.'

I tried and tried as I threw it many times. After 15 minutes, I changed my technique to throw the spiral.

I held the ball with each open palm close to the edge of the ball and then I hurled the ball, jumping in the air. The ball went up in a perfect spiral. I was happy to finally get some spin and spiral. 'Good throw, Ankit,' Viraj laughed as he caught the ball.

As we finished and walked back towards the house, Viraj added, 'You know, there is another part of football. You need to hold the ball like this and run.'

'C'mon. Why would you want to hold a football in your

hand? That is a foul, a yellow card.'

'It is a different game. You will figure it out in time once you start college here. It is a big part of the culture,' he said as he put his arm around my shoulders.

For the next couple of days, the Patels played the perfect hosts. They showed me around Houston and we went to restaurants to eat. I was also able to spend a couple of hours each day on the computer figuring out a plan of action to secure an assistantship. There were three departments I wanted to apply to for an assistantship: The Department of Nuclear Engineering, The Department of Computer Science and The Department of Electrical and Computer Engineering. Nuclear would be the first choice because I had an edge over it due to my internship at the Atomic Research Center. I also figured very few international students would try for a nuclear engineering assistantship. I had carefully tailored three separate resumes for each department, and hence one of them was specifically designed to reflect my strengths in nuclear engineering.

The night before I was set to leave for College Station, Viraj and I were in his room as he was getting ready for bed.

'Ankit, how old are you?' Viraj asked.

'I am 21.'

'So do you have a girlfriend back home?'

'No. How about you?' I quickly moved the spotlight back on him.

'Yes. I have a girlfriend. I have been going steady with her for a long time. Before I met her, I dated a lot of other girls. A lot,' he said with a lot of pride.

'That's great,' I said.

'By the time I am 21, I want to be going steady with one girl and get settled. So, have you dated any girls?'

'Nope, never,' I replied.

'Oh man, really? Are you telling me that you have never gone on a date?'

'Yes, that's right.'

'Damn,' he said.

The contrast in our dating patterns was amusing to both of us. I, at 21, with no dates and he at 14, already bored with dating.

I smiled back, 'Never.'

I wanted to tell him that adversity had stolen my childhood and my youth was already spent fighting it, but instead I said, 'I will have many girlfriends in college when I enroll to play on the college football team. Didn't you see the spiral that I was throwing yesterday? Like this?' I repeated the hand motion from the previous morning. He burst out laughing. 'Hey Viraj, is it okay if I stay up and work on the laptop?'

'Sure, go ahead. Good night.'

I spent a couple of hours on the computer exploring alternative ways of raising money to pay my tuition fee.

The next morning as I sat in the car waiting to go to College Station, via Crockett, I bid goodbye to Viraj and Zarna. I had mixed feelings. I felt gratitude to the family for picking me up and letting me stay with them, but I also felt disappointed that they had not offered me the financial help that I desperately needed. Maybe the phrase, 'will take care of it' had different meanings in different countries.

During the drive to Crockett, I sat in the back seat by myself. I had my right leg over my left knee and I kept staring at the soles of my shoes. After studying the map, I was now familiar with the layout of the college. It was a huge campus. I pledged to myself that I would walk to each and every corner of the campus to get an assistantship in the next three weeks...

We reached Crockett and we pulled into the parking lot of their gas station/grocery store. I greeted the female employee who was working the shift and she smilingly replied with 'Hola,' which I presumed, was an alternative greeting to hello. Most of the customers were buying gas, lotto tickets or cigarettes. Uncle proudly showed me around his store as he talked again about his humble beginnings in the US and how he and Aunty worked hard to be where they were today. As we completed the 'tour', Uncle called me into his back room. It seemed like a secret room away from the view of the customers and staff.

He asked, 'How much money do you need for your education?' A rush of elation ran through my veins when I heard these words. This was the question that I had been waiting to hear since I had arrived in the US. For days, months and years I had been waiting to hear these words from someone.

'I only need enough money to pay for my first semester. I will work hard and I am confident that I will get some kind of scholarship in six months.'

'How much do you need now?' he asked again.

'Five thousand dollars.' That too was something I had thought about on the long flight.

'Okay,' he said as he opened his safe and removed a stack of cash and started to count the money,

'I will return it as soon as possible. I can pay you back with interest.'

'No. What are you saying? This is not a business transaction.' He seemed annoyed at the suggestion of paying interest on the loan.

'Sorry, Uncle,' I said as I tried to take back my words. I did not want to blow my only chance and I did not want to offend him in any way.

'I am doing this for your Dad and Mom. I know about your Dad's struggles and your financial situation even though you haven't shared this information with us. I know why he did not contact me for years. He is a proud man.' He continued with uncharacteristic tenderness in his demeanor, 'You know, Pramod is like a brother to me. You are all family. Sometimes you don't have to be related by blood to be family. Remember that.'

'Thank you so much. This means so much to me.'

'Good luck and study hard.' Aunty had joined us and placed

a comforting hand on my shoulder.

On the drive from Crockett to College Station, I felt wonderful and light as a breeze. I felt as if a huge burden had been lifted off my shoulders. I was finally going to attend college. What an opportunity to study in the US. I looked out the car window and saw that the road was straight as an arrow and there were vast fields on either side. Cows were grazing grass and there were heaps of it rolled up into cylindrical stacks. As I looked out, even the sight of the cows eating grass looked picturesque. In my happy state of mind, that Texas scenery looked right out of a Picasso painting. I asked Uncle if I could open the window. As I put my hand out it got pushed back quickly by the wind. I moved my hands in a wave marveling the clean air and the speed of the car. I put my head out, the window to really get a feel of the speed of the car and open my mouth to feel the full impact of the wind. Finally, I saw a tall water tower with 'College Station' written on one side. That's an appropriate name I thought, since college was my station. It was time to focus on getting the assistantship, so I could start classes immediately and complete the degree without delay. I focused on the plans I had laid out to get the assistantship.

They dropped me off at College Station in an apartment where the Indian Student Association had arranged for me to stay. The idea was that seniors would host the incoming students for a week as part of their orientation and help them find roommates among other freshmen. This was a two-bedroom apartment that accommodated three seniors permanently and the five new students temporarily.

As I entered, it was quite noisy with everyone having a good time laughing and talking. The life of the party was this thin curly-haired Parsi boy. He was cracking jokes and everybody was enjoying his company. I recognized him immediately, since I had met him in Mumbai. I had explored the possibility of being roommates, but my first impression of him when we had met in India was that he was too chatty. Having spent the better part of two years in solitary confinement on the terrace preparing for the GRE and my engineering exams, my disposition was such that I found any social interaction irritating and an intrusion on my thoughts and determination. I needed the fence of dissociation and distance to focus on my future.

'Hi. I am Zubin. Remember me? We met in Mumbai.'

'Of course, I remember you. You are Parveen's friend.' We started to chat about our mutual friend.

'You are late, man. Most of the new students have already found a roommate and they are moving to their own apartments. It seems that all the guys who came from Mumbai had created a mailing group and had already decided on their roommates when they met in India. I did not go to the meeting because I forgot about it,' he laughed.

'Me too,' I said, knowing deep inside that I did not check my emails because I didn't have a computer or the Internet.

'So I'm still looking for a roommate,' he said.

'Hmm.' I still did not want to commit to being his roommate. He was so talkative and I needed my space and periods of complete silence.

'How is the assistantship scene?' I asked, changing the subject to what was foremost in my mind.

'Oh, it's bad. Students have been trying for many weeks, going from one department to the next, submitting their resumes. It is such a big university and walking from department to department is such a pain. And the heat is too much, the Texas heat, man, is way too much. It burns your skin. Look at this,' he said as he showed me his tanned forehead and hands. I noticed the tan lines on his forehead as he had been wearing his cap in the sun.

'So, the process to apply for an assistantship is that you need to drop off your resume at the clerk's office in each department?'

'Yes.'

'Why can't we meet the head of the department?' I asked

because that was a part of my plan.

'There are too many students coming this year and they can't talk to everybody. It's tough, man. You are late. I have been trying for three weeks now without any luck. And I still have to find a roommate. The four other guys are moving in together.'

'Hmm,' I said, still not biting the bait.

'How do I get a printout of my resume?'

'The college is a five-minute walk from here. There is a computer lab with free Internet access. It is very fast, not at all like the dial-up connection in India.' He laughed.

'Free Internet? Wow!'

'And free printouts too.'

'Wow.' Free and fast Internet was a luxury unheard of in India.

'Can you take me to the computer lab?'

'Yes. It is too hot right now. We can do that in the evening. C'mon, let me introduce you to the seniors and the rest of the gang.'

I met everyone. Zubin helped me move my luggage to one of the rooms.

'Currently, it is very crowded. Three of the new guys are teaming together and will move out soon. So it will be better.'

'C'mon, let's chat with the seniors. I was in the middle of telling this funny story when you arrived.'

'You go ahead. I am going to take a walk and come back a little later.' I was a recluse at home and I am here to study not to socialize, I thought to myself.

'Okay,' Zubin was somewhat surprised.

I started to walk around the outside of the apartment. I was thinking about what I needed to do to get a scholarship and what I was going to add to my resume.

In the evening after sunset, Zubin and I walked to the college. Even though the sun had set and it was getting dark, the ground was warm. I could feel the heat coming through my shoes. The warm air was hitting my face.

It was going to be a challenging three weeks' time looking for assistantships. *March on Ankit,* I urged myself to push forward.

Zubin pointed out a building across the road. 'That is the Zachry building and that is where the Department of Electrical Engineering is located. There at the left corner is the computer lab.' My thoughts went back to the resume that I had emailed to myself. I had to make sure that there were no typos and that the indentations on the print out were correct and even. The resume had to be perfect and stand out among the others.

'Have you seen any movies lately?' Zubin asked casually.

'What?'

'Movies.'

'No,' I said trying to end the topic and refocus on how to perfect my resume.

'Do you have a favourite movie?'

I felt irritated. But I had to answer this question so as not to appear rude.

'Ah, hmm. Die Hard.'

'Nice. I like it too. Which is your favourite part?'

I thought this guy is crazy. Who talks about movies when you are on a mission?

'The first one,' knowing that there is always a first part to sequels.

'Me too. There is a video room where you can watch movies. For free. We can go together if you want.'

'Maybe.' In my mind, I was surely not going to do that. Also, he was not going to be my roommate. I thought talking was his way of life while keeping silent was mine.

I looked both ways and began to cross the road.

'Hey, dude, what are you doing? You can't cross the road like that.'

'Why?'

'It's the law here. You have to press this button and wait for the walk sign to appear.'

He pressed the button and we waited.

'Man, when do we walk?' Waiting for a signal when no cars were coming seemed stupid. I was eager to get to the computer lab and start working on my resume.

'When the little running man appears on the sign, you can cross. There's the sign.' Then he imitated the sign and started walking like the little man. He seemed to be enjoying himself, much to my annoyance.

As soon as we entered the lab, I started to work on all the three resumes for the three departments. Paying attention to the smallest details, I checked and rechecked each resume, printing and reprinting until each one was perfect. I looked at the university website and reviewed the faculty of different departments. I wanted to meet the head of each department to increase my chances. I needed to assert myself, rather than just drop off my resumes with the office clerk as the other students had done. I examined the department websites, looked at their photos and noted their office numbers. My resumes were ready and my plan was set.

Back at the apartment, I slept on the floor since there was no extra bed. I did not sleep soundly as I was preparing myself mentally and feeling the anxiety that I have always felt during stressful situations. The next morning, I got up early to reach the Department of Nuclear Engineering at 7.30 a.m., since most of the senior management arrived early. I took my beautiful black project thesis book from my internship at the atomic reactor along with my resume. I sat outside the department and waited for the head of department to arrive. I knew what he looked like. It was just about recognizing him and then approaching him. I had been waiting for almost an hour when I spotted him walking into the building. He was tall and lanky with a long clean-shaven face.

Instantly, I approached him, knowing precisely what to say, since I had been rehearsing this conversation for many months.

'Sir, my name is Ankit Gupta. I am here for the masters

programme. My internship back in India was spent working on nuclear reactors. I am looking for a research opportunity in the Department of Nuclear Engineering. I know we have a nuclear reactor on campus.'

'Yes, we do,' he replied proudly. 'Very few universities have that, you know.'

'I have seen some photos of it. I would love to see it. The one we had in India at the Bhabha Atomic Research Centre was pretty cool as well.'

'Yes, I have heard about that one. It has been in the news.' India had done a nuclear test in 1998 and that had been very newsworthy at that time. 'Do you have your project thesis with you?'

'Yes Sir, here it is.' I handed him the beautiful black book. He perused it for five minutes and looked impressed. He asked me some questions which I answered confidently, thrilled to be having this exchange with the head of the department.

'Okay. We have some funding and there is a research assistantship that I can offer you. I'll talk to the clerk now and you can get the rest of the details from her.'

'Thank you, Sir. It was good to meet you.'

'Likewise. I will talk to you soon.'

As he walked away, I sat on the couch outside the department. An exhalation of relief went through my body…I could see the sign of the Department of Electrical and Computer Engineering, which was the adjoining department. Finally, I will be doing my masters in engineering in the US. I put my hand over my head and took a deep breath. This was the moment I had been waiting for and planning for months and years. I could finally sleep in peace. I just sat motionless, breathing deeply, trying to absorb what had just transpired and the prize of it, this new beautiful academic surrounding.

The office clerk gave me the details of the assistantship. She said that due to the assistantship, the out-of-state semester fee would be waived but I would be expected to pay for the instate fee which was about $1,800. The monthly stipend was $1,200. Wow, 1,200 dollars was a lot of rupees.

I returned to the apartment late morning after the meeting at the university. Almost everyone was just getting up after a late night of fun. I gave them the good news.

'Dude, you are so lucky. You just arrived yesterday. We have been trying for a month now,' Zubin said.

'I don't know about the luck factor, but I am very happy.'

I wish you knew my past, I thought to myself.

I slept very well that night after a long time of restless ones. The next morning, I got up late, around 10.00 a.m. No one was present except for one senior. I was surprised and asked, 'Where is everybody?'

'Everyone left early for college.'

'Why?'

'Because of you. After your successful venture, everybody wanted to leave early and employ your strategy to get an assistantship.'

'Not just the new ones, but also the seniors. Haha,' he laughed. 'I am leaving now. You can grab yourself some food from the fridge.'

'Is it okay if I boil some eggs?'

'Why do you want boiled eggs for breakfast?'

'I just feel like it.'

'Okay, whatever you want.' Then he left.

As I put two eggs in the pot to boil, I got a whiff coming from the boiling eggs. The aroma reminded me of my internship at the Bhabha Atomic Research Center.

During my summer vacation between my third and fourth year of engineering, I had done an internship for about three months. The challenging part of that internship was the very long commute. I used to leave my house at 6.30 a.m., walk 20 minutes to the bus stop, stand in line to catch the bus, then transfer to another bus and reach the Atomic Centre around 9.00 a.m. I would then take an internal bus to reach the office after going through the security check. I generally reached office around 9.30. The three-hour commute was somehow manageable in the morning but was challenging in the evening after a busy day of work and standing throughout the journey in the crowded bus. I didn't arrive home until late evening. When I got off at my final bus stop I would not have the energy left to walk the last few miles to my home. I used to sit at the bus stop just to take a break before I started walking. One day I saw a street vendor, an old man sitting on the curb. He had a huge kettle where he was boiling eggs and selling them. I went and bought one for 25 paisa. He removed the white shell, cut the egg smoothly with a thread and put some salt and pepper on it. It gave me a burst of energy. From that day onwards, it became my evening ritual during my internship at the Bhabha Atomic Research Centre. As I ate the eggs in the apartment, I felt relief and a sense of gratitude for the Atomic Center internship and those roadside eggs that helped me get through the programme and subsequently to Texas A&M.

I felt a strong urge to talk to my parents. I got a phone card and called using a landline. I told them about the internship and how I'd be able to pay the tuition fee. They were overjoyed. I felt very emotional talking to them, but I held myself back from sharing my emotions on the phone. They refrained from sharing their emotions as well. In our family, there was seldom an expression of emotions. Rather it was always about controlling your emotions, fighting the battle and being stoic. So, our conversation centred more on mundane stuff. I wanted to tell them how I missed them and how lonely I was feeling in this new country. But I just told them about the hot weather and how big and clean the place was. I also told them about the stipend and told them I would be sending $100 every month. I would also be sending a personal computer soon for Anamika. I did not want her to face the same issues that I had faced during GRE preparation.

As the minutes of the phone card ended, I felt the emptiness. A lot was left unsaid.

I spent the next few days walking around the campus. There was a small church close to the engineering building and I used to sit inside focusing on my future goals. Zubin also got an assistantship. No matter where I was, he would find me and drag me to meet other students. Sometimes, I would hide underneath a church bench to avoid him, but he would still find me like in a hide and seek game. I would try to remain in my private shell, but he persistently tried to invade that space. Somehow, he felt it was our joint obligation to be social and make new friends. And I could not see the reason why.

He also took me to the video room where we watched some movies. Sitting there reminded me of my childhood when I used to watch movies with Abhishek. It was great to spend the afternoon in the air conditioned room away from the Texas heat.

I was still not completely sure about being roommates with Zubin. He talked too much, but now in my relaxed state of mind I began to find humour in his jokes. He was actually very funny and loved playing pranks. He had purchased a whoopee cushion that made farting noises when someone sat on it. He tried it on everybody, including the seniors. He had got a fake parking ticket and placed it on the windshield of the seniors' and strangers' cars. He always enjoyed seeing their confused reactions. It was funny watching them getting a ticket for doing nothing wrong and trying to figure out what it was for.

In a few weeks, it seemed like all the new students had paired up with roommates. Zubin, I and one more guy who was staying at some other apartment were the only ones left. One night, I saw Zubin in the corner of the room uncharacteristically quiet. He was listening to music on his Walkman.

He called me over, 'Ankit, come here and listen to this.'

Though hesitant, I put one of the ear buds in my ear hoping

it was not one of his pranks.

It was a beautiful Indian pop song about friendship and the lyrics went something like this:

Friendship is a beautiful thing
You would be lucky to have a friend, a true friend
One who is happy at your happiness and sad at your sadness.

As I listened to the song, I realized that behind his jovial exterior there was a calm person. I realized, like me, he too was away from his family and trying to cope by seeking human connections.

'Let's be roommates, Zubin.'

'I always thought we were going to be roommates,' he said.

'Yes, yes, of course. I am just confirming it now.' I did not disclose my earlier reservations.

So, we teamed up with another student, Rajat, who had arrived late and could not find a roommate. We found a two-bedroom apartment further away from the college but cheaper. Rajat got his own room while Zubin and I shared the other bedroom. I wanted to save money, so I went ahead with the cheaper option.

Zubin dragged me to many parties. I was not sure that I would fit in, but they were fun. I also attended some social events organized by the Indian Students Association. When one of our friends couldn't find a lady singer for a duet, Zubin volunteered.

'Zubin, it's for a female voice,' I clarified.

'So what, I'll sing in a female voice then. No problem.'

So he got on stage in front of 200 students and sang in a female voice. Although he sang horribly, it was very entertaining. Not just me, but the whole crowd burst out laughing. It was the most entertaining act of the show.

Before I knew it, our classes started. With the assistantship, I was not required to pay the full amount of the tuition fee, so I immediately returned $2,500 to Vrajesh Uncle and told him that I would return the rest in a few years.

It was an amazing learning experience to attend lectures of

esteemed professors who had extensive practical and research experience. Some of them were authors of some of the textbooks I read in India. The atmosphere in the classroom was casual and there was open discussion among students and professors. They made solving technical problems fun and interesting for us.

Trying to get used to living with two roommates was challenging. Without the help of my parents, I was finding it difficult to get through the daily chores. Back home in India, I never had to cook or do much else around the house as Mom and Dad provided us with everything. Now I had to do everything, from cooking and washing the dishes to cleaning up. Rajat was a bit older than us and he had lived alone in India, so he was more accustomed to taking care of himself. Zubin was very disciplined, and that made me the only one who had to struggle with completing daily chores. When I returned to the apartment after attending classes all day, I would take off my pants and step right out of them, leaving them on the floor. The next morning Zubin would point to them and, just like a school teacher, would ask me to fold them and put them in the drawer. He would do the same about washing the dishes. When I finished eating, I typically left the dishes on the table and he'd tell me to clean up after myself. Cooking was a problem. We would take turns cooking, but since I'd spent all my time in India rushing around trying to get a scholarship, I failed to get some lessons from Mom. In the little time we had, she had taught me to cook just one dish—kidney beans. It was a very simple dish since the boiled kidney beans were available in the can. All I had to do was add some spices, fried onions, tomatoes and boil them together for a few minutes. Voila, the dish was ready and with that I had fulfilled my obligation this time around.

I cooked the same dish every third day when it was my turn. I did this until my roommates became fed up and decided to intervene one weekend. One night, with all of us in the living room, Zubin and Rajat pointed out I was not doing my fair share of household chores. Zubin again emphasized on me leaving my pants on the floor, which struck me as funny. Rajat pointed out that I cook the same dish every three days and that I didn't wash the dishes. He was sick of eating the same thing every three days and said he could not continue doing so. I told them that I was finding it difficult. I told them that my parents had always told me that my primary responsibility as a child was to study and do well and they would take care of everything else. But now they were not here.

'I know. However, that was India and we are here. Here it is different, everybody in the US has to do their fair share of chores,' Rajat scolded.

'I think even the president,' Zubin added with a straight face. I was never sure whether he was serious or joking.

'Point well taken, guys. I will make a concerted effort going forward. I will do my chores properly and learn how to make some new dishes. I can cook a can of chickpeas.' We all laughed.

The nuclear engineering assistantship started with a few meetings with the head of the department. He informed me that the project was at its very initial stages, so we needed to conduct some background research on techniques used around the world.

He said that I would have to visit the nuclear reactor at least once a week. I was excited to see the nuclear reactor, but it was far from the campus. There was no public transportation and buying a car was out of the question. Instead, I bought a second-hand bicycle. It was a 45-minute bike ride along an airstrip to the nuclear reactor. I hated cycling and the Texas sun did not help. When I reached, I was sweaty and my clothes were soaked, but I was very excited to be there.

Once inside, I was absolutely thrilled to see the nuclear reactor. It was an open dome structure with the radioactive material at the bottom of a huge pool of water. It was an experimental facility designed to carry out nuclear research experiments on isotopes. At the bottom, I could see a blue tinge of light coming out from the metal tubes of the nuclear chamber. The state of the nuclear reactor was monitored with huge displays indicating activity levels. My mind was simply blown away. I was unsure what kind of research I was expected to conduct. At the start, I was asked to do research survey on nuclear materials and then write a report.

As I cycled back to the campus, I wondered why the nuclear reactor internship was so far away. I realized that the only way to relieve exhaustion from the distance and the Texas heat was eating a full tub of ice cream that we had bought at Walmart.

I was very careful about saving rather than spending money and not splurging on unnecessary things. I wanted to make sure to send some money home and start building some savings for an emergency. Most of the time I ate at home to keep my costs down. Though I did not spend money eating at McDonald's or Subway, I did buy their soft drinks. Since they offered unlimited refills, I could buy favourites such as Coke and Sprite. Unlimited drinks were unheard of in India, so I indulged in this new opportunity. The meals at these fast-food restaurants that cost $5 or $6 were quite a huge expense for me. I preferred to buy from a man of South American descent who had a food stand and sold jambalaya, a spicy chicken and rice dish for $2. It was cheap and very filling.

On one weekend, Zubin forced me to go to a football game at Kyle Field on campus to watch the college team 'Aggies' play. I agreed and I wore the school team's maroon T-shirt but told him I would not buy the twelfth man towel. I believed that these games were a commercial ploy to get students to spend money. As we reached the stadium, I couldn't believe how packed it was with students and faculty and alumni wearing maroon T-shirts. As the game started, we all got into the football spirit, copying the shout-outs of other students and feeling the same school spirit rush through our bodies. We high-fived with our neighbours when the Aggies scored a touchdown and cheered on the defense when the opponent was on the attack. It was a diverse crowd in the stands; aside from us and other Indians, there were Caucasians,

Chinese and African-Americans. It was no big deal as long as we were all cheering for the same team. We were shouting at the top of our lungs, feeling the infectious excitement of those around us. Watching the students shout and cheer in unison, I realized that the game was not just about winning or losing or for commercial reasons, but it was about creating a sense of community. It was a way for people of different backgrounds to come together and share an experience while having a good time. It nurtured school spirit. I bought the twelfth man towel and cheered on my college team; I was no longer just an Indian student coming from overseas to study, I was an Aggie and this was my school team.

When our team won, it was time to party. We went to Rajat's friends' house where two couples were living. They made some great Indian food and got beer. I had never consumed alcohol in my entire student life up to this point. I felt it was time to start drinking, now that I could relax. As I was about to take my first sip of the beer, I thought about the lecture that Mom had given us when we were kids. The lesson was about the evils of alcohol and she demonstrated it in the kitchen by pouring some whiskey into a steel glass and dropping a lit match into it. As the fire burst out of the glass, she declared dramatically, 'This is how alcohol burns your stomach when you consume it.' We were children back then and really believed it.

Sorry Mom, it was time to burn my stomach. After drinking two or three bottles of beer, I felt a buzz. It was quite a relaxing feeling and my obsessive thoughts about the assistantship, studies and other worries gradually evaporated, and I was able to live in the moment. The music of heavy metal bands such as AC/DC and Nirvana, bands that I had never heard of before, resonated with me. I saw Zubin and the others lost in the music, climbing on the sofa with hands raised, moving and grooving. I followed their lead, as I figured that the music was about losing oneself and reaching a higher state. So, I climbed on the sofa as well.

We laughed about the previous night's fun the next morning and promised to repeat it the following weekend.

Four months into the nuclear engineer internship, the head of the department informed me that the project I was working on did not receive the expected funding. So they would not be able to continue with my assistantship. He said he could write me a recommendation to find another assistantship. I was disappointed but ready for the next challenge. I needed to get an assistantship to pay for the second semester. For the months of November and December, which were surprisingly cold for Texas, I looked for another assistantship on campus. During those two months, I made sure that I continued to wire money back home by hesitantly borrowing from Zubin.

Finally, just before I had to pay for the second semester, I was able to get a research assistantship in the Department of Aerospace Engineering. I was amazed to find out that it was a project for NASA. The professor who gave me this assistantship told me, 'If you are good enough to work on two nuclear reactors, you are ready to work for NASA.'

The professor in the aerospace department at Texas A&M was developing algorithms to identify the location of a spacecraft in space by identifying the location of the stars around it. It was basically identifying the landmarks, in this case the stars, through image processing. To verify the algorithm, we would design an experiment module with a camera and computer that would be placed in the space shuttle and launched into space. When in space, it would take images, process some of the data to identify stars using triangulation techniques, then make estimates on the exact location of the spacecraft and send the calculated estimates back to the NASA base station. I was responsible for designing a networking module for this experimental unit. It would send data from our experiment module to the NASA spacecraft and then from the NASA base station to Texas A&M's computer machines. It was super exciting. I was given access to the aerospace labs and

I had the opportunity to work with some of the smartest people at NASA and in aerospace engineering generally. We had regular meetings with the engineers at NASA and Texas A&M engineers. I got a sense of what made America great. There was a sense of optimism and abundance, a desire to push the limits and an overall environment of looking forward and open communication. 'Be frank, be honest.' I remembered the words from Dad, something he had learnt from his American friends. I began to thrive in my project and in my college courses and a year went by quickly.

In 2001, the US economy was at its peak and all the networking and software companies were doing very well. That was evident from the number of companies that were coming on campus and courting students with freebies. I was planning to graduate in the summer and so I had to start looking for a job.

In February 2001, I went to a career fair that was held on campus. Zubin and I went together, dressed in our formal attire. I felt very confident with my resume. I had taken some of the most difficult and relevant courses in computer science and computer engineering. I had a GPA of 3.85 out of 4. I had two internships at the BARC Nuclear Reactor and one at NASA. I was confident of landing a job with my outstanding experience. Zubin and I moved around the big hall giving our resumes to numerous representatives and collecting the freebies. A company that designed software tools used for design chips caught my interest; it was number one in the electronic design automation field. I thought that was a perfect fit for me since it would require both software and chip design knowledge. Another reason was that the manager showed great interest in my resume. We had a good discussion about the prospects of working at this company and my suitability for the position. We both thought it was a good fit and he said he would set up an interview.

Around 4.00 p.m., things were winding down at the job fair. Zubin and I were exhausted after going from booth to booth talking to the representatives from different companies as we tried to prove ourselves as good candidates. So we sat down at one of the booths that had been vacated. Suddenly a student approached us with his resume. He looked like he was from India and appeared to be on edge. He was applying for an internship.

'Oh. Nah,' I began to clarify that we did not work for the company, but rather we too were students.

'Ankit, wait. I will take a look at the gentleman's resume. He may be a good fit for our company.' Zubin winked at me to play along.

'This is a good resume.' Zubin started asking him questions similar to what we were asked in the morning.

To our surprise, he was answering us. Zubin was surprised and kept at the ruse.

'Do you know the CADMI software?' I looked at Zubin as he had just made up that name.

'No, I don't know it.'

'That is a very important skill needed for our company.'

'Sir, I don't know about it but I am willing to learn.'

'I don't know. It is a key requirement. What do you think, Ankit?' passing the ball to me.

'Mmm. Well, I am from HR. I don't know what that software is, but I do know it is important. Sorry, but we will keep your resume on file. Zubin, give him a freebie from our company.'

'Ok,' Zubin hesitantly gave one of the freebies to the unsuspecting student.

As he left, we laughed and I told Zubin, 'I think we are going to go to academic hell.'

'Will they teach CADMI software there?' he asked.

'I don't know. But I am willing to learn about it,' I said smiling.

The company got back to me very quickly and within a week I had the interview. The people there were great. My only concern was that the job was for a customer support engineer, a position that was responsible for interacting with other companies and solving their problems. I wanted a job in design and research.

At the end of the interview, I let the manager know that. The next morning he called and told me that they were interested. To make it an attractive offer they would enroll me for the first six months in a new leadership programme conducted in the Austin office. General Electric had pioneered the concept whereby they took new hires from an elite university and trained them in leadership, communication and the company's various business interests. I thought this would be a unique job opportunity and so I accepted the offer.

Once I got the offer, I was super relaxed. I took a lot of driving trips. Zubin used to borrow a car from his colleagues and we would drive to different parts of Texas. I was the navigator because I did not know how to drive. I used to struggle trying to read the maps and then fold them neatly. We always got lost during our trips. Once we drove four hours off track mistaking the north for the south on the highway. We travelled to Austin, Louisiana and Florida for a reunion with Arun and Nihar and other engineering friends.

One of the most memorable trips was when we visited New York City in the spring. It was fascinating seeing the skyscrapers that I remembered from the Spider-Man comic strips. The city had a unique energy with crowds hurriedly crossing streets, taxis honking trying to find their way in traffic and street vendors crowding the sidewalks. It reminded us so much of Mumbai.

We went up the World Trade Center. It was amazing to stand at the top of the tower; the view was breathtaking. Standing on top, you could feel the building moving with the wind. As we were admiring the New York skyline against the sunset backdrop, Arun asked Nihar, who lived in New York, 'Which bridge is that?'

'It is the Hudson,' Nihar said with his usual swag.

'Wait, didn't you tell me that the other bridge was the Hudson?'

Nihar took me to the corner, 'Look man, I'm not a tourist guide. Shakespeare said even if you call a rose by another name it would still smell as sweet.'

'Don't make a Shakespearean excuse,' we laughed and enjoyed

the view.

As we walked downstairs to the main lobby, you could see the hustle and bustle of the people who worked there. We were stuck among the crowds of employees who were leaving for the day. Like the crowds in Mumbai, they were hard working people trying to make a living. That also reminded us that this building was not just a tourist spot but a place where people worked. New Yorkers reminded me that if you want a better life, you've got to hustle.

Vrajesh Uncle and Aunty came for my graduation ceremony. Knowing that I would be emotional and overwhelmed and still not comfortable talking about money, I returned the remaining $2500, placing it inside a 'thank you' greeting card.

As I was about to graduate, I wrapped up my part of the Aerospace NASA project. I created a demo with mock NASA servers, showing end-to-end data communication from the NASA shuttle to our college machines. The overall NASA project was moving towards success and was ready to be placed on the space shuttle. Each team member got an Award of Excellence from the NASA team in appreciation and recognition for our contributions to the project. After my last meeting, the NASA liaison asked to briefly speak to me outside.

'Hey Ankit, I heard you are graduating and going to leave the project.'

'Yes,' I said.

'Are you sure you want to leave this project? It's going great. If you want, we can increase your stipend and you can do a PhD.'

'Hmm. Not really. I would like to work in the computer industry.'

'You know, we could get your green card processed very quickly by applying to a special category of visas.'

I thought about it for a few moments. The only thing I cared about was working and contributing to the field of chip design and computer engineering.

'It's tempting, but I can't. I really believe I can contribute to the field of electronics more. I think that is my calling.'

'Okay, as you wish. I hope you are making the right choice,' he replied.

'What I would love though is if you could invite me to the space centre when the shuttle launches with our space module.'

'Cool. I will definitely try to do that. I think it will be at the end of 2002 or 2003. It will launch from Cape Canaveral in Florida.'

It would be so cool to watch a space shuttle launch. I thanked all the coordinators, professors and my colleagues for the great academic opportunity. It was now time to apply whatever I had learned in my academic life to my professional life and immerse myself in it.

The six-month leadership trainee programme started at the Austin office. There was a group of 50 university graduates from the top universities. It was a diverse mix of people from different countries and cultures. It was a fun group of people; there was a lot of camaraderie as we participated in team building events and training in different fields that the company was doing research in and selling its product. Besides the technical aspects, emphasis was placed on communication, leadership, teamwork and ethics.

On 11 September, we were attending a technical seminar when the teacher got a call. Her look of horror was followed by a frantic search on her laptop for news. The World Trade Center towers had fallen. We could not believe what we were seeing—two planes had crashed into the twin towers. We were aghast, there was panic in the air and there were questions about some other airplanes still in the air and the looming threat. Everybody felt scared and was in disbelief at what was happening. Nobody felt safe that day.

At lunch time, I went back to my apartment, which was within walking distance from the office, and I watched the images on the TV. I saw the towers collapsing and people walking disoriented among the rubble. My heart froze when I saw people jump out of the buildings, probably some of the same people I had rubbed shoulders with when we were there a few months before. I had felt a sense of kinship with them when I was there. They were regular hard-working people hustling to make life better for themselves and their families—they were my mirror image. I felt anger against the perpetrators. They might be thinking of themselves as martyrs, but in reality they were the cowards preying in the shadows.

In the ensuing days, people started trying to return to normalcy. We all wanted to show that our way of life could not be changed by such an act of terrorism. But that sad and tragic day left an indelible mark on all of us.

In November, as we were about to graduate from the trainee programme, I was certain that I did not want to go back to work in a customer support role. But, my friend Pavan tried to convince me otherwise.

'Ankit, it is a great position. What is your problem?'

'I don't see myself sitting on the phone and answering customer calls. I would like to do design and make new stuff, bring fascinating things to life.'

'You know, after 9/11, a lot of companies are laying people off. It has started in the Bay Area and soon it will be happening here. This position is going to be safe because our customers will always need support.' He was sounding like Arun, who was in the Bay Area and giving the same advice.

'I know it is safe. But it is not in line with what I want to do. I have to be involved in a more cutting-edge work. We can't make career decisions based on safety, we have to believe in ourselves and pursue our passion. Actually, I have already spoken to our research and design centre in Boston and they are keen on having me.'

'You are taking a big risk. You know if they have layoffs, the experimental team is going to be the first to be let go. Also, the current manager and coordinators of the university are going to be angry because you were hired for the position first and then enrolled for this trainee programme.'

'I have to follow the path of my heart, not the path of fear. I think it is best for me and best for the company.'

I was able to convince the higher management of my decision and they reluctantly agreed. Pavan took my position in customer support and ended up working in that line for the next 11 years. I drove to Boston to assume my risky but exciting R&D job. I also ignored Pavan's advice to leave my second-hand Ford Mustang in Texas. Instead I drove it to Boston.

'It is a rear wheel drive. The Mustang is good for Texas but not for Boston. It will skid in the snow. And you're travelling in December,' my friends cautioned.

'C'mon, it's a short road trip. It's like going to the grocery store, except it's 2,000 miles. I can't miss that experience.'

So, I took all my stuff and loaded it into the Mustang. My small coloured TV was in the back seat and I put the luggage in the trunk, while everything else was somehow shoved inside the car. As I got ready to go, I saw a pile of clothes lying on the ground that I'd left because there was no space in the car. So my friends and I just threw them in the car and squeezed them in one by one into whatever space we could find. The plan was that my friend Nihar would fly from New York to Dallas, and then I would pick him up from the Dallas airport and we would do a cross country road trip together. I would drop him off in New York and then head towards Boston. I saw that he hadn't listened to me. Seeing him at the airport with a suitcase, I said, 'Dude, I told you not to bring too much stuff. There is absolutely no space in the car.'

'It's New Year's. What if we get invited to a New Year's Eve party? I want to be dressed properly for that.'

'Great. Well, there is no space for your stuff. You have to sit with the bag on your lap. Throughout the road trip, Nihar had to sit holding his bag. It was a fun and memorable trip. It took about 30 hours over five days, driving across the American heartland.

We took turns, driving fast and racing with other sports cars or slowing down and enjoying the scenery. We welcomed 2003 at a New Year's Eve party in Washington DC. The driving experience changed drastically as we entered New York City, where I came across some serious car honking and vehicles aggressively cutting in and out of lanes to get ahead.

I reached Boston at around 10.00 p.m., after dropping off Nihar in New York. The plan was to stay in a motel. During the drive alone, it started getting cold and I could see there was a storm approaching. It had started drizzling. Coming from Texas, I wasn't prepared for the extreme cold weather, so I decided to stop at a Walmart to get some gloves and a cap. As I pulled into the Walmart parking lot, the entire complex was white and covered in snow. I could see the snowflakes falling under the golden glazed reflection of the street lamps. As I took a sharp left turn to get into a parking space, my car skidded and went out of control. I was now in the path of oncoming traffic and stuck in the snow. I honked for a long time to indicate to the other drivers that I was stuck and most importantly, in their lane. Luckily, the other cars stopped. I pressed the accelerator slowly for the rear wheels to get some traction on the snow.

Ah, this is why my friends were suggesting against taking a rear-wheel sports car to Boston in the snow, I realized. *Oh well. I am too attached to my Mustang. I am glad I didn't pay attention to their warnings about the cold weather. I'm going to enjoy the snow while I'm at it,* I thought.

I parked the car and got out. I saw snow for the first time; I had never seen snow in India or in Texas. There was hail in College Station which hurt when it fell on my head when I was cycling in the rain, but these snowflakes were soft. I enjoyed looking at their slow graceful dance under the lights as they fell slowly on my face and outstretched hands. It was a great start to this year with a new experience and I predicted that I was going to have a great 2002.

After taking a few days to settle in, I drove back alone to New York City. Ever since 11 September, it was something I had been thinking about doing. I parked my car and walked up to the place where the World Trade Center towers had been. As I stood at the place where the lobby had been, I remembered being at the same location the previous summer and looking above my head and seeing this massive building, which was now just rubbles barricaded by the yellow police tapes. I felt the void deep within thinking of the suffering that people had to endure. All the televised images of that day's horror flashed through my mind. I closed my eyes and offered a short prayer for peace of the departed souls. Then, I returned to Boston.

One of my new resolutions for 2002 was to bring my father to visit me in the US. It would be difficult for Mom to come all the way due to Anamika's studies. The last decade had been difficult for Dad and it was time to change that. It was time to share my achievements with him and bring cheer and joy to his life.

On a spring day four months later, I picked Dad up at Logan International Airport. However, destiny dealt a cruel blow. On that day I was in a state of ambivalence, being happy on the outside but devastated on the inside. Dad was seated next to me in the Mustang, his luggage in the trunk and in the back seat I had a cardboard box filled with my office things, including a red folder with my job termination documents.

8

BATTLE WOUNDS

'Your position has been terminated.' It hit me like the sudden loud ringing of a bell. The echo of the words bounced around in my head for a long time.

That Friday morning, I had come in early to the office to wrap up my work quickly and leave at noon to pick up Dad from the airport. Bob, my manager called me on the cubicle landline at around 11.00 a.m. and asked me to come to his office.

As I stood outside his office, I saw the HR manager staring at a raft of files she was holding.

'Do you want me to come back later?' I asked, thinking he was busy with some HR matter.

'No no, please come in and have a seat.'

As I took my seat, I was perplexed why we would be talking about technical issues in front of the HR. Even before I landed on the seat, the HR manager said with no apathy, 'I am sorry to inform you, Ankit, but your position has been terminated.'

I looked at Bob sitting on the other side of the desk. He had his eyes fixed on the floor as if to say that he was not part of this decision.

My mind went blank. I was completely shocked by this news. She continued, but her words made no sense to me. I was worried about how I would break this news to my Dad in a few hours. How will he feel when he gets to know about this? He has not seen even one place or tourist attraction in the US and now I have this bad news to share.

'How much time do I have before I have to leave the US?'

'I think, in your case, it is two months.'

'Just two months?'

'Your visa expires in two months. But you can check with your lawyer.' She said 'your lawyer', but for me it had been all about working as a team the entire time. Now I was put in an isolated corner with 'your' problems.

The HR manager continued her spiel. It seemed like she had a lot of experience in firing unsuspecting employees. She removed a red file and started going through the documents, pointing to where I needed to sign. She was still talking, saying something about compensation, training and health insurance and Cobra. Did she say Cobra or was it Corba? I didn't care. I was feeling suffocated and wanted to get outside to get some air. I couldn't understand anything written in the document, but I signed on the dotted line.

'These are your copies,' she said as she handed me the red file containing all the documents.

'Bob will help you collect your things from your cubicle.'

'Can I do it next week?'

'No, you have to leave now,' she said.

Damn. What's the rush? As I stood up, the HR manager was already looking at the next file, the next victim for the firing squad. Bob walked me to my cubicle.

'I am so sorry, Ankit. I really am.' I could see that he was sincerely apologetic and full of remorse.

'Was it my work performance? I thought I was doing well. We had successfully completed that challenging project just a few weeks ago.'

'It is not you. It is everybody in our group. Our whole team is being dissolved.'

'Oh no, really?' That made me even sadder.

'Post 9/11, the economy is slowing down everywhere. Our company is focusing only on projects that produce revenues. A lot of the research projects with future prospects are being terminated.

I think once I have helped with this round of layoffs, I will be on the firing line too.'

'Our project has great potential, Bob.'

'Innovation is always risky, Ankit. It's like walking on a tightrope. Failure is more probable than success. I hope this experience does not dampen your spirit.'

As I reached my cubicle, a brown cardboard box had magically appeared on my desk. I started putting my stuff, mostly books, in the box. I looked at the chair. It had been a good four months. The cold weather had been unkind, but the office, my colleagues and the work had been great. I could not believe this was happening to me. Was it a mistake?

I did not want to waste Bob's time with my sentimental musings, so I quickly loaded my stuff and walked out of the building with the box in my arms, avoiding eye contact with my former colleagues.

'I am so sorry again. Good luck and I hope we can stay in touch,' Bob said as we shook hands and he walked back inside, leaving me alone on the sidewalk.

It was an isolating feeling. I was still grasping for my bearing and did not know what to do as I kept looking back at the building. My Mustang provided me the safe haven I needed, so I went and sat in my car and put the box in the back seat.

That spring day had started out perfect. The sun was out, the birds were chirping and the trees were in full bloom. I was sure Dad would enjoy his trip, now that the horrible winter was over. The previous night I had cooked lunch for him and prepared my roommates Ananya and Murtaza. 'My Dad is a great person. Initially, he comes across as a bit strict because of his background in the Army, but you will love him once you get to know him.' Ananya was in a trainee programme in Austin. Four months ago, we had moved into this big two-storey house. It was a huge three-bedroom house with big back and front yards. Murtaza was with me in the engineering programme in Mumbai and I had helped him get this internship in my group.

Was this really happening to me? I wondered again, opening my file and going through the first page again. There was no doubt that it was for real and I had indeed been laid off.

What should I do now? Should I go home first? It was 11.45 a.m. *Forget it, I'll be late.* So I started for the airport, which was an hour away.

What am I going to tell Dad? He will be so disappointed.

The news of my layoff might open up old wounds. It might stir up bad memories of his layoff from the oil company and the horrible things he experienced after that. Our house eviction had put him in an emotionally fragile state of mind. He obsessively worried about something bad happening to his kids. And something had happened now. I had just been fired and my visa was expiring in two months. I didn't know how he would react emotionally. It would be too much to take in considering he would be physically exhausted after his 24-hour flight from India.

After some contemplation I decided I would tell him about it the next day, once he had had a good night's sleep. I hoped I could keep myself together, control my emotions and keep them in check. I had to be strong and absorb the hit. So, I let Dad get some rest before giving him the heartbreaking news.

I was angry at myself for I was about to cause him disappointment. I punched myself repeatedly on my right thigh while holding the steering wheel in my left hand. After I carried on doing so for some time, I pulled myself together and became stoic. Love trumps emotion. *Keep it together, Ankit.* I couldn't reach Ananya, but I called Murtaza and told him that I'd been laid off. Thankfully, Murtaza's internship had not been terminated. Ironically, I had been his mentor at work. Murtaza informed me that Ananya was laid off too.

When Dad saw me at the airport arrival area, he gave me a bear hug. He was excited to see me and so was I. However, the lingering feeling of being laid off tugged at me. As we drove from the airport, Dad was not looking at the beautiful landscape of Boston's downtown, but just kept staring at me as if my face were a piece of art.

'You look healthy. That's good.'

'Here in Boston, it is too cold to go outside and play any sport. Generally I stay at home and eat too much and watch a lot of TV,' I said with a smile.

My eyes were on the road, but I could feel his admiring glances. I just wanted the journey to be over. We were stuck in traffic on the bridge, with the river running underneath. Construction in Boston never ends and the natives always complained that the traffic delays were very frustrating. I was anxious to get home so that Dad could rest and I could go for a walk to clear my head.

'How is Abhishek doing at work?' I asked.

'He is doing well. He is now working in a bank. He works really hard and puts in a lot of extra hours. He got quickly promoted to branch manager.' *Oh great, I'm going to disappoint him big time tomorrow.*

'How are Anamika's studies going?'

'Well. She is in her chemical engineering course. The computer which you sent has been helpful. She also started preparing for the GRE. She is going to follow in your footsteps.' *Oh. I hope not.*

'She is a hard worker. She will find her own path. I advised her to pursue petroleum engineering. That has a great future.' *Better than chip design for sure.* I thought.

'I am glad all my children are contributing to society.'

'All that is the result of how you and Mom raised us,' I said.

'How is your work?' *Oh no, not that question.*

'It's okay,' I uttered the words knowing I would have to take those back the next day.

'You told me about your interesting R&D project, the one that is going to be part of the industry technical standards. Have you completed that?'

'Yes. We finished it a few weeks back,' I said thinking about the last four months. I had not taken a single day off and had worked most weekends. Today was going to be my first official half day.

'How are your marathons coming along?' I asked trying to change the subject. I was happy to know that for the last few years, Dad had taken a keen interest in running marathons and staying active.

'It's lot of fun. I have completed many marathons now. I also received several gold-plated mugs after completing a few of them. I will show them to you when you come to Mumbai.'

'That's awesome.'

'So you were saying you finished that project and...?'

'Look over there. That's downtown Boston where all the tall buildings are. In the US, a city's principal commercial hub is generally located in one area called downtown. It is the same as in South Mumbai.'

'Yes. That work of yours will set the standard for everyone in the industry.' He barely looked outside, still trying to appreciate my face and exploits at work.

'Maybe.' I was so overcome with embarrassment that I felt like stopping the car and jumping into the river. *C'mon Ankit, try harder*.

'I have a work colleague, Akshat, who is also from Mumbai. His mother is here as well. She is a very nice lady. They have invited us for dinner,' I said, hoping to distract him from talking about work.

'Okay,' he said, mildly alarmed by the introduction of this unrelated topic.

'And you will meet my roommate, Ananya. He is originally from Gujarat. His parents are teachers.' *C'mon, keep dragging the topic*. 'He likes to write poetry. And you met Murtaza in Mumbai. We studied engineering together. He is a very nice guy.'

I realized that any silence would bring in the opportunity to talk about my job and the needless lies I would have to tell. So I continued chattering, talking incessantly about everything under the sun except my job. I talked about my roommates, my other friends, my friend's roommates, about their families. I even talked about the weather, the football games and how the local team, the Patriots, had won the Super Bowl for the first time in their franchise history. Finally, we reached home. Dad ate the food I had prepared the day before and went to sleep. With my mission accomplished, I went for a walk and let out a cry of pain.

The next morning, I woke up to the noise of the vacuum cleaner. Instantly, I knew it was Dad and he had started with his cleaning mission. There was also some clanging of dishes. Ah, a nice cup of tea.

Then I heard another voice. It was Ananya. *Oh man, I had not asked Ananya to not tell Dad about my layoff since he had been out the previous day, probably grieving his own job loss.* I got out of bed and rushed downstairs to the kitchen.

'Uncle, even Ankit lost his job.' I heard those words as I reached the kitchen door. My heart sank.

I saw Dad holding the vacuum standing by the kitchen. Ananya was standing next to him. They were looking at the red file on the kitchen table. Next to the file was a cup of dark brown tea and a small plate covering it. I tried to gather what had likely transpired before my entry into the kitchen. My file was still in my car, I remembered. This was Ananya's file. Dad must have seen this file in the backseat yesterday and finding it here now, must have read it thinking it was mine. He must have realized that Ananya was laid off from his job and probably said something to the effect that he was sorry for his job loss. Ananya may have been annoyed and might have defensively answered, 'Ankit lost his job as well.'

As I entered, there was a stunning silence. Dad and Ananya were both looking at me.

'Dad, I found out about it yesterday. I thought I would let

you rest before I told you.'

Dad was still looking stunned. I wanted to quickly lessen the blow. I didn't want him to go into shock.

'It is a usual thing in the US. Companies just lay off employees when they don't need them anymore.'

'Yes, Uncle it is very common,' Ananya said, picking up my cue.

'They say that an average person in the US changes jobs seven times in his lifetime,' I said. He was still staring at me.

At this point I realized that there was no way to lessen the blow.

For the next few days, we did not communicate much except for on basic topics. Dad became quiet and stayed in his room. His door was closed, but I was not sure if he was sleeping or not. I went out for my usual walks, called my friends and searched for a job.

A few days later, we went to the dinner that Akshat's mom had invited us on. It was something I had planned for Dad's visit, so he could meet and socialize with people. But the layoff created a somber mood for the gathering.

Akshat's group was spared. He was a couple of years senior and was offering his guidance. Akshat's mom was a full time social worker back in India. She told us how she worked in a school for the rehabilitation of the visually impaired, helping them learn skills so that they could earn their livelihood. I was very moved by the goodness of her work, so I promised to help her in some way once my current challenge was resolved.

After a sumptuous dinner, everybody started chatting about life in India, reminiscing about the good times, about growing up happy and remarking how cheap everything was. How amazing the food was! Murtaza pointed out that the cost of a haircut was ₹7 in India including a head massage, whereas here in the US it was $12. Over the later part of the evening, the conversation turned serious. Akshat's mother talked about how her husband had built up a big business in India, but when he passed away, their nephew, who was his apprentice, stole the business and the property. Their case has been going on for decades in the Indian courts without any resolution. Ananya told us how his grandfather had established a school in Ahmedabad, Gujarat, and how his parents were denied rights to the school or even an entry, since someone else put an illegal claim on it. He said that the case was still going on and they had sold most of their belongings just to fight their case. Murtaza too shared a similarly tragic story. As I sat listening, I remembered that night when the goons entered our house and threw us all out. But I did not share my story. I knew it would make Dad feel even more miserable, so I kept it to myself.

While driving back with Dad, I took the long way home. I wanted to chat with him and hear what he was feeling.

'Murtaza is such a jovial fellow,' I initiated the conversation.

'Yes, he is. It's tough such a thing happened to him in India, to all these kids. The impact these experiences leave on kids is so profound and sad,' Dad said.

'Yes, it is.' We both tried to avoid talking specifically about our own bad experience. That was never to be spoken about in our family.

'There will always be good and bad people in every country. I sincerely believe that the majority of people in India are good.' I was trying to steer the conversation away from sad memories.

'But it is the bad people who dominate society and hold the power. They spoil everybody else's lives.'

'It will change,' I said.

'India can be so much more. You know, when I was in the Army, the soldiers were so patriotic, ready to lay down their lives for their country. Thankfully for India, we still have such soldiers.'

'Yup, we saw that during the Kargil War in 1999 when we defeated Pakistan.'

'Yes.'

'You know, I did not tell your mom but after the Kargil War

I wrote a letter to the Prime Minister of India. I asked him to accept me as a reserve soldier. I was too old to run around, but my vision was still perfect. I told him that they could put me on a mountain peak and give me a rifle. I could still be useful as a sharpshooter, stopping the infiltration from across the border.'

'Really?' I was a bit shocked. 'We would have never let you go.'

'Once a soldier, always a soldier,' he spoke with military pride.

'No. It is once a father, always a father. We would come to whichever mountaintop you were perched on and take you back home,' I smiled.

'I am not concerned about India or about the enemy beyond the borders. What I am concerned about is the enemy inside, the corruption and greed that is rotting the country from within.'

'Systems are seriously broken in India. There is corruption at every level. You know, I have a theory,' I said, wanting to share my new perspective after living in the US for the last three years. 'Not many people know this, especially people in the US, but from the first to the seventeenth century, India was one of the top three richest economies in the world.'

'Really?' my dad asked.

'Yes. I also read it in an International Monetary Fund report. So for 1,700 years, India was abundant with natural resources, culture and universities,' I continued.

'Then the British came along disguised as traders with the hidden intent to rule. They were just a handful of people, so they used guile and deceit. They adopted a policy of divide and conquer and became the sole ruler, slowly transferring all the wealth of India to England. Since they were seriously outnumbered, they created a system with sycophant Indians. They closed all the original universities and erased all the sources of information and knowledge. At the behest of the British, the Indian sycophants controlled the locals and pillaged the public using a corrupt judicial system and unjust taxation. The sycophants earned their commission and enjoyed a better life than the average person.

With such benefits, these pawns of the British were eager to assume these positions to squeeze life out of their own people. Some were driven by the meaningless titles that the British Empire conferred on them.'

'So when the British left, after more than 250 years of plundering the country, India's biggest loss was not the wealth but this system of sycophants they left behind. These sycophants continue to loot the public coffers and the public remains disillusioned, just trying to survive. That is why in India, people have such a deep-rooted distrust of structures, rules and governments.'

'That is why not many follow the rule and are a rebel in their own way,' Dad chimed in with a smile.

'Exactly. India can be so much more, if only it could recognize the importance and value of a good system of justice. For that, we need officials who possess a strong sense of morality and honesty so that they can win the trust and respect of the people. For example, the Mumbai police in '90s did such a great job of eliminating the mafias once it realized their excesses.'

'Yes. It is one of the best in the world at solving crime,' Dad agreed.

'The system should be treated like God. Everybody follows it and nobody is above it. After its independence, India should have worked on itself the way Tagore imagined it in his poem, 'Chitto Jetha Bhayshunyo':

> 'Where words come out from the depth of truth;
> Where tireless striving stretches its arms towards perfection;
> Into that heaven of freedom, My Father, let my country awake.'

'I guess it will change when people like you come back and change it.' I thought about that for a moment. Did Dad just suggest that I should go back to India? Is he thinking I might not find another job here? My visa was expiring in less than two months. Maybe he was thinking about that eventuality.

'Let's not tell Mom, Abhishek or Anamika about the job. They will needlessly worry.'

'Okay,' Dad agreed.

A few days later, I intensified my search for a job. I contacted all my friends from the bachelor's and master's programmes. Everybody was very helpful and forwarded my resume to their managers and HR. But, it was dawning on me that most of the tech companies in the US were not doing too well as layoffs were commonplace. We were at the beginning of a recession, which was the worst time for hiring because companies were looking at an uncertain future.

I would sleep late and go on long walks around the neighbourhood. I was searching for the right path to follow. With ensuing days, my walks became longer and longer. It was good to see that Dad had taken a great liking to my roommates, especially Murtaza. They talked a lot. I felt more of an outsider as my stress level increased and my mind remained occupied with the job search. Once Dad got his bearings around the house, he took over all the cooking responsibilities and made delicious food for all of us. His contributions let me focus on my job search. I had put together a new resume and was applying to numerous companies, sending my resume wherever possible.

One morning when I came back from my long morning walk, I saw Ananya having a laughter fit. 'Your Dad gave Murtaza a haircut. You should see it.'

Murtaza walked into the room. The only hair he had left was on the top of his head. The sideburns and back of his head were completely shaved as in a crew cut. I laughed my guts out when I saw him.

'So I was telling your Dad how expensive the haircuts were here in the US.'

'Same story again, Murtaza? You are still stuck on that point?' I asked.

'Yes, since I had hair clippers, he offered to cut my hair.'

'I felt it could be good savings. So, I agreed. And I told him to cut it short.'

Ananya chimed in, 'So Uncle took a bowl, put it on top of Murtaza's head and cut the rest of the hair around the round vessel.'

'Ankit reporting for duty,' I said as I gave a big Army salute. Murtaza laughed as well.

Three weeks went by but there was still no progress. I had applied to each and every tech company in the state and I had also started looking out of state. I did not receive any response, not even one interview.

It was now less than six weeks before my visa expired and I would have to leave the US. One morning after intensely thinking during one of my morning walks, I went to Dad's room where he was lying in bed reading a newspaper.

I sat down by the bedside and said, 'Dad, I've been trying to get a job, but it is not looking good. The US is in a recession and companies are not hiring.'

'I read about the US recession in the newspaper as well.'

'Basically, I have two options—accept my fate, pack my bags and go back to India or try harder.'

'Which option will you choose? We have missed you badly for the last three years.'

'I don't mind going back to India. Most importantly, I will get to be with family if I go back. In the US, life is not as comfortable as it looks. You have to do everything yourself, prepare meals, do the dishes, clean the house and do laundry. The weather is severely cold and I have to shovel the snow from the sidewalk every time it snows. Most importantly, you have to do all this alone, without any familial support. So, I don't think there is much personal comfort in America. You find your sense of individuality, but it comes at the cost of extreme loneliness and human connections. Some days when I am shovelling the snow, I miss sitting in a chair at Juhu Beach, drinking coconut water.'

'India has its charm for sure.'

'But it is not about India or the US, it is about my path and my dreams. I really think I can make a contribution in my work. Giving back to society, just as you taught us,' I continued with resolve.

'And I was on the right path until this lay off. I can go back to India but there are no research jobs in semiconductors. The chip design industry is not fully developed there and I might get stuck in some mundane software job.'

'What do you want to do Ankit?'

'I have five to six weeks until my visa expires, at which point I'll have no choice but to leave the country. But before that, I want to give it everything I've got. I have to go to the Silicon Valley in California. It is the hub of semiconductor companies, and I will look for a job in the Bay Area. If there is any possibility of a job in this horrible recession, it is going to be there. If it works out, great, otherwise I will accept my fate.'

'I am sure it will work out,' he said, putting his hands on my shoulder.

'You know, when I go jogging in the evenings in India and I see young children sad and gloomy like you are today, I tell them the story of a courageous boy who travelled to the US without any money because he believed in the power of his dreams. Do you know who that boy is?'

I looked at him and smiled.

'Will you be all right here? I hate doing this to you. You travelled so many miles to spend time with me and now I am leaving you alone,' I said.

'You go write the next chapter of your life. Don't worry about me. I will be fine. Also, I have Murtaza and Ananya for company. You just focus on your job search.'

'Okay. But don't give Murtaza another haircut,' I joked.

'Where will you stay in California?'

'I am going to stay at my friend Arun's place in Fremont for the time being. If I get a job, I will rent an apartment and you will join me.'

I booked my ticket for San Jose, California, and flew to the Golden State.

I stayed with Arun, who'd been a pillar of support for me during the last few weeks. He was renting a two-bedroom apartment that he shared with another roommate. He let me share his room. Arun was working at a start-up company in the Bay Area. It was a fast moving company challenging the groundbreaking technology of Intel. But it was in its initial stages and faced its own funding challenges in this tough market. Arun was a low-risk, fearful person and this fragile environment brought his fears to the surface.

Every morning before leaving for his job he would pray before the idols saying, 'I am going to be laid off today. I have a feeling.' And in the evening, he would pray again, 'I survived this round. But I am not sure if I will survive the next round of layoffs.' A lot of his conversations were either preceded or followed by the words, 'God willing. Job willing.' He used to critique my resume for the numerous jobs that I applied to. But alas, nothing was panning out.

All the old friends we met in the Bay Area had horror stories about layoffs and the recession. Only a few companies were spared. Not being laid off was something to be thankful about. Conversations in coffee shops were about job openings, interviews and resumes. We heard stories of some tech companies asking their employees to take their belongings home every Friday and then they would receive a call over the weekend and were told not to come to work on Monday. Companies were letting go of a small percentage of their workforce regularly, so they did not report it to the media. In some cases, mass layoffs were a trend in the Bay Area. These stories only heightened my anxiety and Arun's paranoia. His respite was food for he loved to eat. We both had a favourite restaurant where we ate chicken tikka masala.

A month went by with no action on the job front. I kept in touch with Dad on phone.

I had 15 more days left to stay in the US. During one of the dinners at our favourite eating spot, I told Arun, 'Dude, I have just a couple of weeks left before I leave the country. I need to do something. No more chicken masala for me and you until I find a job.'

'Why are you taking away my chicken tikka masala?' Arun asked.

'This is serious, man. I have to make it happen.'

'I think we should resolve your visa issue first so that you can get more time to look for a job. My roommate was telling me that there are these consultants who can apply on your behalf for visa extensions. You should talk to them.'

'Hmm. That is a good idea. It is definitely worth trying.'

The next morning, I went to a consultancy company and met with a young Indian guy. He said, 'We are facing the same pinch due to recession. There is no contract work for us. A lot of our guys are on the bench already with no work and no pay.'

'Can you just sponsor my visa with no pay?'

'No. We cannot do that. We already have too many people on the bench.'

'Can you do something? I have only a few weeks left before I have to leave the country. It will change my life forever. I just need some more time to look for a job.'

'I am sorry, man. You need to get some contract work. That is the only way we can sponsor your visa.'

'So you are saying that if I get a contract job, you will sponsor my visa?'

'Yes, we can. We will take a cut from your pay. A pay cut of 30 per cent.'

'That's fine. Money is not my primary concern, staying in the US is.'

'So, I looked at your documents. In your case, you need to get a contract position in 15 days. There cannot be a gap of two months between paychecks from your previous company. It is not legal.'

'Okay. I will find a contractual position. Hopefully such positions are easier to find than full-time jobs.'

'If you find one, we will sponsor your visa.'

During the next two to three days, I searched and applied for contractual positions. On Thursday, I got a call from a German wireless communications company. They were looking for someone short term to work with the same technology I had been working on in my previous job. I spoke to the engineering manager and scheduled the interview for the next Tuesday. I called up Arun and told him about it. He told me he was secretly eating chicken tikka masala at the restaurant before coming home from work.

'This is the only decent chance I have. I have to nail this interview. There are only a few days left before my visa expires. I have to absolutely convince them that I can do the job.'

On Friday, I called the engineering lead and got all the information about the job—the technical details, the tasks and the problems that needed assistance. Over the weekend, I worked on solving the problem. I created a presentation which included the problem statement and the multiple possible solutions and their pseudo implementation. I believed that the best way to get the job was to just do the job. They cannot say no to somebody who has already done a part of their job.

On Monday, I requested the lead to arrange a 30-minute meeting with his team so I could do a quick presentation. I got dressed in brown khakis and a blue shirt and put my presentation on a USB drive. I was extremely focused on making the best presentation and a stellar first impression. The presentation went well. They were all pleasantly surprised and impressed with my proactive approach of solving the problem and there was no doubt that I was the right person for the job. By the end of the interview, they offered me a six-month contract.

I called the consultant and told him to start processing my visa application just a few days before it was set to expire. I gave a sigh of relief when all the visa paperwork was completed, and I knew that I did not have to leave the country, at least not for another six months. I was relieved that now I could finally give Dad some good days to look forward to.

That evening I treated Arun to a meal at our favourite restaurant. He had been a great friend and very supportive during the last few weeks. He was very happy with my success. Towards what should have been the end of our meal, he asked the server for more rice to finish the gravy, so the server gave it to us free of charge. After some time, Arun asked for some extra gravy to finish the extra rice. The server did not know how to handle this new form of dining request. I assured the server that I would pay for the extra gravy and rice. Arun uttered, 'God willing. Job willing' as he always did. 'My good friend Ankit is going to stay and work in the same city as me. I am very happy, so I am going to eat extra.'

'Thank you, Arun. Dude, I really appreciate your help in the last few months. It's been tough. I really did miss this chicken tikka masala over the last few weeks.' We both smiled.

I started my contract work at the German company the very next week. Shortly thereafter I rented a two-bedroom apartment which I shared with another person. It was only a six-month project, so it was expensive to get a separate apartment. I sent a plane ticket to Dad and arranged for my car to be shipped. Next, I made sure I took Dad to all the tourist places around the area. Every weekend when I was not working, I took him to a different place. We went to Reno, Lake Tahoe, Yosemite and Las Vegas. He was enjoying these trips, though he missed the family back home and the socializing he was accustomed to in India. He loved to jog in the morning and the evening. One day when I was driving to work, I saw him running and crossing the street right in front of my car. I stopped on the side of the road and told him it was not safe to do that and was moreover not allowed in the US. I bought him visitor's health insurance though I myself did not have any coverage.

Work was going very well, and I was able to complete my task and do some extra work for the team. The engineering manager liked my work and we got along well. My office was on North 1st Street in San Jose and during lunch, I used to take walks along the avenue. It was sad to see so many empty buildings with 'Office Space for Rent' signs outside. Some days I would see groups of people holding boxes and exiting an office building, feeling dejected and sad. Silicon Valley was collapsing under the weight of this recession. It was a difficult time for a place that was the mecca of technical innovations in the world.

Dad completed his six-month stay and left. He was happy that I had weathered another storm. Before he left for India, I had the pleasure of sharing good news with him—my manager had offered me a full-time position and he was just waiting for the final approval from the headquarters in Germany. I was happy that I had a good news to share with him before he left. We had a laugh about how, when vacuuming, he had found out about my layoff from Ananya. Now we could laugh about the incident and I could finally share with him how bad I had been feeling the day I picked him up at the Boston airport, after my layoff.

I was awaiting the official offer from head office, but it took a long time to come. I checked with my manager regularly, inquiring about the status of the offer. It took almost a month when the manager finally called me into his office.

'So Ankit, I had asked the main office about creating a position for you. I know you have been eager to hear back. I heard back from them today and much more.'

Hmm. What did 'much more' mean?

'You see, at this location, we have offices in two buildings, this and the adjoining one.'

'Yes,' I said.

'Well, all the employees in both buildings, including me, have been let go.'

'What?'

'These are tough times for all of us. I am sorry.'

'I am sorry too, for you and the team. I hope everybody gets through these tough times.' My contract ended that very day and I came back home with my brown box filled with my belongings once again. I could not believe my bad luck.

I was back to job hunting. Since the consultancy had made good money, they did not cancel my visa. They were hoping I could get another lucrative contract position. I tried for months to get a full-time or contract position, but my efforts amounted to nothing.

With no job, I could not afford to stay in the two-bedroom apartment even though I shared it with another person. I decided to move out. Arun wanted me to move into his apartment and share his room. I wanted that too, but I said I would sleep in the hall or on the couch in the living room and not in his room. He agreed to that, but we had a disagreement about the rent. I wanted to pay my share of the rent and he adamantly refused. I did not want to be a burden on a good friend, so I decided to move into a one-bedroom apartment with another friend. I slept in the living room on a $30 foldout couch from Kmart.

One night, I got a call that every immigrant fears. It was around 11.00 p.m. and I was hanging out at Arun's house. I got a call on my cell phone from Abhishek. It was a rare thing for him to call because we never chatted casually.

'Hi Ankit'

'This is Abhishek. Are you outside?'

'No.'

'Can you call me? Make sure you are not driving and you are by yourself. I have something important to talk about.'

'Okay.' I rushed downstairs and started walking on the

sidewalk lined with parked cars. It was a cold night with gusts of wind blowing in my face. *Oh shoot, I should have grabbed my jacket. Forget it.*

I will just call him. It must be urgent. He had never called like this before.

'I have bad news.'

'What?' My heart sank.

'Dad is in the hospital.'

'What happened?'

'He has developed some kind of clot in his neck which is blocking the blood flow to his right arm. He has been having a lack of sensation in his arm for a few days and the daredevil that he is, he did not tell us and went to some cheap hospital. They gave him some painkillers that did not fix the pain but worsened it. The whole arm from the neck down started to darken. When a doctor saw his dark arm, they immediately admitted him to the emergency room and called me. His whole right arm from the neck down is completely dark red and numb. He cannot feel any sensation.'

'What?'

The doctors say it is gangrene and it may spread to the rest of the…they said they need to amputate that arm to prevent it from spreading.'

'Oh God!'

'I told the doctor not to operate and I have moved him to Lilavati Hospital. He will have the best staff and equipment.' Lilavati was the premier hospital in Mumbai.

'What are the doctors saying there? Will they have to amputate his arm?'

'They said they will try their best to save it. But it does not look good.'

'I will take the next flight. I'm coming home.'

'As we were changing hospitals, Dad specifically told me not to tell you. He said you will be worried.'

'Worried? I have to come and be by his side.'

'Ankit, we know that you don't have a job and a secure visa. If you come back to India, you will not be able to return to the US.'

'Who gives a shit about the visa? I want to be with him.'

'He said to ask you to stay on the path.'

'No man, this is bigger than that.'

'Listen, Ankit. I am here. He has to be operated on today. Even if you take a flight, it will take two days before you arrive.'

'At least I will be with him.'

'Listen, Ankit. Do you trust me? I am your older brother.'

'Yes.'

'I will do everything. I will not spare any effort. Trust me. I will take care of it. Just pray.'

'Okay, I will stay. I will transfer money to your account right now. Please, please Abhishek, please save his arm.'

'God is watching over us. It will be fine. Okay, I have to go now. I need to arrange for some doctors.'

'Keep me updated. Please Abhishek, just save him.'

'Trust me. Just pray and hope for the best. Bye.' And so with that goodbye, he hung up.

As I looked up at the dark sky, I could not see God. If there was someone like God, then this would not be happening. This could not be happening. This did not make sense. Dad was so healthy and active, training for and participating in marathons. Feeling dazed, I sat down on the corner of the sidewalk under a streetlight. I gazed into the darkness of the night.

The water sprinklers had just turned on and had broken the silence of the night. I saw the stream of water rushing underneath the sidewalk, carrying with it all the dead leaves from the swaying trees. A brown maple leaf fell on my shoulder from the tree above. I looked at it, it was brown and worn out. I could see dark and infected black spots on it, just like Dad's arm might be right now. I felt the sensation of worms floating through my body and specifically through my arm. I wanted to experience the pain that he was feeling. I wanted it to be me, not him. I took my right hand and bit hard on the webbing between my thumb and index finger. I wanted to feel the same pain that Dad was feeling. I bit harder and harder, my teeth sinking into my skin until I could feel the pain run up my arm and make it numb. Dad's arm was what we had leaned on since we were kids. That hand had raised us and was our strength. Now, that arm would be cut off.

I stopped myself from thinking about an even worse possibility.

'God please save his life. I beg you,' I prayed folding my hands and looking up in the dark sky.

'Please. Please, just this one time. Be on our side.' I put my hands over my eyes, but the tears would not stop.

I called Abhishek the next morning but could not reach him. I called home and got Anamika. She said Mom was at the hospital. Abhishek had been busy arranging for doctors. He was able to assemble the four best neurosurgeons in India. They would operate simultaneously on Dad. The operation was going to take place in a few hours.

I could not be prouder of Abhishek. He had kept his promise and recruited the best doctors in the best hospital in India. Two hours into the operation, I called Abhishek.

'The surgery is in progress. The doctors and staff are working frantically. Not saying anything to us yet.'

I called back again after an hour. No news.

One hour later, one of the doctors came out and informed my family that the gangrene was slowly moving out of Dad's body. This was an encouraging sign. An hour later they said they were in the process of removing the gangrene and they would be able to save the arm. *Oh, thank God.* I was so happy when Abhishek shared the news, but he cautioned me that they were still operating.

An hour later, Abhishek said they were removing the gangrene and had saved the arm, but during the operation a blood clot had formed in Dad's brain. For a few unfortunate but pivotal moments, blood could not flow to one part of his body and he had suffered a major stroke. The entire right side of his body from head to toe was paralysed. *Oh God, why?* My heart sank. I was in a state of shock and disbelief, not knowing whether I should be happy his life was saved or sad for his paralysis.

After a few days I was able to talk to Dad on the phone. He was still in the hospital under heavy sedation. His voice was very slurred and his words were barely discernible. But I understood what he was trying to say.

'I am fine, Ankit. Don't worry about me.'

Even more desperate to find a full-time job and visit my family as quickly as possible, I intensified my job search. In the summer of 2003, I finally found a job opportunity in a start-up company in Irvine, California. It was a small German company with about 10 employees in the US and about the same number in Germany. They were designing computer models and tools to assist semiconductor companies to design their computer chips.

As I started to work there, I realized this start-up had major funding and resource challenges. It was an intense work environment with a tough boss and tight delivery schedules. Our small company was pushed around by larger customers and we were just trying to stay afloat and not fail. All the team members chipped in taking on extra responsibilities, from design to implementation, to doing presentations at conferences to attract new customers. We used to dress up to give presentations at trade fairs at the San Diego Convention Center and other large venues. It was new for me and I felt uncomfortable. Sales was not my forte.

Even after a few months, I could not request for an off since the company was still struggling to survive and I did not want to risk my new job. These were pivotal times for our start-up. Some days the work was very satisfying and I was happy to be part of this promising company, but on other days I could only feel the frustration of no job security.

Updates on Dad's condition were like whiplashes on my soul. Hearing how incapacitated he had become filled me with deep sadness. Imagining Dad endure this torture was infuriating. Six months after Dad had become paralysed, I experienced a period of deep discontent and profound introspection. I was disillusioned with where my life was heading towards and I started to think more intensely about what I wanted it to be.

Finally I could not wait any more and asked the company to apply for my visa, which they reluctantly did. In December, I was able to go to India to see Dad.

I reached Mumbai Airport in the middle of a warm December night. I cleared customs and walked out of the airport. It was around 3.00 a.m., so it was still dark. As expected, I saw Abhishek waiting outside the terminal. He was wearing a formal work suit he wore at the bank. He was now in charge of multiple branches of his bank around Mumbai. He had climbed the ranks very quickly and was rated as one of the promising and rising stars at the bank. As I looked at Abhishek waiting for me, I remembered seeing him in 1999, when he was selling insurance policies on the local train like a street hawker. He had indeed come a long way.

The first thing he did after being promoted was to buy a nice apartment, a two-bedroom condominium in a newly constructed building in a very good neighbourhood. The new apartment was much better and bigger than the previous Juhu apartment. It was Abhishek's dream home for our parents with the hopes it would bring cheer to Dad. I had always had great love and admiration for Abhishek, but over the last few months he had earned my complete respect, largely due to the way he had stepped up and taken charge of everything to do with Dad's surgery. He was my older brother and he showed his love and commitment to our family. As we hugged, Abhishek grabbed my luggage cart and pointed towards a corner.

There, partly hidden by a pillar and underneath a night lamp, I saw Dad sitting in a wheelchair with Mom standing behind him. All I could see was the gleam in his eyes coming from his smile, looking and admiring me from afar. I ran in his direction and hugged him.

As I embraced him with my arm around his shoulder, I felt the stiffness of my Dad's body. It felt like I was hugging a tree.

I moved my hands around his back, moving to different parts of his back. I clawed around his back through the hardened skin. I kept feeling the hardened parts of his back. His whole right side was stiff. His body felt solid like a block of frozen ice; I wanted to thaw it with my desperate fingertips. I felt a surge of anger and a swell of tears. I moved my hand searching desperately where the hardened muscles ended and the human flesh began, which was on the other side of his spine.

Dad then held my hand. I could see all his fingers on his right hand were now crooked and pointing in different directions. His thumb curled inwards and stuck against his palm. He could not bend his fingers at all. His face was a bit twisted but he still had a broad smile. Looking at his condition, I suppressed the anger I felt at our fate. I looked up at Mom, who signalled me to be strong. Her face was wrinkled, and all her hair had turned white.

In every son or daughter's life there comes a moment of truth when they realize that their parents have turned old. They can no longer play the role of super humans. Sadly, that was my unfortunate moment.

Dad was still smiling.

'I am still strong, Ankit. Look.' He took my hand and squeezed it with his right hand. His grip was indeed strong.

'Ouch. That is really strong,' I exclaimed to make Dad feel good.

He said, 'I am fine, Ankit. Don't worry.'

'Let me show you more. I can walk too,' and with Abhishek giving him support, he stood up and walked three steps and then stumbled and kept walking on with Abhishek carrying most of his body weight.

Dad's optimism did little to assuage the sadness that I was feeling, seeing him in this state. I took care of him for the entire week. Still, there was a sense of pain that I felt every time I saw him and his new reality. This impressive former Army person was now reduced to a shadow of his former self. The gold-plated mugs from his marathons were displayed as showpieces in the living room. It was further testimony that what was happening now was not fair.

For this trip, I made no plans to meet friends. I spent every moment with my family. I was thinking very hard and there was something on my mind that I wanted to talk to Abhishek about. Since he was busy at work every day, it was hard to catch up with him. One day I got the chance as we went on a morning walk along Juhu Beach, which was now a 15-minute drive from the new apartment.

'Remember how we used to come here when we were kids, walking barefoot on the wet sand close to the mellow waves of the Arabian Sea?'

'Yup. How could I not? Those were the best days.'

'Yes, running in the rain. Carefree, we were free as birds.'

'Yes. Those were fun times. It was complete freedom,' he said.

'I think we grew up too soon.'

'Yes. We did what had to be done.'

'I have wanted to ask you if you are sure you want to go ahead with the wedding?' A few months after Dad's surgery, Abhishek had agreed to get married under pressure from our relatives. He wanted to counter the gloom of Dad's paralysis with some joy for the family. He wanted to find a simple girl to marry, so he had agreed to meet some girls from Dehradun, known to our uncles.

'I just want somebody who is nice, kind, willing to live together peacefully and who can fit into our family. I think Gunjan is that kind of girl. She said she would love to live together with our family and take care of Papa and Mummy.' Gunjan was Abhishek's prospective bride who was introduced by our relatives.

'I think you should find someone in Mumbai. Someone who has a modern way of living and thinking. Compatibility is very important, not just practicality.'

'A city girl may not be keen to live with our parents in the same house. I can't let that happen. I have to live with Dad and Mom, especially after the surgery. Mom has become very weak and her knees are giving out. With my hectic work schedule, it would be nice to have someone look after them.'

'But still. Are you sure you want to go ahead with this?'

'I am not sure. It is really scary. I don't know what will happen. What I do know is that love demands sacrifice. I can only try to do the best I can under the circumstances.'

'Circumstances. I hate that word. That is all we have been doing since we were kids. We've been fighting our circumstances as we prepared for the future. We were like prisoners toiling in jail so that one day we can taste the freedom of a distant future. And then life just goes by without being lived.'

'Don't say that. Dad and Mom did everything.'

'They did. It is not them. It is the circumstances that is our villain. It stole our childhood and now it is taking away our present. With your decision to get married, it is clearly casting a shadow on our future as well.'

'C'mon, it was not that bad.'

'Really? When was the last time you celebrated your birthday? When did any of us celebrate our birthdays? We used to hide from friends so that we didn't have to spend money on treats for them. It used to be the saddest day of the year for me. Look at Anamika, she was so bubbly and fun. When was the last time she danced or laughed openly? She used to dress up like a doll and now she keeps her hair short like a boy. We have forgotten how to laugh and we couldn't even cry for fear it would hurt our parents' feelings. I feel so sad seeing Dad in this condition, but I have to hold back my feelings.'

'It will get better. Have some faith in God, Ankit.'

'It is not God. It is we who have to rise above the present condition or it will eventually consume all of us, just as it has consumed Dad.'

'C'mon Ankit. It's all right.'

'No, it is not. When Dad first had pain in his arm he chose to go to the cheapest doctor possible. He wanted to save money. That was his first instinct.'

'Yup.'

'This has been our greatest failure. We succumbed to the circumstances. We struggled and survived each conflict, but we lost the battle. Who knows had Dad not been worried about money he would have gone to a better hospital? And it is even possible he would not be paralysed today.'

'We don't know that.'

'I know Dad doesn't talk much, but I can feel his screams of frustration being trapped in that frozen body. We too are struggling rather than living. I want to break this vicious cycle.'

'How?'

'I don't know how. But I do know that I have to break this cycle in my lifetime so that our future generations are not affected by it. I don't want our kids to miss their birthdays.'

'They will not. We are on the path of upward mobility.'

'That's true. But we are still dependent on our jobs. Dad experienced one layoff when we were kids and it changed our lives forever.'

'It won't happen to us. You have a master's degree and I have an MBA.'

'I've had three layoffs in the last four years. I just can't let my kids suffer the same fate as mine.'

'What do you want to do?'

'I want to remove this dependency of life's happiness on our jobs. Our jobs control our happiness, they make us slaves to our circumstances.'

'What do you want to do?'

'I don't want to be just an engineer, I want to be wealthy. I want to be rich so that our future generation will always be safe. Our circumstances should never affect our kids. That is how we can defeat bad luck once and for all. We need to end this vicious cycle of suffering.'

'How do you plan to do that?'

'I don't know yet. I have some ideas. But that is my goal in life now. I know it's not going to be easy. Nobody will hand it to me on a platter. I just have to find a way to do something more than just my job. I have to do more and be more. I have to climb higher. For that, I need to become better, stronger and completely fearless.'

I declared, 'I am going to climb that mountain of prosperity even if I have to risk it all.'

9

WAVE CRASH

I returned to the US in early January 2005 with sadness fueling my soul. I was determined to climb the mountain of prosperity at any cost. I knew it was not going to be easy. There was no free ride to the top. To reach the summit, I had to take risks and fight my fears. Instead of running from fear, I had to run towards it and conquer it. I had to be so strong that fear could not touch me.

When I got back to work after the break, I found the first few days very hectic as I had to catch up. It only got worse after that. Our small start-up boat was feeling the push of the tides. Our CEO called an urgent meeting in the only conference room we had. He gave us an ultimatum—our team had to win a multi-million-dollar contract from a South Korean major semiconductor. We had been working with them for a while as they were evaluating our technology to see how we could expedite their design cycles. If we faltered in any way and did not win the contract in six months, he declared that we would all pack up and go home. We were a small team of very determined and hardworking engineers. Knowing that we were a small enterprise, the South Korean company pushed us hard. A lot of their demands bordered on the limits of what any team of engineers could do, including theirs. We worked until late in the night, sometimes until later than 2.00 a.m. to make sure the work they were counting on was completed on time. I worked six weeks straight without taking a break on the weekends, teetering on the verge of a burnout.

Our hard work paid off; the South Korean company awarded us the contract. Their chief engineer declared, 'We gave you guys a tough time because we like you. Good job!' Champagne was brought into the conference room and we celebrated.

More champagne bottles were opened when it was announced that a much larger British multinational semiconductor company would acquire our small start-up. This Cambridge-based company was one of the most respected companies in the field of semiconductors. Their main product was a microprocessor design that was licensed in millions of computing devices and electronics around the world. They were also expanding into cell phones. At that time, cell phones were slowly but surely replacing landlines and providing more freedom to consumers. However, they were being used mostly to make phone calls.

This British company's microprocessor chip would make phones multifunctional and ubiquitous. They were coming out with features that could take pictures and play music. This company's mission was to make the phone smarter by augmenting functionality, which meant it could perform video playbacks, operate as a camera, play games and provide an audio function. So, besides just acting as a computing processor, the cell phone chip would need to be designed as a whole system of specialized chips with different functionality, all working together to provide a rich set of functionality for the cell phone user. It was called a system on a chip or SoC. They acquired our start-up company to build on our expertise in the SoC infrastructure and software. It was an inspiring technological vision to change the world and we were all on board.

Though I did not reap financial benefits from the acquisition as top management had, it was great to be part of the vision. My work had the potential to change the entire technological landscape. This company was selling more than a billion chips annually.

HR from the new company wanted to retain all the start-up employees. I explained that money was not my chief concern, but I was adamant about getting my green card processed as soon as possible. From my previous work experiences, the fear of leaving the country had caused me some serious anxiety. The HR manager was a nice woman from Texas and she promised me that she would expedite my visa application. I would eventually get my green card in a couple of years.

Once the acquisition was completed, I had the opportunity to attend conferences in Cambridge, England. It was great to travel around Europe and experience different cultures.

A big company offers a certain level of job security and a less demanding and less stressful work experience than working at a start-up. With more free time, I returned to my second pursuit of building wealth. I started to read financial journals and books, including Warren Buffett's, to familiarize myself with how to approach investing. I researched which investments might bring a good return. I did not have much savings to start with, just the regular pay cheques, some intermittent bonuses and company stocks. Given that limitation, the real estate market was out of the question.

In addition to reading, I also watched programmes on financial news channels that featured people who had become rich as the stock market was breaking records on a daily basis.

After years of research, I felt I was ready to make my first stock market investment. It was a scary feeling. I was taking my hard-earned money and putting it some place beyond my control. The value of my money would now be determined by some external set of circumstances. People I didn't know but somehow trusted would be making decisions about my money. But I had to trust my gut feeling and the research I had done. Most importantly, I had to take the risk and start moving towards financial independence. So, I took the plunge and invested in exchange traded funds or ETFs, which was investing in emerging economies around the world. Making my first stock investment felt like burying my money in the ground for a while and waiting for the seeds to grip the soil and grow. I had to be patient and wait for it to sprout and bear some fruit.

Before I began to invest in the stock market, I made sure that Anamika was having no financial issues before moving to the US to get her master's in engineering. I called her regularly, guided her through GRE, the application process and bought her the plane ticket once she was formally accepted. I also kept some money on the side for her tuition fees. I wanted to make sure that she didn't have to endure the fear of financial insecurity that I had experienced when I first arrived in the US. I also made sure that she stayed with me for the first few weeks, so she could settle down before starting her college education in Rolla, Missouri. Those few weeks were fun when I showed her all the tourist spots in Southern California. My friends and I made sure she did not feel too homesick. I bought her a cellphone before she flew to start school. That night I was watching a movie at the theatre when I got a call from her.

'I don't like this place. People are not friendly. I am staying with some senior girls but nobody cares. They don't even care if I have dinner or not. Nobody invited me for dinner yet,' she said. I could sense she was crying.

'It's new and tough initially. Just push through. Be strong. You will be fine.' I knew she would need some time to adjust after Mom's pampering and constant care.

'I don't know. California is so much better. Even the people were so much nicer there.'

I laughed. 'You will find good people there. Just give it some time.'

I called her on the phone regularly and she eventually adjusted to college life. For the next few years, I called her almost daily to make sure she was on the correct path in her career. She got a research assistantship in petroleum engineering, moved to Louisiana State University and published research papers for conferences.

She eventually met some good people and even someone special, a fellow student from India. Within a few years, they got married and moved to Houston, Texas, to fulfil their career goals in the petroleum industry. On her wedding day, as Dad and I sat watching the bride and bridegroom perform all the Indian rituals, Dad with great effort moved his debilitated body closer to me and whispered in my ear, 'Ankit, I want you to do kanyadaan.' It was a privilege and a father's pride to perform kanyadaan.

'Oh Dad, you should do it.'

'Oh, I insist you do it. You have been her friend, guide and teacher. It is only fair that you do the kanyadaan.' Dad was trying to speak softly in my ear but did not have much control over the pitch of his voice. The words were loud enough for everyone to hear. I hesitantly agreed.

As I sat next to Anamika through the ceremony, she looked at me and often smiled at the discomfort she was feeling under the heavy sari and a thick layer of make-up. She was no longer the little girl who liked to play dress up and participate in make-believe fashion shows.

I felt a sense of pride but also sadness as I placed my sister's hands on the groom's.

In the meantime, the seeds of my investment were beginning to germinate. In the first year, my investment experienced growth in high teens. I was happy that my financial selection was good. But my initial investment was low and it didn't give me satisfaction because it was not enough to climb very far up the mountain. Even with a high rate of return, an initial investment of a few thousand dollars was not commensurate with the effort and risks. If I stuck to that small investment and high growth rate, I would become rich only by the time I retired. This was way too slow for my future kids to benefit from. I needed a quicker hustle. I had to take bigger risks.

I was about 27 years old at that time. I felt it was time to expand my boundaries. I could take risks since I did not have a family or children. If I wanted to climb that mountain, I couldn't be cautious. I had to take bigger risks. It was about jumping to the next level to reach the summit. Like a rock climber, I had to leap higher and grab the piton to reach the next level. Stock investment was the ultimate test of financial acumen and emotional strength. I decided to use new experiences to challenge my mind and abilities. For that, I had to be mentally strong and expand the scope of my experiential horizon. I felt I had to train my senses to be steady in uncomfortable uncertainties and come out stronger on the other side.

I identified three fears I sought to conquer in the next few years. My challenges involved air, land and sea. I knew that this would take me out of my comfort zone, but that was the point. Man had long battled the forces of nature and I would do the same.

The first target was skydiving. I was planning to do a tandem jump of 12,000 feet. I went with my cousin, Manav, and his friends to a skydiving centre near Lake Elsinore. After our initial set of instructions, we were all ready to go. We were scheduled to be the last drop, so we could see the sunset while jumping, but for some reason the plane was delayed. The sun had already set. The flying club gave us the option to return the next day, but we chose to jump as scheduled. Driving two to three hours again was not an appealing option. So we boarded the small plane; we were a total of 12 jumpers. When the plane reached 12,000 feet, we were hovering above the clouds and ready to jump.

As I moved to the door of the plane, I looked at the ground where things looked really far and small. As I was about to jump out, I asked myself, 'Why am I jumping out of a plane at 12,000 feet?'

Just because... and boom, I was out of the plane.

Gravity is a force that the body rarely experiences consciously. As humans we like to stay in control of our body and never let go to fully experience a free fall. We read science textbooks and use the equations relating to gravity, but to experience gravity with all its force was an out-of-the world experience. A pure adrenaline rush! I was falling like a bullet piercing through the cold clouds, the force of the wind stretched my face and cheeks and my body picked up speed as it cut through the air.

Then I saw the sun with its wavy shades of red and orange. From that height, the sun had not gone under the horizon yet. It was the most marvellous sunset I had ever seen in my life. It was a satisfying blissful feeling when I set both feet firmly on the ground with a renewed sense of control over my body.

For the land challenge, I bought a second-hand Jeep Wrangler and took long drives in the mountains and near the beaches along the California coast. I also joined an off-road Jeep club, and together with other members I drove the Jeep over the mountains. It was scary driving over rocks on Big Bear Mountain, but the team was very helpful. A group of 12–15 Jeeps would ride along the mountains, sometimes on top of very big boulders. At times, one of the Jeep's wheels would be in the air as I drove it over the rocks. I had to be careful to follow the tracks set up by the team leader. One slip could lead to falling off the cliff. With intense concentration, I had a sense of being alive and away from everyday worries.

Coming back from one of these excursions one day, as I took off my seatbelt and got out of the Jeep, I noticed that my blue sleeveless T-shirt was covered in dirt. Only the part of the shirt that was previously covered by the seat belt was clean and blue. The clean strip across the shirt was like a badge of honour. I folded the T-shirt and put it into a plastic bag and kept it as a memento of my second achievement.

I enjoyed driving all-terrain vehicles (ATVs) as well. One of the trips I took with a friend was to Ensenada, Mexico. It was thrilling to drive the ATV over huge sand dunes. I wanted to drive over the highest sand dune there, but my rental ATV was substandard. I still decided to go for it. As I reached the top of the sand dune and looked down, it looked really steep. Without hesitation, I started my descent, but I could immediately feel that the slope was too steep for the speed my ATV was going at. I was beginning to lose control. To regain it, I pressed the brake. The vehicle toppled over and threw me out on the ground. I rolled over and was flat on the ground with my legs stretched out when I realized that the ATV was rolling in my direction. I knew this could be deadly. It could crush me with its impact if it landed on me. In that split second, I put my hand on my head to protect it and closed my eyes.

The engine fell on my feet, but being on sand my leg was able to absorb the impact. The heat of the vehicle engine was such that I could smell my skin burning. My friend rushed in and tried shifting the engine to free my legs. The skin around my front left shin was burnt, exposing the whitish layer covered in blood. My friends took me to the office where we cleaned the wounds and applied some ointment on it. I felt angry at myself for miscalculating the manoeuvre; I realized I should not have applied the brake so hard. So, I decided to try again. The rental agency was understandably not keen to rent an ATV to me again, so I just took my friend's and went to the top of the same sand dune. This time I adroitly controlled the descent of the vehicle and arrived at the bottom with a satisfactory grin. My friend looked at me as if I was not in my senses. I told him that I had a personal issue against mountains that he would not understand.

For my third and last challenge, I needed to conquer water bodies. Living in southern California near the beach, the natural choice was surfing. Since childhood I had been fascinated by the ocean and was always eager to go beyond the waves washing onto the shore. However, surfing did not come naturally to me. I did not know how to swim when I lived in India. My siblings and I could never learn swimming due to financial constraints. I had taken some basic lessons in college, but my idea of swimming was jumping in the water and pushing the water real hard with my hands until I reached the other end. Surfing was an entirely new activity for me.

Lukas, a colleague who worked at the Cambridge headquarters but had a short summer stint at the Irvine location, was an avid surfer. He was originally from South Africa and loved surfing. He agreed to teach me, so we went together to San Onofre State Beach. Surfing was difficult for me to learn at first. It was quite a struggle just sitting on the board or getting through the initial waves to get into the calm waters. I was often washed ashore. However, by the time Lukas's brief internship ended and he returned to England, I had become confident enough to surf by myself. Although Laguna Beach was close to my place in Irvine, the waves there were not really for beginners. They were big waves and the ocean started getting deep very quickly. However, I had to see how much I could push myself. I loaded my long surfboard onto my Jeep and drove to Laguna Beach. I bought a package of five private sessions with a surfing coach. I was in a rush to learn quickly, so I scheduled them over the weekdays.

My third lesson was scheduled on a very windy day early in the morning. My surfing coach, a man in his 30s, suggested that we should wait for another day since the waves were breaking big and there was strong wind. But I was already there and suggested that we go ahead with the class. We put the long surfboards over our heads and walked to the oceanfront in our wetsuits. The ocean waves were roaring that morning. Looking at those waves, I began to feel somewhat doubtful, but I still went ahead. My coach and I went into the water with our surfboards. The surfboard was not tied to my leg as I was still learning. It was best to let the board go rather than having it tied to avoid the possibility of injuring myself on falling.

The waves had the force of the wind behind them and they were really throwing us around. One strong wave came in and threw me off my board. The coach came to my rescue as my surfboard got swept away. He checked on me asking me to hold onto his boat while he went to retrieve mine. I held on to the edge of his board as he swam along the shore tracking where my board had been swept.

Suddenly, a huge wave came by and hit me hard from behind. I lost my grip on his surfboard and I began to go underwater. As I flapped my arms in an effort to get above the water, a second wave came by. Most of the force of this wave was under the surface—it grabbed me and flipped me around multiple times. I was completely disoriented and had swallowed a lot of salty water. The pressure of the wave was so strong that I couldn't move my arms or legs. The wave was in complete control of my body, pulling me deeper towards the bottom of the ocean. With no air to breath and my mouth filled with water, I felt like I was drowning.

By the time the wave passed by and its pull on my body became weaker, I was completely disoriented. I knew that I had to come up for air and swim, but I did not know where the shore was. I was feeling exhausted and I had to move quickly before another strong wave came in. I could feel myself going deeper and in the darkness of the ocean with no orientation of where the shore was. I opened my eyes and glanced up—there was a ray of sunshine piercing through. That was a divine sign for me.

So, with all the energy I could muster, I pushed the water down with my arms as hard as I could. As my body began to rise, I began to swim towards that light. Luckily, the direction I was swimming in was towards the shore and not further into the ocean. I could soon feel the ground under my feet. By this time, my coach was nearby. He picked me up and dragged me out. I coughed up a lot of water but was happy to be alive. As we walked back towards the shore, I looked back at the ocean. I had learned a lesson to always have my eyes on the waves. Nature always finds a way to make us feel small. I was humbled but stronger after that experience.

After that incident, I had a lot more respect for the power of the ocean. After my five training sessions, I was more comfortable surfing. After that, I started going alone to San Onofre State Beach, paddle through the initial waves and go further into the ocean. I soon learnt that most of the time surfing is actually spent sitting on a surfboard waiting for the right wave. Sitting and watching the ocean, sky and sunset was a spiritual practice in itself. I felt a deep connection with nature as I felt the rhythms of the water. There was harmony in that moment and I felt like I was a part of it.

But my mind with its own preoccupations soon took over. Stocks were on my mind and while sitting on the surfboard I began to realize the parallels that existed between surfing and the stock market. Like surfing, it was all about detecting and catching the right wave or the best stock tip before anyone else. Catching a good wave was a competitive thing among surfers. Whoever caught the wave first and stood up on the surfboard had the right to the wave. Any great wave first manifests itself as a small rise on the surface of the ocean. The expert surfer is able to detect this initial surge in the water at an early stage and move towards it, knowing the exact location at which it will break with maximum force. If you have an eye to detect the right swell and are able to catch a great wave, it is possible to ride on it all the way to the shore. I thought I needed to adopt the same strategy with my stock investments. The key was to detect the right set of events early enough, move into the market and make the right investments before any other investor realized it. I tried to detect the next big trend that was about to hit the financial market. The answer was technology.

The technology sector was going through a major upheaval and it was at an inflection point, completely transforming life as we knew it. Some of the cutting edge work my company was doing to transform the cell phone into more functional personal computing device would contribute to changing lives. In San Diego, there was a company working on wireless technology. The CEO, a visionary person, gave a talk about how wireless technology would change our world. He explained how movies would be broadcast directly on our TVs, that there would be no need for DVDs. At that time, it was hard to imagine how with only waves, air data could be transferred without any wires. That would be a welcome change, I thought, as I dropped my rented DVDs at Blockbuster, late as usual.

Great advancements were happening in chip design in the Bay Area, in Japan and in South Korea. All these changes were swelling in the ocean of technology and it was just a matter of time before they would converge and become an enormous wave. Now was the time to ride this wave into what could be a revolution in mobile space. I started to move my investments into the technology sector.

Over a period of time, my entire portfolio was in tech stock. The more I thought about it, the more I was convinced that that was the right wave to catch. The more I was convinced, the more I invested. I divested all the assets I had and put all my money in technology stocks. As soon as my paycheck arrived, I moved the money to my stock account, leaving just enough to pay my bills. I started finding ways to cut my expenses and investing more and more money in the stock market. I cut down on eating out or taking short trips. I went to work and then came directly home to spend time researching investments on the Internet. I cut down on my recreational activities like off-road driving and surfing. Ironically, I stopped surfing, so I could use that time to go surfing on the Internet or take walks thinking about stocks. I reached a point where I had no money left to invest, but I was convinced that I had made a good move. My stock investments were mostly in technology companies because I was convinced that technology was going to change the world.

In order to convince our Japanese customers of the increasing computing power of our chips and what new functionality they would add to their phones and music players, my company sent me to Japan for six weeks. I visited companies, which had great camera technology but limited cell phone expertise, with our Japan sales team and taught about the new features of our product. The six weeks provided me with a great experience, a new perspective on business models and a new appreciation for cultural differences. I enjoyed travelling with the sales team; they knew how to have a good time. We went to restaurants, bars and sang karaoke. I made some friends and loved the Japanese people. Over the years, I have visited many countries in Asia, North and South America and Europe. I am convinced that there are more similarities among us than differences. A line on the map does not separate us as human beings. Our basic human nature is fundamentally the same and we all feel the need to connect and empathize with the emotions of others.

During 2007, things started to heat up at work. There was a mystery project that everyone in the company seemed to be focused on. We were unaware of who the customer was but what we did know was that this customer was of the highest priority. It was referred to by only its code name. If a task with a code name was allotted, we would drop everything and prioritize that work.

In the same year that iPhone was announced, our managers told us that the project with the code name was Apple and the product was the iPhone. Listening to Steve Jobs announce the product was awesome and I was very excited to get my hands on one. The day it was launched, I went to get one. When I arrived at 4.00 p.m., there were already about 100 people in line at the AT&T store. It was a festive time and people were very excited.

I stood in line by myself whereas most other people had come with friends. I wanted to mingle with them and tell them more about what was behind the new phone—what happens when you touch the screen or press a button, how millions of operations that happen within nanoseconds on hundreds of millions of small units called transistors are responsible for the functionality of the iPhone. All this was unfathomable, such complexity and functionality on a chip the size of a postage stamp. If the iPhone was a beautiful car, the processing unit from my company was the main part of its engine.

I thought about approaching some of the college kids in front of me, but abandoned the idea quickly. *What if they think I am some kind of a geek or a nerd, as they called engineers and techies.*

An hour standing in the line alone got me thinking about why I hesitated to mingle, why I doubted myself about who I am and what my work is. Did I have some kind of 'engineer complex'? Why was it uncool to be an engineer? In today's society, engineers and academics don't get the respect they deserve. Engineers and researchers spend their entire lives creating something that will improve human life, and in some cases, actually save a life. Sitting in a corner cube, an engineer works each day to push the boundaries of human possibilities, yet accolades are not forthcoming. The appreciation and reverence are saved for celebrities and their children.

We were a generation of researchers who had moved the world from black and white television to coloured TV, to the personal computer, to the Internet and now to all the complexity of a supercomputer in just one mobile that you can hold in the palm of your hand. In our lifetimes, engineers had built the information highways that could connect all of humanity and benefit future generations. As engineers, we had pushed away the darkness of ignorance and shed light on what's possible. This sense of contribution was what motivated me. It was why I had worked so hard to become an engineer and it was why I endured the unending hours of studying while sitting under the water tank on the terrace. This was the reason I came to study in the US, even with empty pockets. And this was the reason I stuck around despite being laid off numerous times. I wanted to leave the world slightly better than I had found it. Even if our present society had not evolved to respect engineers, teachers and researchers, I felt proud of my fraternity and the work we did. After the Industrial Revolution, the mobile phone and the Internet had been the biggest technological revolution for humanity. Engineers are the artists of the twenty-first century. I was proud to be a small soldier serving in that revolution and I had the wounds to show for it.

As I held the first iPhone in my hand, all my misgivings evaporated and the sheer beauty of the product moved me. I was feeling a much bigger kick than the time I had seen the Mona Lisa at the Louvre in Paris. It was indeed a piece of art defining my fraternity.

Buoyed by the increasing stock prices and returns in my stock portfolio, I decided that it was time to risk more. My desire for financial security for myself and my future generations inspired me to take bigger risks. Always at the back of my mind was the fact that I had come to this country and into this world empty-handed and that I needed to move beyond this station in life. To do so, I needed to take the biggest risk of all. I took some loans from the investment firm based on the profits and stocks that I had already earned. On the first page of my stock trading account, it was noted how much I could borrow, tempting me just as casinos tempted gamblers to increase their bets. The broker tempted me with the possibility of increasing my profit and I fell into that trap. I started borrowing money based on my increased profits, and as I saw my returns increase, I took on more debt.

I had started with small margin loans but then it was becoming a big number. It was a positive feedback loop and I had to keep feeding into it. I could not control this urge to invest to make lots of money. It reached a point where I borrowed the maximum amount I could and even got my limit increased further; it was the maximum amount that I could borrow against my account. My loan was approaching the $100,000 mark and it was starting to concern me. But the value of my account had increased to more than $200,000. It was safe as long as the stocks I held were in an upward trajectory and did not fall.

In April 2008, we got some news from the head office in Cambridge, UK. Our team in Irvine was asked to come into the conference room. The British director who was our manager informed us that the company had decided to move some of the technology we worked on to a team in England and sell the rest to a smaller US-based company. We had a few months to stay in our present positions after which our division would become part of some other company. It was a complete surprise to us since we had done such good work. He explained that this was part of a corporate realignment and it was best for the company. Everybody was surprised but not panicking. Since we had the option to move with the new company, it was not a lay off. That afternoon at four, I got a call from a manager at the Cambridge, UK, office. We had worked together on this technology for a while and he asked me if I wanted to move to Cambridge to continue working in the same capacity with the same technology. I told him I would think about it. I felt reassured knowing that I had the option to stay and wasn't facing yet another lay off.

For a few weeks, I contemplated my options: I could stay with my current company and move to Cambridge; move to the company that was acquiring our division since they had offered a promotion with an increase in salary; and finally the option to move to the dream company in San Diego which was big enough for long-term career growth. In my current job, I had limited opportunities for career growth given the small size of the Irvine company. Maybe this was the push I had been waiting for.

I rejected the first option because I didn't want to move to England. I wanted to stay in the US, and specifically in California to be close to the beach. So, I called the head office, thanked them and told them I was not interested. The second option, though initially lucrative and secure in the short term, did not offer long-term security or stability. Also, it was basically doing work similar to what I had been doing for a long time now. The third option was more exciting as it offered a new direction and a new challenge. With change, there were always risks involved, but after much deliberation I decided to take the risk. So I declined the offers, from my previous employers and the new company, in pursuit of the path unknown. Part of our original start-up team decided to move to Cambridge and the rest of my coworkers moved to the new company. Very few like me decided to tread on the third path. Luckily, the European company offered a generous severance package that gave me a few months of paid salary to transition to a new job.

During the next few months, I focused on the stock market. With the iPhone wave spreading around the world, technology stocks were on fire. My stock account was hitting new heights, but so was my borrowing. I soon realized that the stock market did not follow a straight line. It was a game of psychology, a game of smoke and mirrors. The big players, the hedge fund managers used media and the so-called financial TV commentators to spread fear, uncertainty and doubt. That created unwarranted stock reactions for no apparent reason. They moved the market up or down to suit their stock positions and the small investors would get crushed. The hedge fund managers would make money in bull and bear market, but the small investors would get slaughtered.

There were some crises in the energy sector which inexplicably brought down the whole market. I did not believe that this crisis had any connection to technology but the technology stocks started plummeting. With my loans approaching their threshold, I put my entire severance package from my company into the technology sector to add as a buffer, but the margin loan was high. I knew I was walking on a tightrope.

I was exhausted, spending the whole day in front of the computer or TV, tracking financial news. My iPhone, with its unlimited data plan, turned out to be a curse in that respect. I would check the US news throughout the day, then at night I checked how the Asian market was doing and then later, I would check the European market. The time differences made me crazy, as I felt that I had to be on top of all the important world markets. I would generally be in a state of panic if they opened negative. Even if one opened up, I would be in a state of anxiety until the Nasdaq opened early in the morning. Then I would spend the entire morning tracking the market until the afternoon. The sad thing was I could not make any sense of why the oil crisis affected the technology sector. If the oil prices were low, wouldn't it allow people to save on gas and free up money to spend on electronics? For an engineer, that made sense. But Mr Stock Market was not logical. It was as if it were bipolar, trying to manage its erratic emotions.

Soon I became manic-depressive. I could not sleep at night suffering from anxiety, and then in the morning I had an unbearable pain in my jaw, which would then spread along the side of my temple to my shoulders and to my back. I suffered intense headaches throughout the entire day. I did not know the cause of the pain and headaches for a while.

When I went to my dentist before my health insurance ran out, he told me that I had been grinding my teeth while I slept. The dentist was a kind Korean doctor and he could see through my mental state. He said, 'Everybody is running up the mountain to get the sunset at the highest point, but when they reach the top, the sunset is already gone. Life and nature wait for nobody, Ankit. You have to take care of your mental and physical health. The way you are grinding your teeth while sleeping, you will not have any teeth left in a few years. Grinding is causing the pain in your jaw. I will make you a mouth guard. You should wear it throughout the night so you don't grind your teeth, but most importantly do something about the anxiety. That is what is causing that grinding.'

'I will try the mouth guard. I'm not sure if I can do anything about my mental anxiety.' I put on the night guard, but it was uncomfortable. As promised, I tried to calm my mind. I bought a guitar and took some lessons. But the instructor and I soon realized it was a futile attempt as my mind was barely focused on it. I also took pottery classes in a local Irvine community college. The spinning wheel and the beautiful shape the clay could create were not for me. While trying new things, my mind would be so preoccupied with stocks that I could not focus. The lack of sleep did not help either as I would be awake the whole night checking the stocks.

I was mentally and physically exhausted. It was eating me up from inside. I had become addicted to checking stock market and I could feel how it was torturing me. I was getting weaker, but I had to persist. I could see the shore through the water—the pipe dream, as surfers called it, the dream of becoming wealthy. I wanted to be able to go home and tell Dad, 'See, we have money now. We don't have to worry about money. See, we won.' That shore was close now and I just had to balance for a little while longer.

With the severance running out, I also began working on getting hired at my dream company. The manager at this company was a family friend of my previous manager who was moving to Cambridge. He gave me a good recommendation. That connection got me an interview. During that time, I had an interview with another group in Austin. It was not as natural a fit as the previous company, but I thought it would be good to explore the opportunity. During that trip I also visited Arun, who had moved to Austin from California. That interview went well enough. It was a memorable evening to enjoy a cold beer with Arun and his wife in an open restaurant in the Texas heat.

It brought back a lot of Texas memories.

The trip was worth it, though I got a good lecture from Arun about risks in the stock market. He told me I was being reckless about my stocks and also about my job. It was better to take the higher paying job in the company that acquired my previous company and then apply for the dream company. I jokingly told him, 'Caesar said, "If you want to conquer the island, burn the boats."' Here I had not burned my boats, but I had burned myself and I was feeling the heat.

Several days later, I was excited when the director of the San Diego group set up an interview for the position. It was a natural fit. The work was something I had done and they were using the technology I had personally worked on. The icing on the cake was the outstanding recommendation. I did not prepare excessively, assuming it was a done deal. However, I was in for a surprise when I saw that there were eight interviews and the director was not among the interviewers. I was informed that he had to leave the office that day and was not able to come. The interview went fine, but at one point an interviewer asked some incisive questions. There were anxious moments, yet I felt confident with my skills and my good references.

In the meantime, I had been in touch with my family over the phone. I was careful not to mention about losing my job or talking about risking my hard-earned money on the stock market. I also made sure to share good news only. The slow recovery of Dad's paralysis was frustrating everybody in the family, mostly himself. He was feeling increasingly agitated. There were moments when he would lash out due to his frustration, mostly at Mom. He could walk a little now, but with a cane. He would lose his balance quickly if the surface was uneven. Mom still believed that he would recover completely. Some of her close friends told her to visit temples to make religious offerings. Mom believed that some divine intervention would fix my Dad's problems and meanwhile Abhishek told me about her interest in travelling around India, visiting temples and performing ceremonies.

I was burning in my own hell and was in need of a divine intervention myself. My soul was completely sapped and my anxiety was intensifying. I was imagining that my stocks would reach a certain value after which everything would be fine. I began to believe in the possibility of that reality and spent a lot of time visualizing it. I seemed to have lost touch with reality and was living in a world of illusion. But the reality of the slow, erratic and ever-changing stock market was terrifying. I felt trapped in this labyrinth like in a constant dreamlike state. In an attempt to break out of it, I told my parents that I would be coming to India to take them to all the religious sites my mother was longing to visit.

Though I was not religious, I wanted this trip to be a retreat or a digital detoxification from the stock market and the Internet. I decided I would avoid browsing Internet on this trip and free my mind from the worries of the world. I would disconnect and give my restless soul a break. I needed to lighten the emotional burden I had been carrying. Being cut-off from my professional burdens while visiting India would do me a world of good.

I went to India and travelled to all religious sites with my parents. My prime focus was to ensure that Dad did not suffer any inconvenience. He still needed someone to be close in case he lost his balance on an uneven ground. In crowded areas, he needed to hold on to someone to move forward. As we travelled from one site to another, I was happy that Mom and Dad could feel the religious fervour, although I found the religious rituals a bit too much. The offerings of milk, sweets and flowers to gods while people starving outside the temples defied logic of human understanding. The same resources could be used for improving the lives of those going hungry. Charity was the truest service to God. But I did not want to think too much and get riled up about it. So, I tried to relax and focus on ensuring that my parents could have the best religious experience.

There was one moment in the Banke Bihari temple in Vrindavan when I felt something divine. It was around 11.00 a.m., and I was somehow able to get through the crowd holding my Dad with one arm. The temple was completely packed with fervent worshippers and there was little space to move. Mom was on the other side of the temple reserved for women. With a little pushing and shoving, I was able to get us to a spot near the idols. Dad was standing, holding the wooden ledge with his right hand and my forearm with his left hand. I was intensely focused on ensuring that he didn't fall down and that he got a good look at the idols, which were behind the curtain and were soon going to be unveiled by the head priest. There were more people than the temple could accommodate, and many were pushing around just to be able to get a close look of the idols.

The jostling kept increasing as the moment of the unveiling came closer. As we were facing the idols, I could see the whole place was now filled with flowers and there were bells ringing all around. Some people were throwing flowers and powdered colours in the air. There were birds flying around the open ceiling, which was only covered with steel bars and netting.

The junior priests blew the shankha (conch shell) to indicate that the doors with the idols behind were about to be opened.

As the conch shell and the crowd's energy reached a crescendo, the priest unveiled the curtains. I caught a glimpse of the idol as the crowd behind us moved ahead pushing us forward. I pushed Dad with my shoulders to box him in the corner, so that his body was firmly held against the railing and the crowd behind us could not impact us. There was more rush with another group of people forcing their way behind us. I was relentlessly trying to hold Dad steady and getting increasingly worried that if he were to fall, he would get stomped on. He tried to be steady. I could feel his fingernails going through my skin and I clenched my teeth to absorb the pain. I knew if I said anything to Dad he would immediately release his fingers from my forearm and would fall down. The ceremony should be only a few minutes long, I hoped, so I could take the pain a while longer.

As his nails dug deeper into my forearm, the pain became excruciating. I clenched my teeth and bit my lips. I closed my eyes as the pain became unbearable. My arm had gone numb but now I could somehow feel the rhythm of the sounds around me. I could feel the energy of the place, the sounds of the conch shell and the hymns that were being sung. At that moment, I could feel sunshine hit my face and then there was something I had never experienced before.

I felt like something had just touched my spirit; it felt like a balm on my wounds. I found myself chanting along with everyone. I felt transported to a different world.

As if in an imagination, I saw a bird's feather emerge and rise up in the air. I saw its beautiful colours, reflecting the sunlight. It had vibrant shades of blue, like one on a peacock's head. This feather was floating up and up in the air, dancing with the wind. It was beautiful and mesmerizing. As my imagination soared along with it, I felt that we were above the clouds with many mountain peaks emerged in it. It was foggy everywhere.

I saw the feather land on a path of a big mountain. I stepped on the trail. It moved further along the path, which was covered in fog. I looked at my bare feet and it seemed small like that of a little boy. The feather just danced in its glorious rhythm and flew even further. I clenched my teeth and followed it. I was curious and entranced by the dance and wanted to see where it was taking me. As we moved along, I could see the feather intermittently, as it would appear and disappear, dancing and floating in the wind. But even when it disappeared, I continued walking along the path.

As I walked higher up the mountain trail, the fog cleared up a bit and I could see the feather soar higher. As I raised my eyes to follow it, it showed me the summit of a glorious mountain. The summit was beautiful as it glowed in an orange colour reflecting the rays of the sun. The feather moved up higher towards the summit, encouraging me to climb further.

As I walked, the trail ended and there was no longer a path. The feather only flew higher in the air. Then I saw there were some holes in the mountain wall and so I started climbing with my hands and bare feet, struggling to maintain a grip. As I climbed the mountain, I was able to go higher and reach closer to the summit. But the air was getting thinner and I started feeling cold and uncomfortable.

As I kept climbing higher, the summit seemed to move further away. The view was closing in like a setting sun and I had to hurry. But my body was worn out. I had bruises everywhere on my body as the mountain had torn through my skin. The air was so thin that I could barely breathe properly. I paused and tried to inhale as much as possible as I held myself against the mountain. It was cold and I felt emptiness all around. But the summit with its golden glow looked beautiful and I knew when I would reach there it would look amazing. I just had to ignore the current state of pain. *Stay on the course, Ankit. You can do it.* I clenched my teeth and I resumed my climb clinging to the mountain, looking up at the feather. As a strong burst of wind came by, it took the feather away, making it disappear. I looked everywhere and then at the summit. I felt alone and nervous now that my only companion was gone. I kept climbing upwards with one thought, *oh how beautiful the summit would be once I get there.*

The journey got more tiresome and with little energy left I had to push myself even harder. My progress was slow and I was not reaching any closer to the summit. I kept trying to hang on because now I was afraid to fall down and inflict pain on my body. After a few moments of further agony, I felt glad seeing the feather come back as it moved along from my right shoulder coming at an eye level. It kept still for a while, trying to get my attention and convey something, but then it fluttered away again. *C'mon, help me to the top, please.* But the feather moved in the opposite direction. It came back close to me again and I heard the whisper, 'Let it go, Ankit.'

I let go of my grip and let myself fall. As I lost sight of the summit, I felt the air beneath me heavy enough to hold my body. I spread my arms and legs to further relax my body and breathed deeply to inhale all the air around. As I inhaled, the air filled every inch of my body. The boundary between the air in and outside my body receded and I was one with the wind. I glided along the strong currents of the wind, enjoying how it moved my body bringing with it the joy of detachment. I felt each part of my body come alive and my mind became free. I felt the infinite space and energy within and outside.

A hard jolt from behind brought me back to reality. It was as if someone had woken me up from sleep, but I quickly got my bearings. I changed my grip to put my right hand around Dad's back, so he could not see my bruised forearm. I asked him to hold my left hand as I moved my right hand behind his back to hold his waist. As I looked at my forearm, I could see deeper white layers of my skin peeled off and the deep red marks of his fingernails.

'Ankit, let's go. It was a great visit.'

'Yes, it was special.' I had never had such an incredibly detailed vision as the one I experienced. I still marvel at how my imagination soared in that temple and I still have no explanation of how or why a force greater than myself took over my mind, but the memory of it remains vivid and meaningful beyond words.

The following morning, I woke up late from a blissful sleep. It was a bright, beautiful day. The windows were wide open and the wind from outside was moving the curtains and ventilating the whole room. The view of the mountains and the rustic ambience added to the feeling of calm. I could hear the birds chirping and temple bells ringing from afar. Looking at the rustic mountains outside and the scenic background, I felt great. I looked around and Mom came over to my side of the bed.

'Good morning. What time is it?' I asked.

'It's 11.00 a.m.'

'Where is Dad?'

'He went for a walk. He told me that he has had enough temple visits to last many years.' I looked at her and smiled.

'He asked me to tell you to relax today.'

'After a long time, I actually enjoyed visiting a temple yesterday.' I took a deep breath.

'Really? But, you are not a religious person.'

She moved her hand over my forearm, where there were deep marks left from Dad's nails. 'Let me put some oil on this.'

'No, seriously. I felt really good in the temple yesterday.'

'It is all right. I know why you are doing this,' she said rubbing my hand with oil hoping to relieve the blood clots.

'Move over. Let me massage your head as well,' she said sitting on the bed. I readjusted my body, so my head was in her lap just like back in the childhood days. She moved back my hair off my forehead and started to put oil and massage my head with her hands.

'After a long time, I really felt good in a temple. Or rather, after a long time, I felt good. Period.' I laughed at my own joke.

'That's good for you, Ankit. I have noticed that you have been very jittery. You are a different person these days. Are you okay?'

'You know I have been tense over the last few years with the stock market.' I had told my parents about the stock market investment, but not about the huge loans I had borrowed and the risk involved. I had also not told them about my layoff from the previous company. I believed that these were temporary matters that would be resolved in time, so why bother them needlessly? 'It's tough.'

'It seems to affect you pretty bad,' she said. 'You often make noises in your sleep as if you are in pain. I can hear you grinding your teeth. Is everything all right with your life in America?'

'I think it is the normal ups and downs of life. You know it is not an easy life in the US. It is more professional than personal. Your work defines your life and there is not much beyond it. I wish I could spend my workday in the US and come back to India in the evening every day.'

'No, there must be something else happening. Your mental state seems to be in turmoil. You seem unsettled.'

'Well, as I said, the stock market takes up a lot of my energy. It is sucking up my mental and emotional energy. I have trouble relaxing as it distracts me from more productive and emotional activities. It is not easy.'

'I hope you are not taking too many risks.'

'I have taken risks. There is no doubt about it, but I think they are manageable and under control. The last few months have been crazy though.' I did not want to get into the details about the loans keeping me up all night, so I changed the topic.

'Do you remember, Mom, we used to lie like this in your lap in the afternoons when we were kids and you used to tell us stories?'

'Of course, I remember.'

'Those were fun days, relaxing with Abhishek and Anamika after morning classes at school. It seems like a distant dream now.'

'You kids grew up quickly,' she said pensively. 'You had to. That is the only regret I have in my life.'

'You don't have to feel any regrets. You and Dad did everything you could. It is because of your sacrifices that we have been successful in our careers.'

'As a parent, I could not be prouder of you kids. One kid has an MBA and two are engineers. You surpassed all my expectations.'

'Yup, we did achieve a lot in our short careers. As a child, I would not have dreamt of becoming an engineer designing cell phones. I wanted to be like Rambo,' I laughed.

'It is not just about achieving the dreams but how you achieved them. For me, you followed the correct principles. I am proud that you all turned out to be good human beings. Only a lucky few can say they have achieved their dreams.'

'Dreams are the weirdest things. Their impact varies from person to person. Dreams have a way of putting some to sleep. But dreams also have the power of keeping some awake at night. In our case, our dreams did not let us sleep,' I said.

'I know it was tough.'

'I think at a materialistic level we got back everything we had lost in our childhood.'

'It is much more than that. All three of you are much more successful than we had ever imagined you would be.'

'But I think subconsciously we lost something that we can't get back.'

'Hmm, what is that?'

'We cannot be free from fear. Our joy has been tarnished by our emotional scars.'

'What do you mean?'

'Events in our childhood left us with fear for the rest of our lives. Fear has become an unwanted companion, like a pack of wolves walking alongside us throughout life's journey. All our actions are designed to keep them at bay.'

'It will go away with time.'

'No, I have tried. I have tried to get rid of this fear. I have driven over mountains, jumped from the sky, swam the oceans, but I still can't get rid of it. It is always there, lurking like a ghost waiting for me to slip from the mountain so it can devour me.'

'What do you mean, Ankit?' she asked listening with attention.

'It's like I am walking on a tightrope and deeply aware that there is no security blanket underneath. I will keep climbing because of my ambition but I am always afraid of falling hard. Fear is always there. Even when I laugh, the fear comes as a reminder of my past sufferings and how it can take everything away in a second. When I try to make friends and mingle in a group, it is there as my insecurity amplified by my sense of inadequacy, whispering in my ear that I am somehow inferior to others, that I don't belong, that I will be thrown out of a gathering because my clothes are worn out or my shoes are torn. It is there distracting me in my work, magnifying the smallest mistake into an immediate threat to my job and livelihood.'

I continued as she held my head and gazed down at me with compassion.

'Recently I had an interview with a company and I had adroitly answered each and every question from all five interviewers, but the sixth interviewer asked one tough question that I could not answer. At the moment when I missed that answer, fear gripped me by the throat. I was just stuck and blanked out. My mind and body were frozen in that moment and I could sense the wolves relishing the carcass of my epic failure. Mom, I wish I could get rid of this omnipresent fear. If only I knew how to achieve that.'

'Everything will be fine.'

A gust of wind from the open window lifted a strand of mother's white hair. I had to continue to unburden my heart to her, now that I'd begun.

'I have never shared this with anyone, Ma, but that night, when we were evicted from our home by the hired goons, when Abhishek and I left to get the police...'

'Yes?'

'When we left the apartment building and all our possessions were being burnt in a big bonfire, there was a picture of us, the three of us when Anamika was one year old holding a comb.'

'Yes, I remember that picture, the one where she is in the middle and Abhishek and you are on either side of her. You must have been four or five years old.'

'As I came out of the building, I saw that photograph burning in the bonfire. I reached into the fire to pull it out with a stick, but I couldn't get a hold of it; it was just burning in front of my eyes. To this day, I still get nightmares about that. In my nightmare, I see that picture burning and I am trying to reach it, trying to pull it out. I am stretching every inch of my body, trying to stretch my fingertips just a little bit further, struggling to somehow pull it out of the flames. I see my image fading in the scorched picture and then I see Anamika's image disappearing as well. I try harder to reach, but I can't. I feel that I can't move forward, that something is holding me back. I see these dark demons emerge from behind and pull my legs, grabbing my body with their black tentacles, dragging me back. They relentlessly continue mauling me for their demonic pleasure. I see that Anamika's image is also burned and then Abhishek's. I keep fighting and trying hard. I match the fury of the demons with the fire in my soul, but I can't do anything to save the photograph.'

I let out a sigh of despair and kept talking.

'The photograph keeps burning. I look back at these creatures pulling me and the ruthless ferocity in their eyes. I fail to understand why this is happening to me. I look gently in their eyes and ask them, "Why me? What have I done to deserve this? I am the good guy." Like a fish caught in a hook, I keep reeling and twitching in bed through the night…It makes me hate the skin I am in. It leaves me feeling nothing but failure.'

'It's okay, Ankit. It's okay.'

I felt a strong tug on my forehead as my Mom tried physically to break my emotional state. Her grip tightened as my head was about to fall out of her lap. I came out of that state, sweating, my legs stretched out on the bed.

'We are all fine now. We are all fine now.'

'That fire still burns in me and continues to char my soul.'

'It's okay now, Ankit.'

'Nightmares like these have kept me awake for a long time. I fight my battles to reach my dreams when I'm awake and I fight them when I'm asleep. I don't want to dream. All I want is to sleep peacefully without fear. I am like an injured bird that keeps flapping its wings endlessly with the fear that it will fall. I don't want to struggle anymore. I just want to be home. I just want to sleep peacefully, Mom.'

I took a deep breath to come out of this agitated state. I had to escape from this negativity. Complaining about my childhood would just hurt Mom's feelings. I tried suppressing the emotion and changing the course of the conversation. So, I got up and turned around to face my mother who had a shocked expression on her face. I held her hand,

'Yesterday, I had a beautiful vision at the temple.' I said with a smile.

'Really, what was it?'

'I felt the intimation of a higher dimension where I felt free. It was peaceful and refreshing and there was no struggle. I could trust the feeling and just let go and be myself.'

'Maybe that is the sign, the silent voice. Maybe it is pointing to a new destination. Listen to your heart Ankit and not to the fear in your head. Your destination now is one of peace. All your paths should point in that direction.'

'I think so too. I think it was a new calling for me. I would love to pursue a path of peace and happiness.'

'You definitely should, Ankit.'

'Yes, the stock market is surely not a peaceful thing. I don't want to pursue that anymore. I have made a respectable profit. I am going to take all my money and get out of it as soon as I get back to the US.'

'That's good. Money is just a false pursuit,' Mom said wisely.

'Yes, but it does give you the freedom to enjoy life's experiences.'

'But that is not happening in your case.'

'Yes, that is true. It is not currently. In fact, it is the opposite. I have to change it.'

'Good.'

'I had an interview with my dream company in San Diego,' I revealed to her. 'I will join that company and maybe buy a house with my profits from the stock market.'

'Yes. That is a great idea. Also, you need to start a family soon. You are approaching 30.'

'Hmm. I am not sure if marriage will bring me peace,' I laughed.

'It will. No more delaying.'

'I'm just joking. I have been thinking about it as well. I also feel that it is time to start a family.'

'Really, you think about anything besides stocks?' Mom teased.

'Not all the time. But sometimes I do think about it.'

'Tell me what all you think about.'

'Well, I think about having a family, about having a child, a chubby child, who will crawl all around the house in diapers. Mind you, in my own house. I don't want to raise my child in somebody else's house. I want a big house that has a backyard with an open view of the skyline. So my child can just wander around everywhere, without a care in the world. Like a free bird.'

'And you will run behind, without a care in the world.'

'I don't know if I deserve that. Peace is a not a gift bestowed on me. I hope so though. Someday.'

'That is a beautiful dream worth pursing, Ankit.'

'Yes, it is, Mom. I think once I cash out my stock investments and start the new job in the new city, I will buy an apartment right next to the ocean and take walks in my flip flops like a California dude. It will be a good start to a happy and relaxed life. The future looks calm but exciting.'

I was barely balancing myself on the surfboard of opportunity with the maximum amount of life risks I could handle. But now, with a newfound understanding, I got a glimpse of the shore of a happy life. I was ready to start anew. I thought I was approaching the finish line of this stage of my life.

But destiny was not yet done with me.

Upon my return to the US, I was blindsided by a tsunami in the form of the financial crisis. On that September day in 2008, I was simultaneously hit by two waves. One was getting rejected for my dream job in San Diego and the other was losing my entire life's savings in the stock market collapse and being in serious debt. I was facing impending financial ruin while being jobless. This tidal wave sent me into a brutal panic attack.

I found myself knocked out on the floor of my apartment.

10

RISE, WARRIOR, RISE

In the stillness of the moment, I could not hear a thing. It was so quiet. I looked up at the sky with my eyes wide open. The sky was clear. There were no winds to disturb the beautiful silence of the night. I saw the moon clearly, a three-dimensional sphere floating unhinged in the sky, as Earth's loyal companion in the whole galaxy; its dusty surface lit partly by the sun. In the past, the moon seemed like a two-dimensional object in the sky, but at that moment I could appreciate the full round structure of this soft globe. Wait, where am I?

I looked around the dark room. Oh, phew, I was in my apartment. I checked the time on my phone. It was around 10.30 p.m. I had slept for more than 10 hours. I moved my fingers. I was able to do that and I was able to hear as well. I wiggled my toes. Putting my hand on the chest, I tried feeling my heartbeat. The mad gorilla was now in a quiet state of rest like a sleeping child. I inhaled deeply and felt the air circulate through my entire body. I took it as a sign of relief, knowing that there was no physical damage from the meltdown.

I recollected a moment around three years back in 2005, when I had visited the centre for the visually impaired in Mumbai. I had kept my promise to my friend Akshat's mom to help out with her charity work. The centre offered vocational training for the visually impaired to become self-sufficient. I dropped off a cheque to sponsor books and uniforms for an entire batch of students and was about to leave quietly because I did not want to overwhelm myself with grief looking at the students' struggle. I was still struggling with the aftermath of Dad's stroke. Before I could quietly sneak out, Aunty caught me and called me to meet the students who were in the class.

Contrary to my expectation, all the students looked happy and full of energy. Even with their partial vision, seven or eight of them came to the front of the classroom to shake my hand. They enthusiastically showed me the candles they had made and gifted me some. They thanked me for my donation and one of them said, 'Thank you. We are happy to learn new things in this school. We are grateful for a chance to fight.' Those words stayed with me, especially in moments of personal grief. If these kids despite being barely able to see were happy, then how could I as an abled-body person complain? Just having the ability to fight was reason enough to not give up.

It was clear that I had to push beyond the darkness and tackle the struggle head on. If the past chapters of my life were a guide, each page was marked with the grit to stay on the path and never back off. What I had thought would be the doorway to the 'happily ever after' was now an entrance to a tumultuous battle for survival. I had to change from being a peaceful monk to being a warrior. Adversity has come and gone, but my determination has never waned. As Rocky said, 'Nobody is gonna hit as hard as life. But it isn't about how hard you hit, it's about how hard you get hit and keep moving forward.' Warriors fight. It was time to get back into the ring. It was time to conquer the challenges that life was throwing my way. This darkest hour could be my defining moment. I wouldn't be able to escape my demons, but I would have to slay them with the sheer power of my will. The storm had brought me to my knees and now I needed to respond by walking through it.

Before I got back into the battle arena, I reflected on my defeat. Why was I brought to my knees this afternoon? I had to understand the reason for my failure so I could come back stronger. The dual voices of wisdom returned.

I had a physical and mental reaction to the stock market crash today when I realized that I had lost all money and that I am in serious debt.

Why did that happen, Ankit?

I was not expecting it.

Why?

I wasn't checking the news. I was not staying abreast with the financial news.

Why, Ankit?

The mental pressure of the stock market overwhelmed me to the point of no return. It pushed me to the breaking point. I had to take a break and at the same time, I wanted to fulfil my parents' wish to travel. This prevented me from being on top of the stock market news.

You think your failure is related to your situation, but it is not. It is only tangential.

Tangential?

Reality is something else. You are trying to escape from it using your own projections of it.

What?

They are two different things. One is your conditioning, your sense of self, your history and your feelings about life events. The other is the reality, the ever-changing present moment when everything happens. Life is rooted in reality and not in your thoughts and emotions. When the stock market crashed today, it was a moment of reality. Reality is objective and feelings are subjective. You think reality will blend or bend according to your emotions, but it does not. Reality does not give a hoot who you are or what you have been through. Emotion—the origin of this word means disturbance, a distortion of what is. Reality is. It is not what you want it to be or think it should be, it is what it is.'

But what I feel matters.

There may be a time for emotions and your past stories, but not in the heat of battle. In the battlefield, things happen quickly, and you need to be sharp to understand and react on the spot. In the ring, emotions distract you.

For all your senses to be sharp, you need to immerse yourself in the moment. Forget about your sense of self. Observe even the slightest movement and pay attention to each beat. Dwelling on the past is running away and escaping reality.

In the reality of your life, you must keep an eye on the next wave or the next storm. If not, it will take you down as it did today, as it did during the surfing accident. Complete understanding requires complete immersion in reality. Complete engagement is possible when you are free from your sense of self and its projections. An emotional mind is not a fresh mind as it is burdened by thoughts and past emotions. An emotional mind is not a rational mind. The latter is free of emotion.

I got off the floor and readied myself to fight, but this time with a commitment to rid myself of any emotion and feeling. It was time to run back into the fog of the battle to reclaim my path.

There were two opponents ahead me: the financial situation and my employment status. My debt required immediate action since it was mandatory to repay the money within a few days.

I sat at the table, dusted off my laptop and started researching the current market crisis. For the next seven hours into the night, I examined every article I could find on the current financial crisis carefully. It was clear to me that this crisis was the result of a systematic problem in the country's financial system. It was encouraging to read that the Federal Reserve was planning to introduce a bailout package in response to the subprime mortgage crisis that had been largely responsible for the market's crash. Before the market opened at 6.30 a.m., I was confident that the market would open positive because of the jolt of confidence based on the bailout. Generally, when the market drastically declines, a small bounce is likely the next day—in financial jargon this is called the dead cat bounce. This bounce could be my small window to get out of the market. I was counting on these two factors for the indices to rebound marginally. There was the possibility of stock indices closing lower, which was likely if negative news tipped the market into further losses. I believed that this response was improbable. In the back of my mind I knew if the market declined further, I would be in deeper debt. I owed almost $100,000. I could immediately sell everything and keep my debt limited to $25,000, or risk being in debt for more than that as it could even be a $100,000 debt if the market goes into a free fall. I believed in my research and decided to hold till the end of that day.

I waited and breathed deeply as I counted the minutes and seconds until the market opened. It was as if time stood still. It felt like waiting for the space shuttle to launch and I was hoping it was not going to crash and burn.

The liftoff was successful. I gave a sigh of relief when the market opened in the positive. At the close of the day, I was less than $10,000 in debt and there was the possibility of a bigger rebound tomorrow with news that the bailout was taking effect. It would be great if this happened. I would not only wipe out the remaining debt, but also retrieve my investment. It would be great if I could recoup what I had lost and end up even.

No wishful thinking. Remember, no emotion. Stay objective, Ankit. A voice in my head reminded me of the new battle rules.

I slept in the afternoon after the market closed and woke up again late evening. I spoke to Anamika in Houston and told her my flight back had been fine. I told her that Mom and Dad were doing well and that it was a good trip. When she asked why I sounded so down, I told her, 'I did not get the job in San Diego, the one that I really wanted. I am in debt from the stocks I bought on margin. I am hoping that the market opens positive tomorrow as it did today so I can clear the debt. If not, I am in major trouble.' I held back from telling her about the panic attack. That was enough bad news for one phone call.

'It is going to be okay, Ankit. We will fight it out,' she tried to reassure me.

We said goodbye and I continued researching why the market behaved as it did. I was trying to get a grasp on the source of the current financial crisis and what exactly was the meaning of the credit default swap. One thing was clear—it was difficult to understand what that term meant because the primary purpose of these instruments of financial engineering was to obfuscate. These were just distortion curtains so nobody could see how blatantly financial institutions were risking money they did not have. The current financial crisis was based on an overly leveraged credit system. If there was one actual dollar bill, the financial institution based on ownership of small pennies were borrowing, lending and betting a dollar each. So, for one actual dollar there were more than 10 virtual dollars in play. It was like a house of cards built on virtual money. The moment one card fell, and an actual dollar was taken out of the system, all the other institutions would be exposed as well and the system could crumble. The Federal bailout did not correct the problem because the credit institutions and individuals were overleveraged.

After spending the entire night analysing what had happened, it was clear that the wound was deep and that the stimulus package was basically a band aid solution. It was going to get much worse before it got better.

Unexpectedly, the market opened up higher yet again as traders reacted to the optimism of the previous day. The margin debt in my account went down to zero. At that moment, I thought maybe my analysis was wrong. I should just wait for a few more days. What if the system is resilient enough to absorb this blow? The Federal Reserve can continue to print money as long as they want. Maybe I will be able to break even and get my original investment out without suffering a loss.

Ankit, remember that it is not a subjective thing. Be rational.

What if your analysis is correct and the market goes back down and you are in debt again? There is no way you can repay the debt if this happens. Just sell off everything now while you are debt-free. That will give you steady ground to launch your fight back.

I can wait till the end of the day. At least I could retrieve $10,000 for surviving the next few months, being jobless. The greed in me was licking its chops.

Be objective. This is a systematic problem. It will definitely worsen. Sell now so you can fight another day. If not, you will sink deeper into the quicksand.

With that thought, I sold all my stocks that day. No more margin debt to pay. But no more money in my account either.

My life's savings were wiped out with just a click of my mouse. At one moment, the account had a value of $200,000 and now it was nada. The zero reminded me of the circle of life. You are born with nothing and you leave with nothing. Is that why they call it the circle of life?

After that click, I felt a void in my heart. The small platform of financial security had just been pulled out from underneath me. I had to hold steady so as not to sink further until some help came.

The decision to sell that day would later turn out to be the correct decision as that moment was just the beginning of one of the biggest financial depressions in the history of the stock market. In a couple weeks, the Dow Jones Industrial Average fell 778 points, the biggest drop in its history. Within a few months, the market would lose 50 per cent of its total value.

As I shutdown my laptop that day, I was free of any emotions. I stared blankly into the empty space. I was happy that my debt was erased and sad to lose everything, knowing that there was no way to get the money back. Whatever I felt did not matter anymore. My feelings and emotions no longer mattered, as it was time to launch my attack on the next challenge.

I had to focus on getting a job. One easy course of action

would be to return to the company that had acquired my previous group. They would be happy to take me back and I would be able to steady my ship for a while as I tried to recover from a major financial loss.

On further thought, I decided to stay the course and pursue my dream job. Giant ships don't change course when hit by a storm. I did not have the responsibility of children or a family, so this was the time to take risks while I still had the freedom to do so.

I sent an email to the group's director of my dream company in San Diego, requesting another interview. I also inquired about the interview I had had at the Austin branch of the same company. I knew my chances were slim to be hired there, so I started to think about the company in San Diego that I had earlier set my mind on. I had to remain solvent for the next few months for my new plan of action to come to fruition.

I put my Jeep and my surfboard for sale on Craigslist. The following morning, many prospective buyers called and came to my apartment to inspect and possibly buy the Jeep. A lot of the initial buyers were mechanics who frustratingly made low-ball offers to my already low price. They would inspect the Jeep and point out multiple issues as a way to get me to lower the price. I was happy to finally sell the Jeep to an African-American gentleman who bought it for his teenage son who was going to college. As I handed the keys to the kid, I told him, 'Take good care of it. Make a lot of memories. And be safe.'

I went back upstairs to my apartment and from the closet I took out the plastic bag containing the dusty T-shirt I had saved as a memento from my off-road trip a few years ago. Through the transparent plastic, I could see the T-shirt and the clean strip from where the seat belt had been. I took the T-shirt out of the bag and threw it into the garbage downstairs. No memento. No memories. No sorrow.

When I deposited the cheque from the sale of the Jeep, the

receipt showed an unexpectedly high balance in my account. I looked at it closely. It was definitely a lot more than I expected to see. Where did that extra money come from?

I went home and checked my account online. I saw that $15,000 had been transferred into my account a few days earlier. Where could it have come from?

Was it one of the financial institutions apologizing, 'Sorry for stealing all of your life savings. Here is a little bit back.' I snickered at the ridiculous idea. If banks were that moral, I would not be in this position in the first place.

Looking at the details, I soon figured it was Anamika who had transferred the money. I called her immediately.

'I can't take this money from you, Anamika.'

'Why can't you? You could use it at a time like this, at least until you get another job.'

'I just can't.'

'Look brother, ever since I can remember, you, Abhishek, Mom and Dad have always shielded me. You have always sacrificed to protect me from the suffering that you all faced. When I watched everyone go through pain, I always felt helpless not being able to do anything. Now it's my time to help. Don't take that away from me. Please accept it.'

It was difficult to argue. Also, all emotions aside, I really needed the money to stay solvent to fight for my dream job. So I took it with gratitude.

I tried to correspond with the managers and HR of the previous interviews, but was met with cold responses; I lost two promising positions. I was not given the chance to interview again. My next plan was to apply for various other positions in that company in San Diego. These positions were not exact matches, but there was an overlap between my skills and the requirements of those positions. I knew if I prepared, I could learn the skills. Also, my good technical background and education might be sufficiently impressive to convince them. The next day I was informed that I would have a telephonic interview. I searched the Internet for information about the job requirements and I went to Barnes and Noble to purchase books and learn about the new technical aspect.

The interview went well and I was subsequently invited for an on-site interview.

Don't screw this one up, Ankit. Work hard. For the next two to three weeks, I prepared hard for the interview. I felt confident thinking, theoretically, I knew everything about the skills that were required. But putting that knowledge to practical use was more challenging since I had not worked on any of those technologies before. There were eight long interviews on the schedule for that day. I did well answering most of the technical questions and came out feeling confident that I would get the job. I drove around San Diego. I loved this place. There was something about the beaches and hills that viscerally attracted me. I felt that I belonged in San Diego and in this company. I just needed a lucky break to cross the finish line.

But the next day I received an email stating that I was not a good fit for the position. *No emotion. Don't fret about this failure. Keep moving forward, Ankit. Try again.* I told myself. I revisited the company's website and started to apply for other openings.

I got a telephonic interview for another position. Once again, my job requirements only tangentially matched my skill set and that was exposed in the interview. I applied again and got yet another interview for a different opening, failing that one as well.

By that time, I had failed five different interviews in the same company, but I wanted to continue trying to somehow get my foot in the door. Maybe my previous unsuccessful interviews would negatively impact my future chances, particularly if the people interviewing me knew the results of the previous phone interviews through the common company database. They might think that there was something wrong with me. I created a new candidate profile for myself, hoping the new position would not be negatively affected by my previous unsuccessful attempts. Within one day I received a warning email from the company's IT engineers stating that I was not allowed to create a new profile and that I had to stick to my former profile. My previous five failures would stick with me and interfere with any prospects. I didn't back down and shortly thereafter I secured another telephonic interview.

Once again, I did well and was asked to appear for an on-site interview. To improve my chances, instead of driving the long distance in the morning and trying to keep alert during the long interviews, I decided to stay overnight at the hotel on the company's San Diego campus. I thought this would help me relax and stay more alert.

From the window of my hotel room I could see the company's buildings and the company's neon sign. I was reviewing my notes and rereading some chapters from books I had brought with me. I was listening to motivational songs on my headphone and I was walking around the room looking at the sign. I was listening to 'Lose Yourself' and 'Remember the Name', two rap songs that really spoke to me. This was my moment to make it happen. I was so worried that I couldn't fall asleep until early morning.

The interview went well and I answered most of the technical questions. But when some of the interview conversation addressed my previous work experience and the job specifications, there was an enormous gap. It was like a valley in the middle of the road that was inevitable and impossible to avoid. I felt the gap was not too big, but was not sure that the interviewer shared my perspective. I tried to keep the conversation focused on my achievements. I pointed out the impressive references I'd received from my managers and my stellar performances in my career so far. I highlighted the amount of dedication I would bring to the job and told them I was a quick learner. I had worked on much more difficult projects, so I was very capable of quickly learning any task at hand. The interviewers were not seeing it that way since they wanted some hands-on experience.

Within a week I received another email rejecting me. This one stung quite a bit. I tried to suppress my emotions, but knew this could be the end. *C'mon warrior, just one more try.* Lucky seven, I thought. I tried again, but didn't get a single interview in November. The recession was spreading like a disease and every technology company was ailing and freezing any further hiring. I tried some other companies but there too the positions were pulled off after my interview.

It was a cold and lonely November. I was exhausted. There was still the easy option of going to the company in Irvine, but I didn't want to concede as I thought there was still something left to fight for. I needed to recharge my batteries and come up with a new strategy for 2009. A charismatic African-American was going to become the president of the United States in January that year and that was another reason to be hopeful.

The hiring freeze made finding a job slower if not impossible in December. I decided to go to India for a few weeks. Spending time at home with Abhishek's angelic baby girl would be a welcome change from the doom and gloom. I did not tell anyone about my financial predicament. I did not want any of them to worry, so I told them that I had some vacation days left and decided to come home for a relaxing visit.

In January, I came back to the US energized and ready for the next round of battles. But the recession continued well into January. There were not many openings as hiring for full-time positions had come to a standstill. A friend of a friend who worked at my dream company in San Diego confirmed that. I had to come up with an alternate strategy.

This new strategy entailed taking a different approach to get my foot in the door. When companies stop hiring but work needs to be done, they start employing short-term contract workers. If

I could get in as a short-term contractor, I was certain that with my skills and commitment to excellence, I would convince my employers in time to convert the short-term job into a full-time position. Also, the interview bar for contractors was low, so even if there were issues with my horrible interview skills, I believed I could get through the process. I applied for a short-term low-key technical position. I again had to appear for a telephonic interview which was followed by an on-site one. The latter, to my surprise, comprised eight long interviews.

As I sat through eight interviews, I could see the same script playing out. 'You have done good work but your profile does not match with what we are looking for. You have more hardware skills and we are looking for software skills.' Interview after interview seemed to be revealing the poor match, stopping me from putting an end to my joblessness. But I kept at it, answering all the challenging technical questions to the best of my ability. I was showing genuine interest, but the game was just slipping away. It was not about the 10 questions that I answered, but the one I could not. That was the issue for each interviewer; it created doubts in their minds whether I could meet all the expectations of the job.

My last interview of the day was with the technical team leader. It seemed like other interviewers had briefed him on my shortcomings, so his interview was not very technical but rather a casual conversation. I found this very frustrating. As the minutes passed, it was dawning on me that I was losing the battle. Any possibility of working at my dream company was disappearing before my eyes. I was thinking, *C'mon. Hit me with a technical question. Give me a chance.*

Towards the end of the scheduled time, he said that he recognized that I had a good profile, but my expertise was in hardware and chip design and that the team was more interested in hiring someone with a software skill set. I said, 'Look, Sir. I know it appears that I am not the right fit for this position. And

I know that I don't have good interview skills and that I don't interact well with people. I become tense during interviews and I am not able to think on my feet. But I can assure you that I can do the job. I have a masters degree from a top university in the US, I have done projects for NASA, I have worked long hours helping a start-up get off the ground and I have worked at a company whose design went into the iPhone. I can do any project if I set my mind on it. Please just give me the chance to prove myself. I can work for free if you want. Please let me work for free for a few weeks to prove myself.' My hands were raised up into clenched fists. I was so overwhelmed by emotions that I was literally trembling.

At that moment I became aware I was pleading with my hands in the air. I quickly resumed my professional posture. The manager was sympathetic, yet continued to be professional. 'We will definitely consider your skill set and talk with our group internally and I'll let you know.' He stood up and showed me to the door.

I shook hands with him and left. I trudged out of the building and collapsed onto one of the chairs a few feet from the door. The umbrella on the table was providing shade from the intense sun in the afternoon. I was shaken up, disappointed and surprised at my emotional outburst. I was thinking about how I had decided to bottle up my emotions a few months back and then, seemingly from nowhere, my emotions surged to the surface at a professional meeting. I never expected that from myself. I had kept my emotions in check since childhood, when I learned the importance of displaying fortitude in adversity. So this over the top reaction was a definite surprise.

It's okay, Ankit. Let's try to be objective. There's a recession going on. It's a tough market and the jobs you interviewed for were not a good match. It didn't work out, but it's not about you.

No, it is about me. I am the one who failed in those seven interviews. I am solely to be blamed. Seven bloody interviews. What a loser! Who in this world has failed seven different interviews at the same company? C'mon man. That is disgraceful.

I thought as I grimaced with my hands rubbing my forehead.

And this one was for a short-term contract, not even a full-time position. It was a contract for making testing tools for verification engineers who are testing software on the chips made by the hardware engineers. How unqualified and bad do you have to be, Ankit? How bad an engineer are you to fail seven freaking interviews?

Maybe I am not as bright as I thought I was. Maybe the stock market had blunted my brain and now I couldn't think clearly or quickly enough. You wanted to be a jack-of-all-trades, and now you are the jackass of all trades. Be it in the world of engineering, socializing or financing, you are a well-rounded failure, Ankit.

I looked at the road facing me. Then I looked back over my shoulder and glanced at the building's closed door and the company's sign and I knew it was time to hit the road for good. It was time to give up on my obsession with this company.

Nobody wants me here. If more than 50 employees who have interviewed me are convinced that I don't deserve to work at this company, then I don't deserve it.

Shame. The word kept echoing in my head. I tightly squeezed my hands around my head with fingers locked in the back of my head and forearms pushing into my forehead. I bent forward and put my elbows on the table. I pressed as hard as I could but I could not suppress these echoes of shame in my head.

I sat there for a while with the troubled feeling. I had to accept this new reality. I hit the highway quickly and avoided the city that was not meant for me.

By the time I returned home, my mind had given up but my soul was still restless. That night, I sent a thank you email to the last interviewer, attaching my references from previous jobs. I kept pestering the consultancy company to keep on top of the employer for any news about my interview. I also told them to convey my willingness to work without pay for a few months as a trial period.

There was calm for a week. Then a miracle happened!

I got a call from the consultancy company that I had been hired to start next week on a six-month contract. I was elated at the news. Finally, I got a foot in the door, a chance to fight.

I had to make a quick move from Irvine to San Diego. I had not accumulated many material possessions and the few that I did have, I'd sold over the last few months. I rented a one-bedroom apartment next to Bird Rock Beach in La Jolla. The apartment was very small but only a few steps away from the beach. Though it was only for a few months, I was excited. Finally, my dream of living in the finest city was being fulfilled. In the afternoon of my move, I drove a rented U-Haul to La Jolla from Irvine.

There was a steep downward sloping road as I approached the final turn to my new place. As I drove the U-Haul to the very end of this slope, I slammed on the brakes. The ocean was right there in front of me greeting me. Huge waves and winds were welcoming me at the door. Seagulls were smoothly gliding above the water. I knew I had arrived home.

With complete motivation, I started my six-month contract period. I knew that I had to march towards a full-time position and I would only achieve that if I demonstrated excellence in my performance. Every day as I drove to work, I listened to motivational songs on repeat and arrived fully charged to put in my best effort.

A few months prior, during my trip to India in December, Mom had introduced me to Tripti, a girl who was known to us through a common relative. That relative was one of the misguided youth that my Dad had helped. He had stayed at home with us in Mumbai for many years. His wife was Tripti's aunt. Tripti was an intelligent and good-looking girl who had studied mechanical engineering and was planning to do an MBA in the US. Initially, we had exchanged emails, so I could help her navigate the different colleges that specialized in her field. Our email communication evolved to phone conversations and then to video chatting. What I liked about Tripti was that she was a simple person and had a gentle heart. She lived in one of the religious holy towns near the Ganges in North India. Her life was uncomplicated and had not been tainted with bad experiences like mine. Conversations with her took me to a different but simpler world devoid of complexities and struggles. After a few months, we mutually agreed to get married, much to the satisfaction of our parents. At work, I got an extension of my contract in the fall of 2009 and things were looking smooth.

Tripti and I got married in India and she moved to the US with me the following year. I moved from my bachelor pad on the beach to a more family-style rental apartment to make sure that she had access to public transportation. Tripti was accepted into an MBA programme.

The initial period of married life was a big adjustment for both of us. Tripti had not only gotten married, but was living in a new country without any friends or family. I was almost a stranger to her. I had been by myself for a long time or most of my life, so being with her felt like taking time away from myself and my thoughts. Also, I was prone to hiding my feelings and emotions, so sometimes I came across as if I had none. I recognized that I had my responsibilities as a husband and hence I made sure she was comfortably settled in her new life and studies. There were moments when I felt I should have talked about my past with her, about my childhood and family struggles, but then I would decide not to taint her optimistic view of the world. So, I never told her much about my past. I wanted to leave everything behind and move forward as I started a new phase of my life.

'Why haven't I seen any pictures from your childhood? You have seen my childhood album.'

'We lost them when we moved,' I would lie.

'Why are you so tense? And why do you overthink all the

time? You don't even sleep peacefully. I see you at night, lying awake and staring at the ceiling.'

'It's nothing. I am thinking about work and how I can do better.'

'It will be okay. No use worrying. You should relax and enjoy the moment. Life is short.'

'I can't relax. I am always waiting for an unexpected turn in this journey called life. There is a storm waiting for me at the corner and I have to be well prepared every moment to fight it.'

'There is no storm. It is your illusion. Things have a way of working themselves out. Have trust in God.'

I was careful not to burst her bubble. I kept focusing on my contract job. There were days when I used to come home late from work and my shoulders and wrists would ache from the constant typing and stress. Tripti would apply herbal ointment on my back to relieve the pain and help me relax. I really wanted to believe in her optimism and conviction that things would get better, but as it turns out, they would not. Dad had another stroke. He had still not recovered from the first one and with another one now, he had become completely paralysed. I was devastated, but I determinedly pushed forward.

My hard work at the office was soon rewarded and in May 2010, I was offered a full-time position with the same group I had already been working with. The position was one level below what I had held at the British company and two levels below the position I was offered at the acquiring company in the summer of 2008. Nevertheless, I was elated and relieved at finally becoming a full-time employee at my dream company.

Before I could finish celebrating and entertaining the thought of finally settling down mentally, within a few weeks of being hired full time, the company announced that our whole division would be closed down. The products that our division was designing were not doing well, so the company had decided to shut down the division. I could not believe my bad luck. It was like crossing the finish line of a marathon and then realizing that the finish line had been moved. There still remained more hurdles and many miles to cover.

The silver lining in this dark situation was that the company's CEO said that it would do right by the employees who were affected by this realignment. They would be accommodated if there were opportunities in other groups. All engineers were expected to interview with groups that had openings.

I had two interviews, but my inability to perform well at such interactions resurfaced and I was rejected by both groups. From our division, all the engineers were looking for jobs and some who were involved with more relevant work were readily hired. My work at that division was not considered tier one, so other groups were justified in selecting more qualified engineers. After a few tense months, there were a very few of us left who were still unable to get hired. I knew time was running out and that I had to change my strategy. I was working with software but my real background was hardware engineering. I knew that I had to return to my earlier work profile and find a job as a chip designer.

With that changed profile and resume, I was granted an interview with a team that made tools for the distinguished system architecture group. Eight people interviewed me and it was apparent that they were not entirely convinced that I was a good fit. Since I was now an employee, I could speak directly to the interviewers. I asked them to allow me to work with them for a few months on a trial basis. The director of my current division approved the decision and that team had no problem since they were getting a free resource. So, I started working for them in this transition period.

After a few weeks of working with the tools team, I made some contacts within the system architecture organization. I sent an email to one of the group members who forwarded it to the director, who showed interest in my resume and my previous works. He told me to meet two of his best engineers the very next day.

Neither of those interviews felt like interviews at all. We talked about technology, my past work experience, the skills required in the job and where I could fit in. I had finally found a team which was interested in what I had done. They were asking me relevant questions instead of throwing me a curve ball that I struggled to field as all previous interviewers had done. I felt really good after the interview. The next day the director met me and explained how pivotal the system architecture team was to the overall company as it was the most elite one. It was this team that provided the direction and analysis that determined and defined all the chips being produced at the company. He showed some of the presentations and analysis the team had done. I felt inspired and my mind was blown away. This was the work I had been dreaming of my entire professional life and I enthusiastically expressed my interest. He offered me a position on the system architecture team that day.

My dream was coming true. It was the perfect job. This was what I was meant to do.

In the new team, though I had doubts about my abilities and questioned how I would stack up to the brilliance of my team members, I tried to give it everything I had. My goal was to leave my mark at work and in turn impact the entire world. I worked as hard as I could. Being in an elite team, I got to interact with some of the best engineering minds around the world. I learnt that you need to push multiple dimensions of your personality—skills, hard work and attitude—to be successful. Every engineer had something unique one could learn from and enhance oneself. I was on the constant pursuit of improvement and excellence, and two years just flew by.

It was around January 2012, three years into our marriage, when Tripti and I talked about starting a family.

'What do you think about starting a family? I am ready to

have a baby,' she said coyly.

'Ah, I think we should buy a house first,' I said.

'What?'

'House prices are at an all-time low because of the recession. This is a great time to buy.'

'Well, but first let's have a child.'

'The housing market will not wait for us. It will pass us by. Now is the time.'

'But do we even have the money for a house?'

'No, but I will arrange for it somehow. I want to buy a house before we have a baby. Just give me some time.'

I had always dreamt that my baby would live in his/her own house, not a rental apartment. There would not be any landlord pestering us for rent. The baby would not grow up in a cramped place like the apartments in which I had grown up. It would be a big house, with a backyard and a view of the sky, like the openness I had experienced on the terrace. It was the vision I had shared with Mom—my child running in the backyard under a big blue sky. To fulfil that dream, I had to find a way to make it happen.

I had some money saved from the previous few years and there were stock grants from my company that I could sell. It would amount to $30,000. I knew I needed more money to make a down payment.

After the 2007 housing crisis, the lending rules had tightened, raising the initial down payment required to purchase a home. The houses in our price range were not to our liking and the houses to our liking were not in our price range. I was adamant about having a house with a yard. So it was a stalemate and I needed to break the cycle. The only way to purchase a home we liked was to arrange for a bigger down payment. I explored ways to raise more money.

One obvious way was to work hard and get a promotion. Even with that, I thought I would only reach around $35,000 to

$40,000 in the next couple of years. To be able to purchase a big home, I would need double that amount. In the expensive San Diego housing market, I would need to put down about $60,000 to $70,000 for a decent house.

How could I grow that pile of money?

There was something in my past skill set that could be useful now. I knew I had to make a visit to my friend turned foe, Mr Stock Market.

Over the last five years, since the 2008 crisis when I was completely wiped out, I had not invested in the stock market. But I had remained abreast of the financial news, especially the stocks that I had owned but was forced to liquidate. The stock that was the major part of my holding in 2007 had gone up seven times in value and the British company stock, where I used to work, had increased more than 60 times since I had held them in my portfolio. If that economic crisis had not hit at the exact time when I had taken the maximum debt, I could have just waited it out and held onto my stocks through the economic crisis. My stocks would have been worth more than a million dollars. I would have become a millionaire instead of struggling to find a way to put 10 per cent down on a house. But alas, as the old adage went, 'I'd rather be lucky than good.'

The question in front of me now was whether I should invest the $30,000 in the stock market to raise money for a down payment? What if I got wiped out again? This time I had family obligation and a baby on the horizon. Should I take the risk? Did I want to go through the mental ordeal of investing in the erratic stock market? Was I prepared to go through the sleepless nights, the grinding teeth and the pounding headaches and stress again?

At that time, I didn't think I had the luxury of choice. People like me had to hustle hard if we wanted something worth having. The fact of the matter was that I did not have the money to buy a decent house. Nobody was going to help me get it except myself. There was no other way. I had to risk the thousands that I had to get more and I thought I did not have the choice. I had to hustle.

But this time I did have the choice to be judicious about my stock investing. I noted what I had done well and what mistakes I had committed the first time I invested in 2005. I did not want to repeat the same mistakes. One prominent mistake was being overleveraged and taking loans. They added to the risks and pressure, so no margin loan. I had to trust my instincts, believe in my judgement and be patient. I decided not to worry about short-term daily gyrations and not to trust everything the media reported. With those assertions fixed in my mind, I heard an old Hindi song playing in my car with lyrics translating to, 'Fix the fault in your stars, if you believe in yourself, then bet it all.'

I decided to enter the stock market again. For the second time, I placed the boat containing all my life savings into the violent ocean for another voyage into the stock market.

Six months into 2012, my diligence at work was rewarded. I was promoted and given a bonus and stocks. I sold those stocks as well to invest along with whatever I was saving from my monthly salary.

This time, my style of investing was more reflective than reactive. I was quick to identify the FUD—fear, uncertainty and doubt disinformation—strategy, which was to ignore the noise and zero in on the good stocks. The key was to identify the undervalued stocks before others would find out about them in the next few months. My strategy worked and I had significant returns in 2012. While continuing to look for houses, I increased my risk in early 2013 and then cashed out from all my positions when my stocks peaked in March 2013. Now, I had more than enough to pay 10 per cent down payment on a decent house.

In April, we conceived our baby.

In May, we, including the baby in Tripti's womb, looked at a house that sat on a mountain, on one of the highest peaks in San Diego. From the family room, one could see the beautiful backyard and open sky. Out front there was a beautiful canyon with lush trees that served as a bird sanctuary. Also out front was a path that led to a trail into the dense trees. As I stood in the backyard facing west, I felt the refreshing breeze coming from the ocean. At that height, the sky seemed to converge into the horizon as if it were a dome. I heard the birds chirping in their sanctuary and I saw a small feather float by me as it flew up in the sky. I knew this was what I had envisioned for my house and this was where my baby would be brought up.

This was the first day of the open house and the owners had put a high and low range for the bidders to know what an acceptable offer would be. Lots of people came to the open house and there were many who seemed interested. Our agent informed us that there had already been 30 bids on first day of the open house. I listened to him, but I was not going to let anyone take away my baby's new home. I instructed the agent to bid $10,000 more than the top end of the seller's range. With convincing and counter convincing, the seller agreed to accept our bid.

The day we moved into the new house, Tripti was three months pregnant and we were thrilled with the knowledge that we were going to be blessed with a baby girl. I missed having my parents, brother and sister around to celebrate this big moment of my life.

I could not help but feel gratitude for the help I received from my biggest financier.

Thank you, Mr Stock Market, I thought as I entered the house.

And now, Sir, we are even. I smiled remembering what a wild ride the stock market had been for me.

My daughter Trisha was born the first week of January 2014. Tripti had to endure intense labour pain. Before the delivery, I had set up my cell phone to record the moment of Trisha's arrival, but the little one was in no hurry. It took so long that the cell phone's battery ran out. After many failed 'deep breath and push' attempts, the doctor decided to use a suction device to pull the baby's head out. My heart was skipping many beats as I was trying to look strong throughout holding Tripti's hand. Childbirth proved to be very painful for Tripti, hours before and after the delivery. I could not help but admire her grit in those moments.

When Trisha finally came into the world in the early hours of the morning, time stood still. Covered in what looked like dried white chalk, she was the purest thing I had ever seen in the world. All the light in the room seemed to be pointing in Tripti and Trisha's direction and reflecting from their glow. I felt blessed.

We stayed one day longer in the hospital since the delivery was not routine. That night as Tripti rested, the baby slept swaddled in a blanket in a crib and I slept on a couch next to the bed. During that night in the hospital, I woke up hearing the baby cry. Tripti was sleeping and I did not want to disturb her as she was exhausted.

I freed the baby's arms from the blanket and picked her up. I sat on the couch with my legs resting on the edge of Tripti's bed and I put the baby in my lap with her face towards me. She looked at me with her beautiful eyes, still adjusting to her new world. I moved my hands lightly over her head and forehead a few times to soothe her. She seemed to like it and became quiet right away. She stared at me. There was a glow emanating from her that seemed to blend with the early morning light. She was not of this world, but she was making her first adjustments to her new world.

'Don't worry, baby. I am here.'

As I touched her face, she smiled and held my index finger with her little hand. She kept shaking my finger while looking into my eyes. After a while, I tried to shake her grip but she held my finger tightly. I was a bit confused attempting to decipher what she was trying to do or convey. She again shook my finger, looked into my eyes and smiled. She was trying to tell me something.

'Ah…you know.' A rush of tears almost came to my eyes at the sudden realization. It was my birthday.

For more than 20 years, since Dad had lost his job, I had tried to hide my birthday from everyone. I was afraid of my friends asking me for a birthday treat or a party. To avoid the embarrassment of not being able to pay for these things, I did my best to hide that information. I also tried to avoid my birthday, which was a few days after New Year's, in an attempt to dodge the New Year parties we could not afford to go to. This tradition continued when I came to America. I never felt that birthdays were a reason to celebrate.

As a result, the entire first week of each year would be my week in hiding. I would use that time to take stock of my life. During that week, I would come up with a new resolution to work harder than the previous year and to evaluate what milestone I wanted to achieve. I made sure that each year I worked harder than the previous one.

Now this little angel, tugging on my finger, was born just one day before my birthday. Her birthday would always remind me that the first week of the year was not for escaping but for celebrating life. God did have a great sense of humour and timing, I thought.

I rested my head on my baby's chest for a few moments of tranquility and felt her little fingers tap my head. It was like she was playing drums on my head, along with my birthday song.

Old habits die hard. At the beginning of 2013, I made another resolution to work harder so that I could provide the best care for my little angel.

With my baby to look after, I felt my financial situation was still tenuous and I used that insecurity to inspire me to work harder. I felt I could lose my job and the house in a flash. Bad luck could be lurking around the corner. I kept working harder and proving to my team members that I was not only capable but very dedicated. I worked beyond my capacity, even when there were things I thought I could not do. I would dare to take on the work and give it my best. I would have sleepless nights trying to think of ways to solve the problem. Tossing and turning in bed all night long, I would try to think of a plan to attack my problem and break the barrier. Having the baby sleep on our bed with us did not help my erratic sleeping pattern.

Trisha slept between Tripti and me on the same bed. On some nights, she would wake up and shout some orders in her sleep like an Army general and go back to her sweet slumber. But once I was awake, I couldn't go back to sleep as a result of work stress. I used to ponder and walk around, thinking about my job and how to advance my career while the little general readily went back to sweet snoring. Sometimes, she would sleep all tucked up into Tripti's embrace and sometimes she would be sleeping on the top of her tummy with limbs spread in a V shape. Tripti did not mind this at all. In fact, she loved it.

Working with some brilliant minds brought out the best in me. Participating in those meetings, I realized that amazing discoveries were made when great minds were able to traverse freely through the depths of the problem and diverse points of views were explored. The amazing thing was the culture of teamwork. It seemed that everyone was pulling in the same direction. Even when there were disagreements, people would air their differences politely. Even with the diversity of the best minds from different parts and cultures of the world, we shared common objectives. With new technologies and innovation, we were creating the best chips in the world that were powering at least a few billion phones around the world. Hanging in the office corridor was a picture of an old rural Indian woman standing in a paddy field looking at her smartphone and smiling. Our work was about impact and we shared the desire to make the world a well-connected place. I played an important role in some of the company's ambitious chips, which turned out to be very successful. During one celebratory party, our team leader complimented the teamwork. He said the work we do was not a nine to five job, but was about creating a legacy. We were building something that would be remembered long after we are gone. The advent and development of the wireless technologies and smartphones was our legacy for mankind. That day, I felt rewarded with a sense of pride and satisfaction for the artistry and contribution that I was a part of.

A few months later my manager called me into his office. I went there circumspectly, fearing the worst and hoping for the best. From past experience, I never looked forward to such surprise calls to the manager's office. I went there with bated breath hoping for no bad news.

'Ankit, do you want to be the lead engineer of our team for the premium tier chip?'

'Do you think I can handle it?' I asked cautiously because this was the top-of-the-line chip the company was planning to make in the next few years.

'Yes.'

'Okay. Yes then.' I was never one to back off a challenge.

'Thanks.'

'Cool,' I said, quickly stepping out of his office.

As I was walking down the hall, the significance of what just happened dawned on me. I would be the lead performance architect of what would be the most advanced mobile chip in the world. This chip would be in hundreds of millions of top end phones in the world.

'YES. YES,' I thought. I curled my fingers into a fist. And I looked up.

'Yes. I did it.'

'Finally, I did it.' I felt like running and sliding on the carpet and taking a victory lap like a soccer player does after scoring a goal.

'Thank you. Thank you so much,' I said joining the palms of my hand over my face in gratitude. At that moment, I thanked life for its kindness. I knew that over the next few years, the work would be very challenging. But more than anxiety, I was feeling a sense of validation and affirmation as an engineer. All my past dreams and hard work had built the foundation for this moment. This was the mountain peak I had envisioned and had been climbing towards with blinders on for the last 15 years of my career. I was so overwhelmed with emotion that I could not sit down in my office chair. My legs were restless. I wanted to sprint down the hallway shouting, with my hands raised like Rocky, 'I did it…I finally made it!' I wanted to take that soccer slide on the carpet. But my sensible professional mind prevailed and I had to be satisfied with just taking a walk.

I went to the same chair outside the building where I had sat with despair after my unsuccessful bid to be hired as a contractor. I sat at the same table, but this time facing the door. I stared at the door. A nearly failed contractor is about to be the lead performance architect at the company. From failing 10 interviews to coming in as contractor and now leading premium tier chip was a remarkable ascent. What a journey it had been! I wanted to tell the 80 people at the 10 failed interviews that I was not a bad engineer and that I did deserve to be a part of this company.

To that young boy reading engineering books under the water tank on the terrace, I wanted to say, 'We did contribute to this world. Our life's work did bring value to this world. We did matter.'

Sitting on the chair, I called Mom and said, 'Mom, good news. I have been assigned as the lead engineer for the most advanced chip in the world.'

'Wow, Ankit. That is amazing.'

'It is, Mom. It is a big deal.'

'Yes, you did it finally.'

'No, Mom. *We* did it finally. This is a dream come true for all of us, especially for you and Dad. But I still can't believe it. From that kid in our one-room house in Mumbai, I have become one of the top engineers in the world.'

'I am very proud of you, Ankit.'

'I mean, I have been chasing this dream for decades. Today,

I might just have exceeded my dreams. I stuck to my path tenaciously, but I never believed I could go so far. Lead architect for the most advanced mobile chip in the world! It feels good even saying that. This is more than what I had ever imagined when I had decided to become an engineer.'

'Wow Ankit. Just wow. Abhishek is close to becoming a general manager in his bank. Anamika is doing great research in field of petroleum in Texas...You...kids,' she said as she started choking up.

'We just stuck to our paths, Mom, and worked as hard as we could. It is the result of the hard work that you and Dad taught us.'

'I knew that with the right values and ethics, one day all my kids would achieve great success. Life put so much pressure on you kids. And look, just look at you. You all came out as diamonds.'

'Mom, thank you for holding the door for us,' I said thinking of the time my mother sat down on the bedroom floor along the door during my first engineering exam to protect us from the mobsters after the home invasion.

'Which door, Ankit?'

'All of them, Ma, all of them. It is because of you and Dad that we had this opportunity to achieve so much. Your lives have been tough like a tapasya. Our success is due to your tapasya.'

'Not just us. It has been your tapasya too, Ankit.'

'Yes. Life has been like a tapasya.'

'It's been tough.'

'I wonder about the meaning or the wisdom that can be derived from my tapasya. Since Trisha was born, I have often thought of what wisdom I want to pass to future generations. I still don't have clarity on what it is.'

'There should be something.'

'There surely is some knowledge that I want to pass on. But my understanding is so clouded by my past scars. I cannot find the truth until I let go of the fear inside me. The truth I speak will be just a projection of my insecurity.'

'What do you wish for her, Ankit?'

'I want her to have the best life, to enjoy more and be more successful than I will ever be. I want her to experience life in all its colours and shades. I want her to travel around the world and assimilate the best things from each culture. I want her to experience life in all its rich glory, with its full spectrum of emotions, the sunrises, the sunsets, the oceans, the rains. Ah, a few months ago, it rained in San Diego…and I took her outside my garage all wrapped up in a red blanket. Then, I pulled her little hand out. As raindrops fell on her little hands, she felt tickled by the sensation. She looked up in the sky to see where the water was coming from. I looked at the sky as well and felt the same as I used to in the Mumbai rains. After a few moments, when I looked back at her, she had her little tongue out. She was trying to taste the rain.'

'Oh…my sweet child,' Mom said.

'Mom…I want her to be free and fly high but...'

'But?'

'But I don't want her to fall and get hurt. That is the part I don't understand. I want her to fight and tackle her battles head on and never back off. But I don't want her to suffer and get hurt like me. How can we humans fight destiny, something that is more powerful than our limited capacity and still come out unscathed? It is this paradox that I can't understand. There is a truth that is beyond me. I know the answer waits for me somewhere beyond my limited perception, but I can't grasp it until I am free of my own fears. This true understanding of my life is what I still seek.'

'Give it time. You will find your truth and it will set you free.'

'Like moksha,' I smiled.

'That can come later. For now, focus on your current job, Ankit. Now that you have the title, you know the right thing, right? Titles are not important. It is the fulfilling of responsibility and the genuine contribution that matters. If the company has entrusted you, you have to do your best to justify their belief.'

'I know, I know Mom. I will work harder,' I said conceding to her moral lesson.

The new lead role was daunting at first. I overstretched my limits to put in extra hours along with working till late in the night and constant walks around the house. I constantly marched through the empty living room and kitchen and sometimes in the backyard solving problems in my head. Sometimes my little girl followed me around as I walked. For her, the walks were a fun game with Daddy and sometimes she held me as if I was the front bogey of a train and played 'train-train'. When she became tired, she grabbed my leg and I took her up in my arms and continued walking and thinking as she napped on my shoulders.

In the next few months, Abhishek became the general manager in his bank, one of the youngest in India. He owned three properties in India, each much bigger and more expensive than the apartment we were evicted from. After Mom told him about my nightmares, Abhishek went to our relatives in North India and found and sent me the copy of that childhood picture that was burnt on the night of our eviction. Meanwhile, Mom and Dad lived with him and enjoyed their time playing with their grandkids. They were very content with their kids' achievements. Despite having three domestic helps to aid in the household chores, Mom still found a way to stay busy. In Houston, Anamika would rejoice when her daughter Samika would doll up and put on makeup.

I toughed it out and completed my chip design project successfully. But my real reward was experiencing Trisha's childhood. My little girl was a joy, a pure gift full of life as she ran hippity-hop around the house and the backyard shouting 'galle galle'—something she coined in her one-word vocabulary. She ran around moving her head and curly hair from side to side with carefree bliss. Often, she pulled on my hand and asked me to accompany her on her 'galle galle' runs. I ran behind her as she ran forming a random arc with her arms. As I ran with her, I kept thinking of all the obstacles that could hit her on her path as she ran laughing and enjoying.

One day as my little girl was running in the backyard, she tripped on the grass. I was a few feet behind her and I held my breath as her little body hit the ground with a sickening thud. She lay motionless, her body limp. I rushed close to her and my heart skipped a beat as I saw her still body.

'Oh God, did she hit her head? Why is she so still?' I touched her head and her body to see where she was hurt.

'Trisha. Trisha, are you okay?' I was scared as I waited for a response.

She opened her eyes, looked at me and quickly closed them again. But she could not hide her impish smile.

I breathed a sigh of relief when I realized she was okay and it was not a bad fall. But she continued to lay quietly with her eyes closed, still acting. I lay down on the ground next to her.

I was quite shaken up by the realization of life's fragility. Nothing is more frightening than seeing the still body of your child. I felt a pull in my heart thinking how everything can be taken away in an instant. A single moment can destroy what took a lifetime to build.

Is destiny still not done with me? Are more battles coming my way to take me down?

I felt a rumble in the ground. As I looked up in the sky, I saw dark clouds beginning to gather again, as though the demons of my past were coming back to haunt me. I felt the cold wind hit my skin making me shiver. There was the same anxiety that caused my panic attack in 2008, when I was lying doomed, jobless and bankrupt on my apartment floor. As the clouds of memories opened, sad thoughts flooded my mind. And then, memories of my difficult childhood dripped through, the pain of seeing my mother pawning off her jewellery to fund our education, the humiliations that accompanied poverty, the despair in my father's eyes seeing his children go through adversity and suffering, the torturous days of being evicted mercilessly from the apartment that was our home, the anxiety of travelling to a new country with no money and an uncertain future, the sorrow I experienced from so many layoffs. I remembered my father suffering through physical and emotional handicap, the agony of losing all my savings, the dejection of failing so many job interviews.

But then I reminded myself that though I had known intense struggle and suffering, I had also come out of them successfully to achieve my dreams. I had to be grateful for my beautiful present. Despite the odds, I had forged far ahead of what I could have imagined as a kid, personally and professionally. From a kid living in a one-room apartment in India to having this big house with a view in the US, from a kid not being able to afford a computer or college fee to becoming the lead engineer of the most advanced chip in the world, I had truly made it.

When the initial barrage of negative thoughts subsided, I realized that my life was not about my emotional scars or me anymore. It was about this child and the lessons and values I wanted to pass on to her just as my parents did. It was about lighting her lamp with the burns of my life.

My child, I want to pass on the gift of grit to you, the ability to march forward towards your purpose come what may, the knowledge that if your belief and desire to achieve exceed the barrier in front of you, then you will always overcome any hurdle.

Your talents and circumstances may be different than mine, but the key to having grit is an unwavering belief and connection to your purpose. When your moral compass is aligned with a higher intelligence, your inner voice will guide and point you to your true calling. Like a beacon of light, it will be distant but shining bright. So, find that and connect with your deepest passion.

Your path to your goal may sometimes be foggy and dark. You may be stalled by uncertainty and your own doubts. But when the storm calls for you in the arena, don't run away but fly into it. Walk that distance with your deepest fears. The battlefield, though daunting, is also the field of possibilities. The second fundamental thing about having grit is never backing off from your share of battles and doing whatever it takes to reach your goals. Take the hits but still move forward. Have hope, focus all your energy on realities and its possibilities, and watch great things happen to you.

The third principle I learnt is to rise whenever you fall and never give up. Adversity only wins if you don't muster the courage to rise up. If you get up and get back in the fight, then the suffering recedes like a tide to just become a passing emotion. If you persist in challenging times, it will be something that you will look down upon from the top of the mountain. So, never back down and always keep fighting. Trust me, my child. There is no more glorious sight in this world than seeing a warrior rise back up from blood, sweat and tears.

Yes, that is the lesson I wanted to pass on to her someday. At that moment, I just opened my eyes ready to tell my baby girl to forget about the fall and to rise and shine.

But I saw that my toddler was no longer lying on the ground. I could see her tiny bare feet right next to me and could hear her loud giggles.

As I looked up at her radiant face, the dark clouds floated further away to expose rays of sunlight. It was as if heavens had arrived for their opening act. Everything around me seemed to have come alive in perfect harmony; the sky, the wind, the trees, the blades of the grass and my little girl with her resonating laughter, wavy curly hair and her outstretched hands towards me were part of this ethereal symphony.

I suddenly became aware of the walls of my own mind. Why was I separate from all this? This moment was trying to teach me something that had eluded my understanding for so long. I closed my eyes again, absorbing the presence of divinity at play.

The toddler with her simple act of falling and getting up with a gleeful smile already knew the lesson of falling and rising up. It is I who had failed to comprehend it as a natural flow of life, a manifestation of its intelligence. Night precedes dawn, darkness precedes light and there are different shades in between, with the ebbs and flows in the rhythm of life.

There is an unfathomable intelligence that created the whole cosmos, the beautiful Earth, nature and the human body. Our mind, limited to survival, may not fully understand its way but needs to have faith in it and trust it. There is an infinite energy around and within us that can nurture and guide us.

This is what the feather on the terrace and my vision at the temple had been trying to tell me all along. The feather danced in ecstatic motion because it trusted the winds. It was just not about reaching your destination but trusting, loving and living every movement and moment of the way. It was about plunging into the present moment and enjoying its every beat rather than being burdened by it. It was having faith in the grand scheme of the universe and believing that you are part of it. One could have grit without gritting one's teeth.

We humans are nature's work of art, its masterpiece of engineering. Through the challenges that life brings forth, it is trying to evolve us into better versions.

The battles life brought me did not break me, they made me. They were on my side. The demons were not there to hurt me, but to mould and chisel me into my better self. The waves of adversity that I faced were not there to drown me. They were the forces on my side to push me and take me through the sacred passage towards my true destiny.

There was and there is only one true meaning and purpose of each human being's life. And that is to find one's best and true self.

Each battle I fought transformed me into a better person than when I started. Each pushed me hard so that I could be better and move to the next level of my true calling. My battles were my teachers throughout my journey. My battles deserve my gratitude and love in making me the person I am and was meant to be.

The fourth pillar of grit, I realized, was having an openness towards life and acceptance of battle as an opportunity for growth and transformation towards your true self. Life is not what happens to you but what it is going to reveal about you.

With this new-found connection, I felt the embrace of the space around me and a serenity within. I was finally at peace with my battles.

I rose and held my child's hand to connect with the joy around. I was ready to greet life, eager to engage with whatever would unfold.

Blaze to the beat of your heart
Embrace the compass to a higher path
Flow through the fire of fear
Carve your path through mountains like a gentle river.
Rise every time you fall, my friend
To reveal your better self at the other end.

ACKNOWLEDGEMENTS

When an engineer tries to write a book, he needs a lot of expertise and encouragement around him. I was lucky to find those among my friends and family and the lovely literary editors I sought help from. I would like to thank my friends, Thirty Kasad, Zubin Irani, Arun Narayanan, Harsha Jagasia and my brother-in-law, Samarth Tandon who read the early versions of the manuscript and gave me valuable feedback. Editors like Marni Freedman, Lynne Feldman, Tristine Rainer, Rajni George and Saswati Bora helped me learn the art of writing and create a better version of the manuscript with their valuable feedback.

I would like to thank my siblings Abhishek and Anamika for guiding me and being part of this journey. I would like to thank my wife Tripti Aggarwal for supporting me through this difficult process of writing. Lastly, thanks to my daughter Trisha Gupta for providing the inspiration to write this book.